FORCES OF NATURE

A volume in the series
The Environments of East Asia

Series Editors: Ann Sherif and Albert L. Park
Editorial Board: Anna L. Ahlers, David Fedman, Eleana J. Kim, Micah Muscolino

This timely series brings an interdisciplinary lens to the study of the environments of East Asia, approaching questions of human-environment relations by bringing together scholars from social science, humanities, and STEM fields to challenge entrenched paradigms about East Asian societies' relationship with the environment. The series interrogates past and present societies, cultures, and environments with the aim of imagining and forging ways to a more sustainable and equitable future. The series is freely available in open access through the generous support of the Henry Luce Foundation.

A list of titles in this series is available at www.cornellpress.cornell.edu.

FORCES OF NATURE

New Perspectives on Korean Environments

**Edited by David Fedman,
Eleana J. Kim, and
Albert L. Park**

Foreword by Ann Sherif

CORNELL UNIVERSITY PRESS   ITHACA AND LONDON

First published 2022 by Cornell University Press

Library of Congress Cataloging-in-Publication Data

Names: Fedman, David, editor. | Kim, Eleana Jean, 1971– editor. | Park, Albert L., editor.
Title: Forces of nature : new perspectives on Korean environments / edited by David Fedman, Eleana J. Kim, and Albert L. Park ; foreword by Ann Sherif.
Description: Ithaca [New York] : Cornell University Press, 2023. | Series: The environments of East Asia | Includes bibliographical references and index.
Identifiers: LCCN 2022034304 (print) | LCCN 2022034305 (ebook) | ISBN 9781501768781 (hardcover) | ISBN 9781501768798 (paperback) | ISBN 9781501768804 (epub) | ISBN 9781501768811 (pdf)
Subjects: LCSH: Human ecology—Korea—History. | Human ecology—Korea (South)—History. | Human ecology—Korea (North)—History. | Nature—Effect of human beings on—Korea—History. | Nature—Effect of human beings on—Korea (South)—History. | Nature—Effect of human beings on—Korea (North)—History. | Human beings—Effect of environment on—Korea—History. | Human beings—Effect of environment on—Korea (South)—History. | Human beings—Effect of environment on—Korea (North)—History. | Nature and civilization—Korea—History. | Nature and civilization—Korea (South)—History. | Nature and civilization—Korea (North)—History. | Korea—Environmental conditions. | Korea (South)—Environmental conditions. | Korea (North)—Environmental conditions.
Classification: LCC GF659 .F67 2023 (print) | LCC GF659 (ebook) | DDC 304.209519—dc23/eng20221122
LC record available at https://lccn.loc.gov/2022034304
LC ebook record available at https://lccn.loc.gov/2022034305

In memory of Aaron S. Moore,
scholar, mentor, friend

Contents

Foreword

The Korean peninsula, dominated by mountains but spanning varied ecosystems and climates, shapes the human activity and imagination of its people, even as people seek to harness and define nature. *Forces of Nature* places front and center the dynamic interactions among forces of Korea's biophysical landscapes and the competing social forces that have sought to define the cultural, ideological, and social meanings of Korea's environments.

Situated at a crucial crossroads of land and water in northeast Asia, Korea's landscapes have been particularly altered by extended periods of warfare and foreign occupation. In the twenty-first century, the two political entities that govern the Korean peninsula mobilize differing eco-nationalist discourses and policies to promote sustainability and resilience, even as the north and south share soil nourished by the same rivers and global climate change encroaches national boundaries. A range of disciplinary facets—from art history and anthropology to history and geology—illuminate Korea's webs of ecological and social connections as they manifest in the pasts and present of forestry, agricultural practices, and food cultures; conservation and energy systems; artistic expression of climate change and environmental anxiety; and social movements. *Forces of Nature* makes available the achievements of Korean ecological scholarship and environmental thought to English-language readers. Grounded in inter- and cross-disciplinary research, this book advances innovative scholarship and theoretical perspectives essential to understanding East Asia's environments and to proposing paths to sustainability moving forward.

Ann Sherif

Acknowledgments

This volume was born of a conference convened at the University of California, Irvine, in the spring of 2018. We are grateful to the Center for Critical Korean Studies at UC Irvine, EnviroLab Asia at the Claremont Colleges, the Office of the Dean of Faculty at Claremont McKenna College, the Pacific Basin Institute at Pomona College, and the Asian Studies Program at Pomona College for their institutional support. Our initial meeting would have been far less international if not for a grant from the Northeast Asia Council of the Association for Asian Studies. For their unwavering support of this book since its inception, we thank Amanda Swain and Joo Hoon Sin.

The input of many friends and colleagues improved the book immeasurably. In particular, we would like to acknowledge the collaboration and support of Char Miller, Patrick Fox, Wenjiao Cai, Tessa Braun, Sunyoung Park, Joseph Jeon, and Yeonsil Kang. Robert Oppenheim and Aaron S. Moore read an early draft of the entire manuscript, offering critical interventions that transformed everything from chapter flow to framing. Though Aaron did not get to see the finished product, its pages reflect his vision as much as ours, and the book is better for it. It was our great fortune to receive research assistance from Juwon Lee at the final stage of preparing the manuscript, and we thank him for his sharp editorial eye.

Unfazed by the challenges presented by a global pandemic, our editors at Cornell University Press were superb. For her enthusiasm and bold vision, we thank Emily Andrew, without whom this book would not have gotten off the ground. Alexis Siemon shepherded us through the production process with patience and grace, improving the finished product in myriad ways. Ann Sherif, our series editor, was unflagging in her support, even when it was just a kernel of an idea at Irvine. We would also like to thank our two anonymous peer reviewers, who offered incisive comments and suggestions that are now reflected in the very arguments and organization of the book.

The preparation and publication of *Forces of Nature* would not have been possible without the financial support of EnviroLab Asia at the Claremont Colleges (a Henry Luce Foundation–supported initiative) and the Core University Program for Korean Studies through the Ministry of Education of the Republic of Korea and the Korean Studies Promotion Service of the Academy of Korean Studies (AKS-2021-OLU-2250006). We are also grateful to here acknowledge publication subventions provided by the Humanities Center at UC Irvine and the Gould Center for Humanistic Studies at Claremont Mc-Kenna College.

Note on Transliteration and Terminology

We use the McCune-Reischauer romanization system to transliterate Korean words into Latin script, except for instances in which a common transliteration is in wide usage, for example, Jeju instead of Cheju. Names in Korean follow the cultural convention of family name followed by given name, except for those of individuals who publish under or who prefer Western conventions. We forgo transliteration in favor of Korean script (hangul) throughout the text when the meaning might be enhanced for readers familiar with the Korean language. We also forgo romanization for Korean-language bibliographic sources but include the English-language translations. When writing about the time period after the division and establishment of two Korean states in 1948, the authors use South Korea or ROK to refer to the state and territory of the Republic of Korea and North Korea or DPRK to refer to the state and territory of the Democratic People's Republic of Korea. Unless otherwise noted, all translations are those of the author of each chapter.

FORCES OF NATURE

WHOSE NATURE? CENTERING THE ENVIRONMENT IN KOREAN STUDIES

David Fedman

For nearly four decades, a water fight has gradually escalated along a short stretch of the Bukhan River, a waterway that transects the Korean Demilitarized Zone (DMZ). There, not twenty kilometers apart, stands a pair of dueling dams—"twin brothers, born at the same time, facing each other across the DMZ."[1] North Korea was the first to break ground, commencing work on the Imnam Dam in 1986. Almost immediately, South Korean officials began to sound the alarm about an imminent North Korean "water offensive." Whether by accident or design, they warned, the Imnam Dam was bound to burst, a failure that would inundate everything downstream, Seoul included. In keeping with the Cold War rhetoric of the times, South Korean politicians suddenly spoke of a North Korean "water bomb," the power of which was likened to an atomic blast.[2] To forestall such a disaster, the South Korean government launched in 1987 a dam construction project of its own: the Peace Dam, a rampart against North Korea's supposed riparian aggression.[3]

The tidal wave never came. Whatever urgency had initially impelled the Peace Dam project gave way to doubts about the actual threat, prompting officials in South Korea to suspend construction in 1990.[4] In actuality, South Korean hydrologists soon found themselves confronted by the opposite of what they had feared: a suddenly lethargic river. Where North Koreans observed newfound abundance, South Koreans saw a serious infrastructural impediment. Farmers fretted over irrigation shortages. Engineers warned of reductions in hydroelectric power generation. Residents of Seoul faced the prospect of drinking-water shortages from the reservoirs on which they had long depended. Having structured so much of South Korea's economic growth around waterways like the Bukhan, officials now had to reckon with a watershed management scheme partly beyond their control.[5]

The burgeoning "water crisis" on the Bukhan escalated further in 2002, when the South Korean government released satellite photographs that revealed apparent cracks in the Imnam Dam. North Korea's assurances of the dam's structural integrity did little to allay fears in the south of an impending breach. This breathed new life into the Peace Dam project. To the tune of US$429 million, the South Korean government contracted out a massive expansion of the project, which was completed in 2005. Now it was North Korea that was staring down the prospect of a deluge. With its height elevated and structure reinforced, the Peace Dam raised concerns of a hydrological "back-rush": a sudden and forceful reversal in floodwater that would wash across North Korea, Pyongyang included. Their fortunes fixed to the same watershed, officials on both sides had little choice but to call for joint management of the river and mutual inspections of each dam—coordination that lives or dies with the broader politics of denuclearization and inter-Korean relations on the peninsula.[6]

Simply put, watersheds do not abide geopolitical divisions. No matter how heavily fortified the DMZ or how vast the ideological gap between north and south, Koreans across space and time have been bound by the same stubborn realities of the physical environment on the peninsula. Before there were two dams, before there were two Koreas, there was a single catchment basin, which has structured life and labor in the region for centuries.

We begin with the sibling dams on the Bukhan precisely because they illustrate the contested terrain of the natural environment in Korea—a reality that has long animated politics on the peninsula. Insofar as these dams represent monuments to environmental engineering, they speak to both the promise and the perils of state-led efforts to impose order on the landscape. As a conflict ensnaring not just north and south, but also engineers, urban planners, soldiers, farmers, and city dwellers, the management of the Bukhan reveals the social frictions created by enduring questions over access to and use of precious natural resources across the peninsula. For every dispute over a waterway, there have been struggles over other environmental issues such as woodland use, waste disposal, and wildlife protection.

Not every facet of the environment in Korea is contentious. The Korean landscape, after all, is far more than an array of habitats, resource pools, and land titles. It is also an *idea*, one tightly bound up with long-standing efforts to define the very meaning of Koreanness. Consider, for example, the historic summit in April 2018 between Moon Jae-in and Kim Jong-un, a moment of rapprochement that raised hopes for inter-Korean relations. What did these heads of state do when they came together? They did what generations of Koreans had done before them. They planted a pine tree. Placed into a mixture of soils provided by both countries and nourished by waters drawn from rivers north and south, the pine served as a symbol of not only a peaceful future but also a common past. To Koreans across the peninsula, it was a powerful reminder of shared roots, of the environmental heritage that transcended national division.[7] Indeed, whatever the daylight between the two Koreas on issues related to denuclearization, both sides cling to strikingly similar ideas about a distinctively Korean landscape. In the "land of mountains and rivers embroidered in silk," as one popular saying has it, nationalistic ideologies of nature have found fertile soil.

Look no further than the 2018 Pyeongchang Winter Olympics, where the invention of Korean nature was on spectacular display. One need only have watched the opening ceremony to appreciate the centrality of nature myths to the self-image on offer in Pyeongchang. Tacking between imagery of hypermodern green cities and pastoral hinterlands, this carefully curated event took pains to showcase South Korea's enduring tradition of environmental stewardship. The star of the show was an animatronic white tiger—animal protector of Korea and mascot of the games—that, though long extinct, testified to how Koreans had supposedly lived in harmony with nature.[8] Beamed into televisions across the globe, the Pyeongchang games conveyed a portrait of a grandly green Korea, a land of pine-smothered mountains that had been protected by a nature-loving society.[9]

Yet behind the facade of artificial snow and bucolic uplands lay a much messier reality. For months, in fact, resentment had simmered in the shadows of the highlands of the host province, Kangwŏn. At issue was the felling of forests to transform the slopes of Mount Gariwang into a ski run. What to provincial officials was a simple measure to bring the area's mountains into conformity with the standards of the International Ski Federation was to environmental activists an egregious exercise of government overreach. "It's shortsighted, illogical and worst of all, irreversible," decried one pamphlet circulated by opponents.[10] It flew in the face of the notion of an "eco-friendly" Olympics, long touted by organizers, and did irreparable damage to a "forest genetics protection zone," as spelled out in the Forest Protection Act. By one estimate, no fewer than fifty-eight thousand trees were sacrificed to make room for lifts, stands, and runs that were used for only sixteen days of competition. While some local residents welcomed the ski run as a potential source of tourism and economic stimulus, others decried the destruction of a "sacred" forest, old growth that, since its enclosure by the Chosŏn state, had been left undisturbed for more than five hundred years.[11]

Provincial officials responded with a survey of the proposed site, enlisting botanists and other experts into an extensive investigation of the ecology of the area. Their findings yielded a markedly different portrait of these slopes. Far from a pristine forest, they concluded, much of the mountain was covered in trees only seventy years old. To bolster their case, provincial officials also pointed to evidence that shifting cultivators had previously inhabited the area. Accurate or not, in the traces of this "fire-field" farming, officials found counternarratives of land use and exploitation—grounds on which they justified another phase of development.[12]

Though the battle over Mount Gariwang has largely faded from public view, disputes over the control of Korea's environment remain alive and well. Where there are golf course greens, nuclear power plants, and projects of urban renewal, there have been "site fights" over their environmental impact. This is hardly a feature only of the present or recent past. As John S. Lee and Sooa Im McCormick each make clear (chapters 1 and 3), such conflicts stretch back deep into Korea's preindustrial history. While the meanings and ideological valences of nature have shifted over time, the negotiation of these competing interests has been a fixture of local politics across generations. Questions of who gets to define nature, and on what terms, are of profound importance to people in Korea. They bear on everything from food security to ecotourism, labor rights to public health. Just as importantly, they are central to how Koreans have historically understood what binds them together and what sets them apart.

Hence our title for this book, calling attention to the forces of nature in Korea in multiple senses of the phrase. We show, at one level, how geophysical processes across timescales have continually shaped the course of events on the peninsula—how floods, droughts, climatic oddities, famines, fires, and pests have inexorably impinged on human affairs. At another level, we illuminate how different forces have been mobilized by states—preindustrial, colonial, authoritarian, or otherwise—and their corporate and civic partners to variously control, protect, develop, and showcase the Korean landscape. Needless to say, these forces were met with resistance at every turn. This book accordingly devotes considerable attention to state-planning as well as local responses, to national enterprises as well as community projects. Considered together, the chapters reveal the myriad ways in which Korean communities have shaped, and been shaped by, physical landscapes, with implications that reverberate well beyond the peninsula.

Old Questions, New Lenses

The past three decades have witnessed a flowering of the field of environmental history and, more broadly, the environmental humanities. Self-described "environmental historians" populate academic departments the world over, specialized scholarly bodies have proliferated, and canonical works in the field have been translated into dozens of languages. Meanwhile, collaborations between environmental historians and scholars working in anthropology, political ecology, and science and technology studies (STS), among other disciplines, stretched and blurred the boundaries of inquiry, pushing the field well beyond its native soil in the American West. East Asia is a case point. Whereas scholars a generation ago could count the number of environmental histories of East Asia on one hand, they today scan entire library shelves.[13] The creation of national and even regional academic societies devoted expressly to the study of East Asian environmental history have all but assured that these trends will continue well into the future.

And yet, only recently have scholars working in the environmental humanities begun to claim residency in the house of Korean studies.[14] In part, this lag can be attributed to the focus on human subjects in Korea's history. This is especially true of *minjung* historiography, a deep well of research that has foregrounded the role of common people in shaping the arc of Korea's history.[15] Agency, in this view, rests principally in human subjects and systems. Intentionally or not, in their efforts to highlight the collective struggles that attended colonial oppression, national division, and authoritarian rule, many South Korean writers have cast the environment as a mere tableau, a stage on which the human drama unfolds. Something similar can be said of prevailing narratives in North Korea, which tend to highlight how farmers and factory workers have historically overcome material constraints to "master" the natural realm.[16] After half a century of foreign occupation followed by national division and a ruinous war, it is only natural that commentators in both Koreas would set out to highlight the resiliency of the Korean people themselves.

With a few recent exceptions, English-language scholarship on Korea has similarly portrayed its physical environment as a passive backdrop.[17] Scattered throughout the growing body of research on the globalization of Korean cuisine—a driving current of the so-called Korean Wave—are references to Korean agriculture and foodways.[18] One would be hard pressed to find an account of the Korean War that does not call attention to the bone-chilling winter conditions that defined the lived experience of this conflict.[19] The Korean landscape, in short, is at once everywhere and nowhere in Korean studies. Although scholars across fields have long gestured toward the importance of Korea's climate, topography, and biota, they have only recently begun to focus their attention on how these environmental factors—real and imagined—figure into Korea's history.

Forces of Nature takes the flora, fauna, soil, energy systems, and climate events that have long been confined to footnotes and puts them front and center in analysis and argumentation. In setting our sights on the Jeju horse, the icefish, and the tapeworm, we seek to cast familiar events and themes in a new light. We do not so much de-center human actors as more firmly embed them in their physical and material surroundings, revealing relationships often taken for granted.

In this, we follow the lead of a pathbreaking community of Korean environmental writers, philosophers, and intellectuals. It may be true that Korean scholars have only recently begun to self-identify as practitioners of "environmental history" (環境史, *hwan'gyŏngsa*), but they have for decades staked out a place in the broad but vibrant field of "ecological studies" (生態学, *saengt'aehak*).[20] Galvanizing this intellectual movement were the agricultural and industrial policies of Park Chung-hee, the authoritarian dictator who ruled South Korea from 1961 to 1979. Guided by the logic "grow first, clean up later," Park's breakneck heavy industrialization resulted in pollution of all sorts.[21] What to international observers was an economic miracle on the Han River was to many Korean communities a toxic trade-off—a "poisoned prosperity," in the words of Norman Eder.[22] With growing alarm, South Korean activists and political dissidents warned of a mounting ecological crisis with dire public health implications.

For evidence, many simply pointed to the Onsan Industrial Complex, a densely packed compound of factories that became the hub of the South Korea's rapidly growing chemical manufacture sector, a pillar of Park's industrial plans. There, in the early 1980s, local residents began to take note of a growing list of mysterious illnesses: rashes, eye irritation, neuralgia. Scientists eventually traced these maladies to wastewater runoff from surrounding non-ferrous-metal plants. They dubbed this, appropriately enough, Onsan disease (温山病, Onsanbyŏng), which is now recognized as a form of cadmium poisoning.[23]

Incensed by the lack of government accountability and, following a moratorium on fishing rights, the blow to local livelihoods, civil society rallied into opposition. Their activities dovetailed with a broader push following Park's assassination in 1979 toward democratization, a movement that brought new energy and institutional resources to bear on South Korea's environmental problems. Although these efforts failed to force the government and its corporate partners to admit wrongdoing in Onsan, they did result in a state-funded rehousing program for tens of thousands of area residents. This did little, however, to assuage the concerns of many working-class Koreans, who began to question whether industrial production quotas came at the expense of their own bodily and communal health. More and more, ordinary Koreans began to view environmental justice and democratization as two sides of the same coin—a point illuminated in many of the chapters to follow.[24]

It was not toxicity alone that arrested the attention of South Korean environmentalists. The city itself also became the subject of intense scrutiny, as rapid urbanization and a corresponding rural exodus fundamentally transformed South Korea's environmental politics. Faced with grueling labor conditions in rapidly expanding urban areas—Seoul chief among them—many city dwellers began to perceive an erosion of their connection with the natural world. In polluted, overcrowded urban slums, they saw not only a degraded state of nature but also the fraying of Korea's social fabric. Gone were the trees, waterways, and (as the poet Kim Kwang-sŏp lamented) bird life that had once symbolized Koreans' intimate connections with the natural world.[25] In their place stood concrete buildings, shantytowns, and trash dumps—monuments to the social inequality inscribed in the urban built environment.

To a small but growing group of intellectuals, spiritual adherents, and young people, the antidote to this urban squalor was to get back to the countryside, to rediscover agrarian connections that had been corroded by the pursuit of profit. Yet, rural Korea presented myriad environmental problems of its own. For one thing, decades of state-imposed farming initiatives rolled out as part of Park's rural revitalization push had introduced a wide range of pesticides, fertilizers, and other hazardous agrochemicals into rural ecosystems. Hardly a problem particular to industrial zones such as Onsan, toxic runoff touched the lives of agrarian communities across South Korea. Where farmers had once battled the state over land tenure rights, they now asserted their right to a clean environment, one untainted by corporate or state interests. So began, in the words of Nancy Abelmann, a shift in rural activism from "a politics of land (*ttang*) to a politics of earth (*hŭk*)."[26] Adding to their woes was the push during the 1980s toward the liberalization of trade: structural reforms to the agrarian economy that dealt a decisive blow to farming incomes. If these economic reforms accelerated the rural exodus already under way, they also spurred the growth of alternative visions of agrarian life. It was indeed against this backdrop that, as Yonjae Paik shows in chapter 8, South Korea's organic farming movement set its roots, giving rise to communal cultivation arrangements that persist into the present.

Such back-to-the-land movements both reflected and promoted new ideological currents shaping how people in Korea understood their relationship with nature. Some looked abroad for models on how to better protect the Korean landscape. One after another, works by Henry David Thoreau, Aldo Leopold, Rachel Carson, and other influential American eco-philosophers were translated into Korean, offering bridges to newfangled ideas about deep ecology and bioethics. Others spurned these foreign ideas, calling on Koreans to draw on their own traditions of ecological thought, those born of the particularities of the Korean landscape. Where commentators had once plumbed the depths of Thoreau's *Walden* (a bestseller in Korea) for insight into nature's transcendental plane, they now turned to the poetry and prose of writers such as Ch'oe Sŭng-ho and Kim Chi-ha.[27] Blending, among other things, Buddhist imagery, Taoist philosophy, Eastern Learning (Tonghak) principles, and anticapitalist sentiment, these writers put forward a searing critique of the vulgarization of life under Park's developmental dictatorship. Each in their own way, they worked to broaden conceptions of community to more fully encompass the biotic world. Together, they laid the groundwork for what came to be known as a new "life" (생명, *saengmyŏng*) philosophy, an outlook that celebrated interconnection over individualism.[28]

By the 1990s, many commentators spoke of a distinctively Korean approach to interpreting, valuing, and conserving nature. At a time of considerable economic and ecological insecurity—underscored by South Korea's IMF crisis and North Korea's catastrophic famine—such ideas took on newfound urgency. Public awareness of environmental issues in South Korea rose sharply. Whereas only 24 percent of South Korean respondents to a 1982 survey expressed disagreement with government environmental policy, by 1997 this figure had climbed to 51 percent. The registration of environmentally focused nonprofit organizations (NPOs) in South Korea similarly surged, growing from only seven such organizations in 1987 to 175 by 2001.[29] Of particular importance to the expansion of environmentalism in South Korea was the 1992 United Nations Conference on Environment and Development (the Rio Earth Summit), a landmark meeting that forged lasting alliances among NPOs, religious organizations, and other civic groups.

With increasing frequency, South Korean newspaper coverage made references to a bona fide "environmental movement" (환경운동) and "anti-pollution movement" (공해추방운동)—terms that made their way into the popular vernacular. By the turn of the century, once obscure green philosophies had begun to garner broad popular interest and political support. This was not lost on the South Korean government, which since the early 2000s has gone to great pains to style itself a leader in eco-friendly development.[30] To offer but one high-profile example, in 2009 the Lee Myung-bak administration inaugurated to much fanfare the Four Rivers Restoration Project, a massive investment in riparian improvement unveiled as part of a Green Growth Policy. Though the government touted the project as a source of stable water supplies, climate resilience, and green jobs, local communities saw things quite differently. Government malfeasance, mismanagement, and overreach beleaguered the project from the outset, opening up new fault lines in resource politics across South Korea.[31]

If this swelling environmental consciousness sparked popular interest in a more sustainable future, it also spurred efforts to more fully understand Korea's environmental history. Believing that, as Kim Tong-jin has put it, "the answers to future [ecological] problems lie in the past," a growing group of scholars began to mine the historical record for any insight it might offer into how Koreans across generations had adapted to environmental change.[32] From the writings of Yi Kyu-bo, the twelfth-century master poet, they resurrected ideas about "the essential oneness of ten thousand things" (萬物一流, *manmul illyu*)—what many saw as the wellspring of Korean ecological thought. In the *Annals of the Chosŏn Dynasty*, the centuries-long chronicle, they located ample evidence of future-minded "pine policies."[33] Geomancy, shamanism, and *kye* (local guilds) of all sorts were all identified as tributaries to a uniquely Korean set of conservationist ideas and practices.[34] Never mind that, as John S. Lee shows in chapter 1, Korea's premodern landscape bears the traces of multiple layers of foreign influence, the Chosŏn period (1392–1910) was routinely cast as the cradle of an authentically Korean environmental worldview.

To no small degree, this work was animated by a desire to dismantle twentieth-century allegations of premodern stagnation. In a manner not unlike the "sprouts" theories of Chosŏn-era proto-capitalism, Korean scholars have gone to great lengths to unearth the roots of agricultural productivity and forward-thinking resource conservation.[35] Korea's nineteenth century—a period of ecological upheaval, civil unrest, and foreign incursion—has proved particularly contentious in this regard. While few dispute that the late Chosŏn period witnessed a succession of environmental crises (flood and drought chief among them), the degree to which this hastened the decline of the Chosŏn state is subject to debate.[36]

Casting a long shadow over these debates is a defining fact of Korea's modern history: its colonial subjugation by Japan. Following decades of competition and military conflict among imperial powers for control over markets and politics in the peninsula, Japan declared Korea a protectorate in 1905 before annexation in 1910. From then until the collapse of Japan's empire in 1945, the colonial government ushered in far-reaching programs of environmental rule that spelled profound changes for the Korean landscape and its inhabitants, both human and nonhuman. The environmental impact of Japan's colonial occupation has formed yet another major arena of scholarly inquiry. Understandably, the lion's share of this literature has set out to assess the extractive nature of colonial rule—the bushels of rice, board feet of timber, and barrels of charcoal harvested by Japanese settlers and capitalists. A growing number of scholars both in and outside of Korea have likewise taken up questions related to state power and social control.[37] Woodlands, rice paddies, and dams have all become sites of investigation into not just the material impact of imperialism but also the scope of colonial authority and nature of technical expertise. Joseph Seeley offers in chapter 2 one such case study, showing how Japanese efforts to modernize riparian environments spawned a technocratic logic—what he calls "piscatorial developmentalism"—that outlived the empire itself.

To many Koreans, the only real legacies of colonial rule were exhausted forests and depleted resources—the result of the material mobilization of the peninsula to wage a ruinous war across the Asia-Pacific. Yet, the environmental degradation wrought by colonial rule in many respects pales in comparison to that of the Korean War (1950–1953), a cataclysm that, in addition to causing massive loss of life, laid waste to the peninsula's physical environment.[38] To date, scholarly attention has been riveted to the principal material legacy of this still-unresolved conflict: the DMZ. To travel to the DMZ is to come face-to-face with one of the most militarized borders on the planet. It is also to bear witness to one of the world's most unlikely wildlife sanctuaries. There, amid land mines and concertina wire, exist thriving populations of rare and endangered species, including Asiatic black bears, red-crowned cranes, and Amur goral.[39] On its face, the DMZ appears, as some environmentalists have dubbed it, "a green ribbon of hope," a material reminder of the unlikely ways that nature can reclaim the soil.[40] Yet, if we look beyond these surface-level descriptions, we can also see, as Eleana J. Kim has argued, how South Korean unification politics have leveraged ideas about biodiversity and wildlife conservation to advance their broader political agenda.[41]

As much as research on the Korean War has elucidated the unexpected ecological consequences of military conflict in the peninsula, it has also set the stage for investigations into South Korea's economic ascent under Park Chung-hee. How did South Korea transform from a war-torn country into an economic juggernaut, and to what effect on the environment? To answer this question, many scholars have turned to Park himself, situating him in an uninterrupted stream of enlightened stewards that stretches back to the Chosŏn period.[42] Onsan disease notwithstanding, Park is recognized by many in South Korea for ushering in sweeping projects of reforestation and rural revitalization, twin pillars of his New Village Movement (새마을운동, Saemaŭl Undong). Behind these grand schemes of environmental reclamation lay a host of state-led interventions—in fuel economies, fertilizer production, and industrial management—that drove economic growth.[43] In chapter 4, Hyojin Pak draws attention to one of the more revealing but understudied by-products of the period: waste. Far from being mere graveyards of consumption, dumpsites such as that at Nanjido are dynamic spaces of reclamation, illuminating class dynamics, labor relations, and urban poverty. A similar point can be made about South Korea's nuclear power plants: a dense network of reactors that, as Nan Kim reveals in chapter 10, have been at the center of grassroots opposition to state-led energy policies. In the uneven geographies of waste and nuclear energy, in short, we find deeply ingrained socioeconomic inequities that structure exposure to toxins, natural disasters, and other forms of risk in South Korea.

For reasons both intellectual and political, research on South Korea's environment has been strikingly partitioned from the north—a trend reflective of Korean studies more broadly. Even as the DMZ has garnered tremendous interest as a case study in the peace dividend, the broader environmental linkages between North Korea and South Korea—shared weather events, pollutants, and disease vectors, to name a few—remain largely unexplored. What has instead monopolized scholarly attention is the place of nature in the ideology of North Korea's ruling regime. As both a source of political authority and a force of social cohesion, stories about the landscape have occupied pride of place in the founding mythology of the North Korea state itself.[44] More materially minded scholars have also set out to make sense of the environmental implications of North Korea's pursuit of economic autarky and resource independence on the world stage.

Two particular topics predominate this scholarship. One, predictably, is North Korea's nuclear weapons program, a project that has placed a tremendous strain on the DPRK's already limited natural resource portfolio.[45] The other is the Arduous March famine of the 1990s, a period of intense flooding and mass starvation that claimed hundreds of thousands of lives.[46] While such research has gone a long way in revealing the ecological insecurity faced by the North Korean people, it has hardly explained the resilience that has also defined the regime. Nor has it, as Ewa Eriksson Fortier and Suzy Kim remind us in chapter 5, critically assessed the limits and possibilities of international aid in North Korea. Decades of humanitarian relief efforts have yielded little more than stopgap measures, leaving North Korean communities acutely vulnerable to disease, drought, and natural disasters. Now more than ever, they argue, North Koreans need community-centered, long-term environmental policies—approaches that have often been held hostage to the broader politics of denuclearization.

The presence of aid workers in Korea is but one of many expressions of the peninsula's interconnections with the wider region and the globe. The circulation of dust storms, capital, and laborers through the Korean peninsula testifies to the tangled web of ecological connections between Korea, the Pacific Rim, and beyond. Consider beef. In a country as compact as South Korea, where pastureland is sparse, how has beef become a staple of the diet and a fixture of the agricultural economy? The answer, as Anders Mueller shows in chapter 6, lies overseas. Owing to a series of trade liberalization measures, South Korean corporations have been able to offload much of the land-use burdens of the beef industry overseas. Lindsay S. R. Jolivette extends this analysis into the present by showing in chapter 7 how anxieties over the "meatification" of Korean agriculture have found expression in popular culture, including a string of zombie films with not-so-subtle ecological messaging. By blurring the boundaries between the dead and the living, Korean commentators have heightened awareness of the potential perils of consumption in an age of industrial agriculture.

Forces of Nature in many ways builds on the foundations laid by Korean scholars, but makes a conscious effort to push the field in at least two new directions.

First, insofar as it slides the scale of analysis, the book makes a concerted effort to rescue the Korean environment from the nation. For all its depth and breadth, extant scholarship is often beholden to essentialist notions of eco-nationalism. The nation-state indeed retains a strong grip on claims to the meaning and management of Korea's environment. The chapters in this book, by contrast, largely eschew the national framework, opting instead to highlight ground-level complexities and regional variations. We offer portraits of how particular communities—from ragpickers to aid workers to agrarian communes—have interacted with local environments to forge distinctive patterns of labor, modes of activism, and intellectual traditions. Nowhere in this book are these dynamics more clearly at work than in chapter 9, Jeongsu Shin's study of *gotjawal*, forests native to Jeju that reflect the island's fraught relationship with the rest of Korea.

Second, as a collaboration of researchers across disciplines, *Forces of Natures* strives to integrate multiple methodological approaches—from visual studies to eco-criticism to agronomy—to arrive at a truly interdisciplinary approach to the Korean environment. Rather than limit ourselves to a particular set of scholarly perspectives or predilections, we have here set out to showcase the range of tools available to scholars interested in the Korean environment. We interweave climate proxy data, archival research, filmic interpretation, object studies, and ethnographic fieldwork, among other things, to arrive at a fuller understanding of the limits and possibilities of environmental analysis. In the same spirit, we establish a wide range of vantage points—from the forests of Jeju Island to the headwaters of the Yalu—that allow us to appreciate the peninsula's variegated terrain.

These vantage points necessarily take us beyond the peninsula. Some of Korea's most pressing environmental issues, after all, transcend national and regional boundaries. One such challenge is anthropogenic climate change, the implications of which spell dire consequences for the two Koreas. Rising sea levels threaten the livelihoods of coastal communities across Korea.[47] Extreme weather events stand to grow more frequent and more destructive—no trivial matter in North Korea, where the threat of malnutrition and famine is already acute.[48] Cooperation between north and south to mitigate these effects (and lower carbon output) is of course important, but so too is international engagement.[49] Neither country can address the problem alone, raising important questions about the prospects of joint action on climate issues. Something similar can be said of the COVID-19 pandemic, a public health crisis that has thrown into stark relief the degree to which the Korean peninsula is enmeshed with the societies that surround it. Just as efforts to understand Korea's environmental history must draw out linkages between the human and nonhuman world, so must they embed Korea within the global systems of capitalism and circulation that define our world.

Roadmap

Three basic facts of Korea's geography are essential to understanding the arguments advanced in the pages to follow. One is Korea's location at a crossroads of Asia. Situated between a number of powerful state actors in northeast Asia, Korea has long negotiated competing geopolitical and economic interests in the region. This has both integrated the peninsula into networks of circulation and exposed it to a steady string of foreign incursions, all of them shaping the peninsula's environments in distinct and long-lasting ways.[50] A second salient feature of Korea's physical geography is obvious enough to anyone who has ever set foot on the peninsula: its mountainous topography. Upland areas, constituting over 70 percent of a landmass roughly equivalent to the size of Great Britain, predominate the Korean landscape, posing particular challenges for food production, forest management, and flood control.[51] To traverse the alpine spine of Korea is also to come face-to-face with the third defining feature of the landscape: its regional variation.[52] As Marc Los Huertos and Albert L. Park make clear in the chapter that follows, the Korean peninsula is marked by climatic, ecological, and regional variation, making it difficult to speak simply of a single Korean environment. These and other key features of Korea's environments are all elaborated—and visualized—in more detail in their biogeographical sketch of the peninsula that lays the groundwork for the analysis to come.

The book proceeds in four parts, each of which examines the forces of nature in a different thematic sense. Part 1, "Imperial Interventions," offers two case studies in how Asian empires—Mongol and Japanese—etched ecological signatures on the Korean landscape. Though separated in their analysis by many centuries, both chapters reveal enduring dynamics in state-led efforts to seize control over Korea's natural resources and channel them into the developmental agenda of the ruling regime. Part 2, "Crisis and Response," explores how environmental emergencies—whether fast-moving floods or the slow creep of climate change—have shaped Korean society and how Koreans have adapted in the face of these challenges. The chapters ask us to consider what scarcity (and abundance) means in the Korean context and what effect it has on the lived experience of ordinary people. Taking us into pasturelands in and beyond the peninsula, part 3, "Processes of Dispossession," provides two strikingly different assessments of what Korea's dearth of agricultural land means for Korean food production. Here, we encounter not just the environmental impact of agricultural production, but the far more subtle ecological shadows cast by Koreans' changing consumption patterns. The final section, part 4, "Reclaiming Life," maps the contours of local disputes over conservation and development, adding new texture to our understanding of how ecological changes have breathed life into Korea's environmental activism.

Taken together, these chapters reveal not only a wide range of physical environments, but also a striking diversity of land-use traditions and eco-anxieties. They show Korean nature to be a construction of the human mind as much as a set of material conditions—an arena of competing interests and changing meanings that has evolved in tandem with Korea's remarkable transformation across centuries.

A BIOGRAPHY OF THE KOREAN PENINSULA IN MAPS

Marc Los Huertos and Albert L. Park

Constructed Narratives of Nature

With lush and vivid language, creation tales of the Korean peninsula have been passed down from generation to generation. Similar to foundation myths in other cultures, Korean creation tales have featured sacred beings who used their powers to generate areas of land and water that would function as the living spaces for humans. The tales commonly personified these sacred beings by giving them humanlike features and presenting them as characters who formed the world and the Korean peninsula through humanlike acts. Take, for example, the Magohalmi myth, which presents an elaborate and detailed story of the giant Magohalmi who was responsible for forging the intricate details and features of the Korean peninsula. In scratching the earth, Magohalmi created the mountains and valleys. She next went on to relieve her bladder and, in doing so, "caused a huge flood whose strong force made the seas and rivers on the land."[1] As she walked the land, her feces dropped from her body and became hills, islands, and mountains. According to the myth, Magohalmi spat out rocks, which she had consumed, because they were too hard, and they became the highest mountains in the northern and southern parts of the peninsula. Interestingly, Korean creation tales frequently credited female deities, like Magohalmi, as the forces behind the creation of the geographical features of Korea, while male deities, such as Mirŭk, were known as the makers of the universe, including the sun, moon, heaven, and earth. They gave more weight and value to male deities because they created more "significant" entities than female deities. As such, in the course of the transmission of the myth over time, the Magohalmi story became less valued than creation stories that featured male deities and were excluded from research on creation myths. Korean creation tales, in this sense, should be viewed as constructed stories that reinforced gendered, patriarchal views and norms of Korean history.[2]

Offering an origin story for both the human and nonhuman worlds, creation tales have been imbued with significance from the premodern to modern era of Korea. They maintained their value in different ways in Korea's modern era, but, in the face of modern science, they lost their weight as authoritative narratives to explain the formation of the nonhuman world. Based on rigorous methodological approaches rooted in observation, empiricism, and critique, modern science, especially theories of evolution, furnished very precise and technical information on the physical and biological development of the peninsula. Voluminous research from the fields of biology, chemistry, physics, and geology put Korea and its nonhuman world under the microscope, offering granular explanations of complex geophysical phenomena. Researchers have illuminated characteristics, rhythms, and patterns of nature, as well as the relationship between biotic and abiotic entities. In the process, they have traced biological and physical continuity and the origins and pace of change in the biophysical world of the Korean peninsula (figure GI.1).[3]

Modern science has clearly distinguished itself from creation tales based on the principles of the modern scientific method (observation, hypothesis, experimentation/testing, and refinement). Yet, despite these differences, both share the very same quality of being constructed narratives. They have been assembled, in other words, through a selective process of emphasis and de-emphasis within a particular social context. Whether a creation tale or a scientific theory, such narratives derived their authority from different networks of actors and institutions that have organized around them at different times. The creation tale and scientific theory thus both assume the role of being mechanisms that selectively map and chronicle connections, experiences, and events. In this sense, they have allowed their human creators to visualize happenings and occurrences, orient and direct themselves, and ground their existence. Insofar as creation myths and scientific surveys have been created, authorized, and powered by social networks, they embody and display the same narrative qualities.

This brief profile of the natural features and nonhuman world of the Korean peninsula offers its own biographical account of the natural world that exists in the space shared by South Korea and North Korea today. Far from being comprehensive and definitive, it offers snippets and salient details that foreground topics and themes explored in subsequent chapters. Unavoidably, it frames nature from the human perspective. This account nonetheless serves as a platform

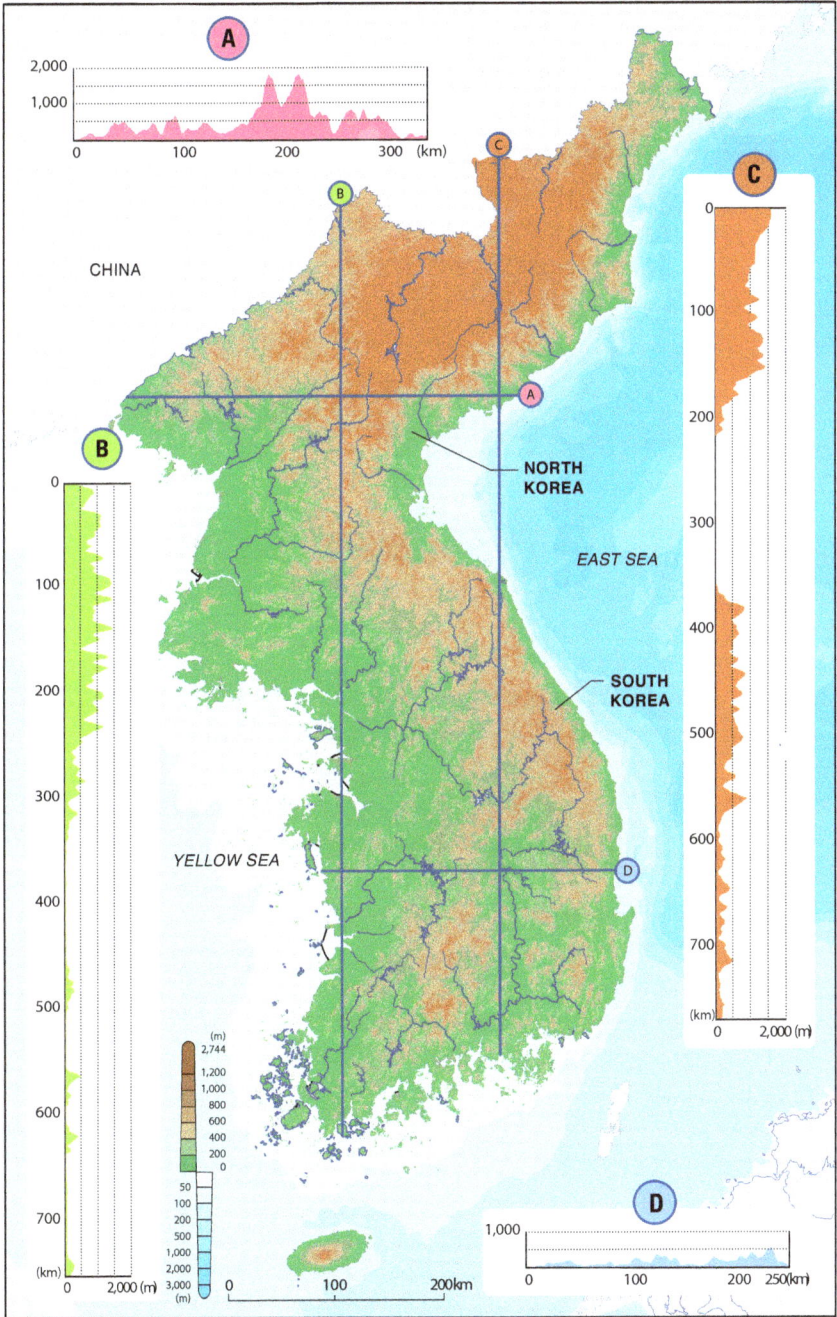

FIGURE GI.1. Topographic relief and profiles of the Korean peninsula.
Source: The National Atlas of Korea II, http://nationalatlas.ngii.go.kr/pages
/page_661.php.

for assessing and framing the relationship between nonhumans and human thought, behavior, practices, and systems, in addition to helping readers to visualize the dynamic features of the Korean peninsula. It serves as a starting point for understanding the formation of the peninsula and the various forms of life that exist within it. Ultimately, it is a platform from which to think about how entities of the biophysical world and human and human-constructed realms in Korean society have interacted and influenced one another.

Physical Geography

Works such as Stephen Jay Gould's *Time's Arrow, Time's Cycle* and Amitav Ghosh's *The Great Derangement* have shown how the field of geology has been an arena of contestation over the construction of narratives about the past. Explaining physical time and changes has historically been centered in the "geological theories of gradualism and catastrophism."[4] That is, explaining physical changes has been driven by the question of "which . . . has primacy in the real world, predictable processes or unlikely events?"[5] In explaining the case of how the Korean peninsula was formed and has changed over time, the answer may lie in both. As a quick glance at any map makes clear, the Korean peninsula extends from the East Asian continental margin and forms the boundary between the Yellow Sea and East Sea (Sea of Japan). While the east coast is characterized by a jagged coastline and shore islands, the west coast is best described as a coastal plain that arises from the ocean with gentle increases in elevation. In spite of this east-west contrast, the peninsula is characterized by unquestionably rugged terrain or rumpled geomorphology. This terrain is the result of a rich geologic history creating a peninsula of contrasting features.

The Korean peninsula is an extension of the Asian continent, but the continent is not made up of one homogeneous piece of the Earth's crust. It is composed of cratons, which are large stable blocks of the Earth's crust that form the nucleus of a continent. Driven by tectonic forces deep in the Earth's mantle, cratons are stitched together (sutured) as they collide, torn apart (rifted), or forced under other tectonic plates (subducted). Material scraped off a subjecting plate may also accrete on the margin of the plate (accreted). Finally, cratons are subject to volcanism, mountain building, faulting, and erosional processes that add to their complex history.

Contemporary geologists recognize that Korea is composed of an amalgam of two cratons, the North China Craton (NCC) and the South China Craton (SCC) (figure GI.2). One hypothesis suggests that the division of the two cratons may fall roughly along the lines of the political division of the Korean pen-

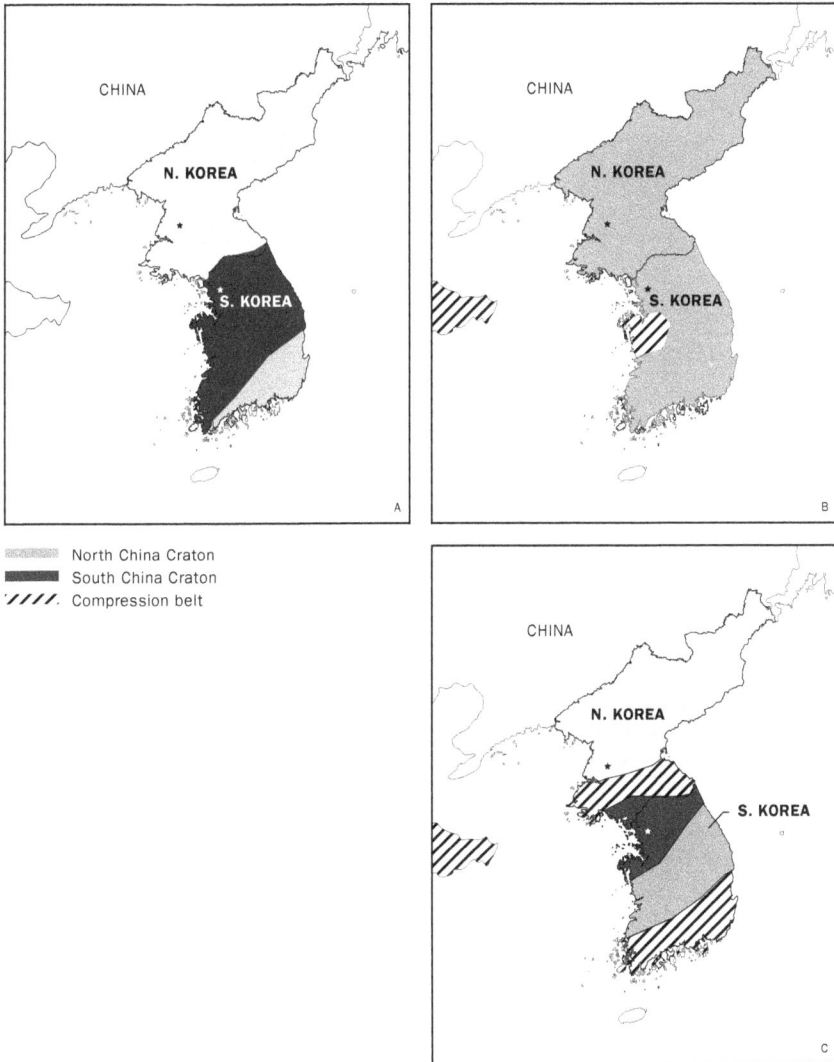

North China Craton
South China Craton
Compression belt

FIGURE GI.2.   Different interpretations of the layout of craton configurations on the peninsula. Image by Leah Nichols and Marc Los Huertos.

insula (figure GI.2A). Other geologists maintain that most of the peninsula originated from the NCC (figure GI.2B). Yet another theory holds that the NCC wedged into the SCC and that a part of the SCC can be found in the northern and southern areas of the peninsula (figure GI.2C). Although questions regarding the complexity of the collision process will remain unanswered, researchers continue to find new forms of evidence, paving the way for new interpretations.

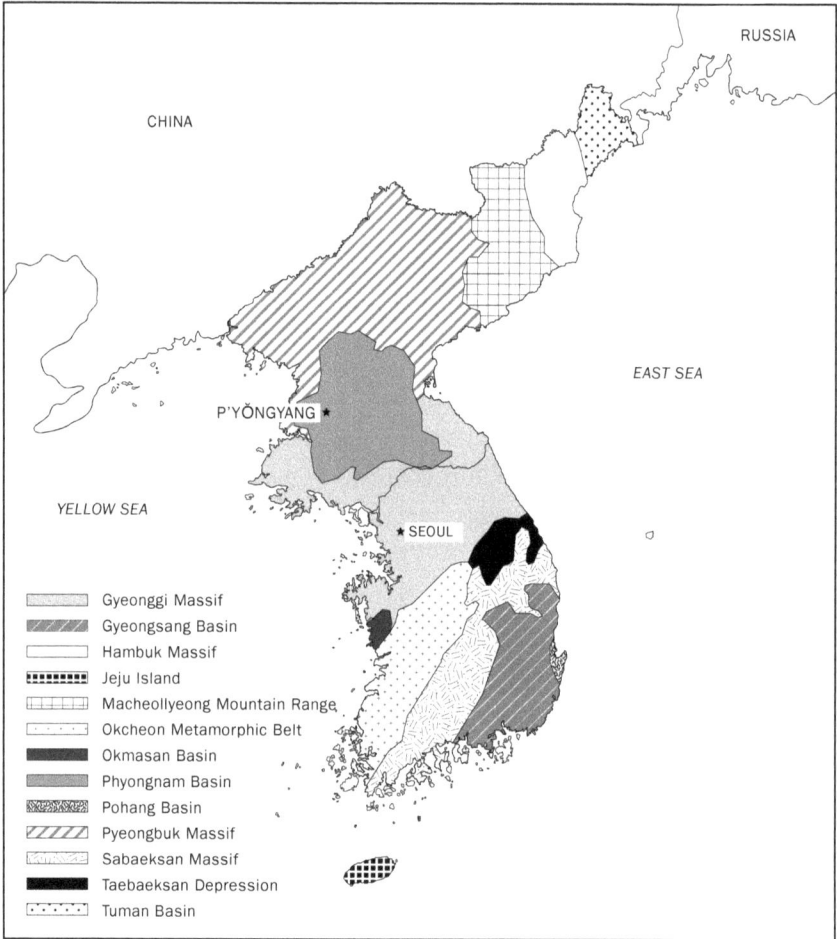

FIGURE GI.3. Geological formations on the Korean peninsula. Image by Leah Nichols and Marc Los Huertos.

The outcome of tectonic activity has created a patchwork of geological formations—with distinct rock types and histories (figure GI.3). The first geologists to evaluate the peninsula identified dominant rock types and histories as tectonic provinces, and created maps with particular consistencies and discrepancies that evolved over time. Of signal importance is the geological composition of the landscape: two-thirds of Korea's landmass is made up of granite gneiss, a thinly foliated metamorphic rock that results in slightly acidic and therefore more erosion-prone soil. Koreans are reminded of this fact each summer, when monsoon rains swell rivers and wash away hillsides. The prevalence of upland areas also means that cultivable lowlands are relatively scarce. What arable land is available is concentrated in the alluvial plains of the west and south, historically the rice basket of Korea.

Ore formation is partially related to supercontinent fragmentation and assembly. The formation of a certain type of ore is restricted to a specific period, and the minerals are formed in relation to tectonic processes. A variety of metallic and nonmetallic minerals and natural resources have been found on the peninsula, petroleum being a major exception. Among the most significant—and coveted—of these natural resources are tungsten, zinc, mica, kaolin, copper, gold, silver, lead, graphite, iron, anthracite, and coal (figure GI.4). Because

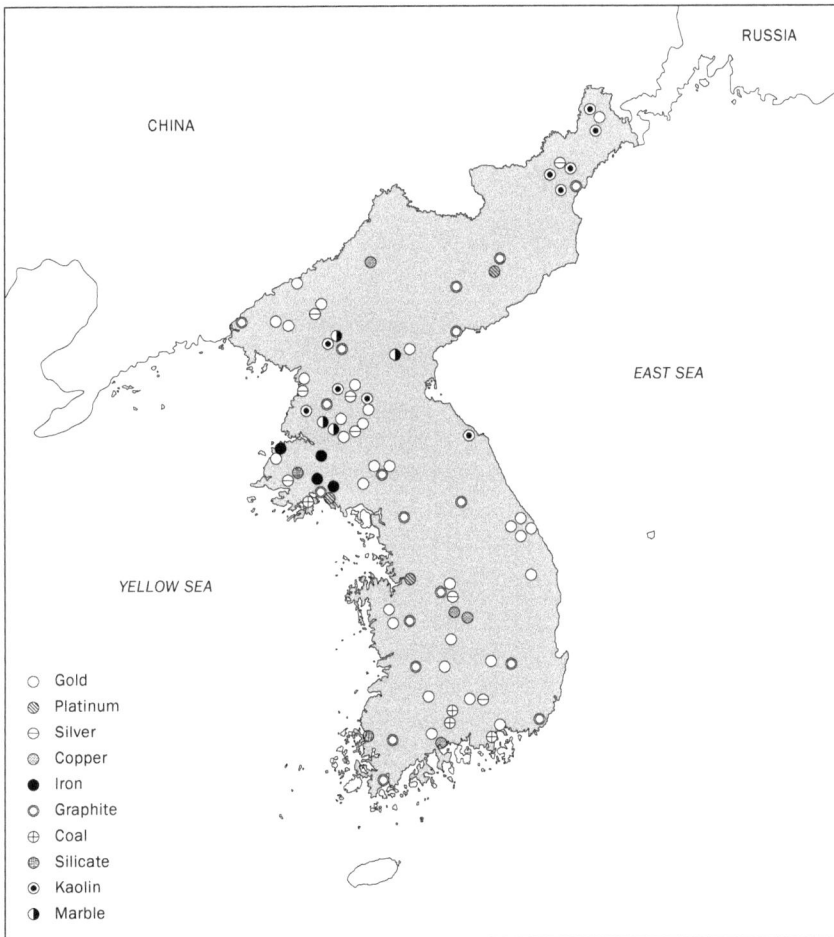

FIGURE GI.4. 1929 map of location of mines in colonial Korea based on records of the Office of the Government-General. *Source*: Hoon Koo Lee, *Land Utilization and Rural Economy in Korea*. Image by Leah Nichols.

of the complex tectonic activities within the peninsula, the ore deposits are also quite rich, but unevenly distributed. Consequently, northeast China and the northern part of Korea, which are likely part of the NCC, have featured a higher concentration of geological resources. These minerals, ores, and natural resources have been mined and refined for human use since the premodern period. The modern period, especially since the colonization of Korea by Japan, has featured concentrated and extensive efforts to locate, identify, and extract these resources for industrial development and the production of energy to fuel the economy. The concentration and extraction of important geological resources in the northern part of Korea has helped to explain, in part, how the region became the center of industrial development during the colonial period. The lack of petroleum, in particular, and drive for meeting energy needs, has been the backdrop for the push for nuclear energy in both Koreas, but especially in South Korea (as laid out in Nan Kim's discussion in chapter 10).

The Peninsula's Climate

The Korean peninsula has a temperate climate with four distinct seasons. It is largely affected by high-pressure air masses from the north and monsoons from the south. In the winter months, high-pressure air masses form in Siberia and produce powerful northerlies that draw cold and dry air into the Korean peninsula.[6] The East Asian monsoon is divided into a warm and wet summer monsoon and a cold and dry winter monsoon. Summers are short, hot, and humid. Winters are usually long, cold, and dry. Spring and autumn are pleasant but also short. Seoul's mean temperature in January is between −5°C and −2.5°C, while the mean temperature in July is between 22.5°C and 25°C (figure GI.5). The northern areas tend to be dry and colder, whereas the southern areas have been more wet and warmer. Over the centuries, the peninsula has, at times, encountered extreme temperature fluctuations, especially during the period of the Little Ice Age on the peninsula, from the sixteenth century to the late seventeenth century (a topic covered by Sooa McCormick discussion of the production of art in the aftermath of the Little Ice Age in chapter 3). Over the past thirty years, South Korea, in particular, has been experiencing rising air temperatures (figure GI.6). In addition, mostly due to domestic industrial and chemical production, air pollution has increased dramatically in the country, making Seoul's air some of the most hazardous among the major cities in Asia.[7] This development is the latest addition to the long history of environmental issues in the history of Seoul since the start of the age of fast-paced industrial capitalist development (which Hyojin Pak touches on in chapter 4).

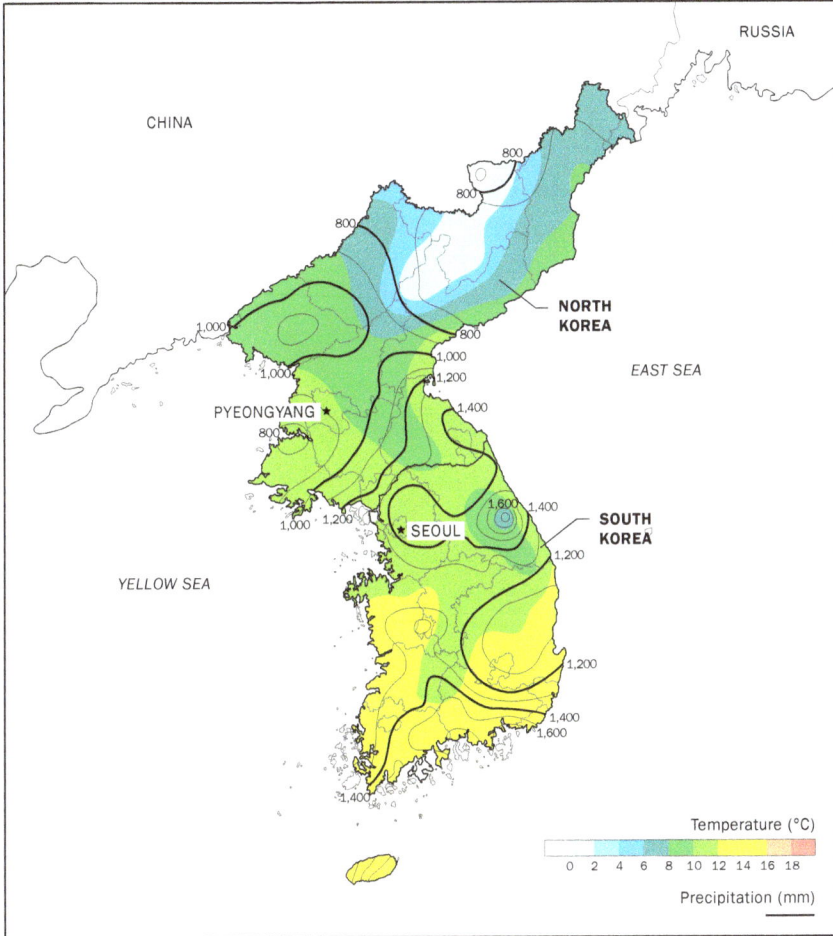

FIGURE GI.5.   Annual mean air temperature and precipitation on the Korean peninsula. Image by Leah Nichols and Marc Los Huertos.

Detailed records of rainfall on the peninsula have been kept since the beginning of the Chosŏn period (1392–1910), starting with the creation of the world's first rain gauge (*chugugi* in Korean) in 1441.[8] In order to measure and record rainfall, the government at that time distributed rain gauges throughout the peninsula and established a meteorological network that produced reliable data on patterns of precipitation. In general, the monsoon follows a predictable pattern, with winds being southeasterly in late June, bringing significant rainfall to the Korean peninsula. This leads to reliable precipitation patterns, wherein about two-thirds of the annual precipitation occurs between June and September, enough rainfall to sustain forested landscape and provide ample water supplies

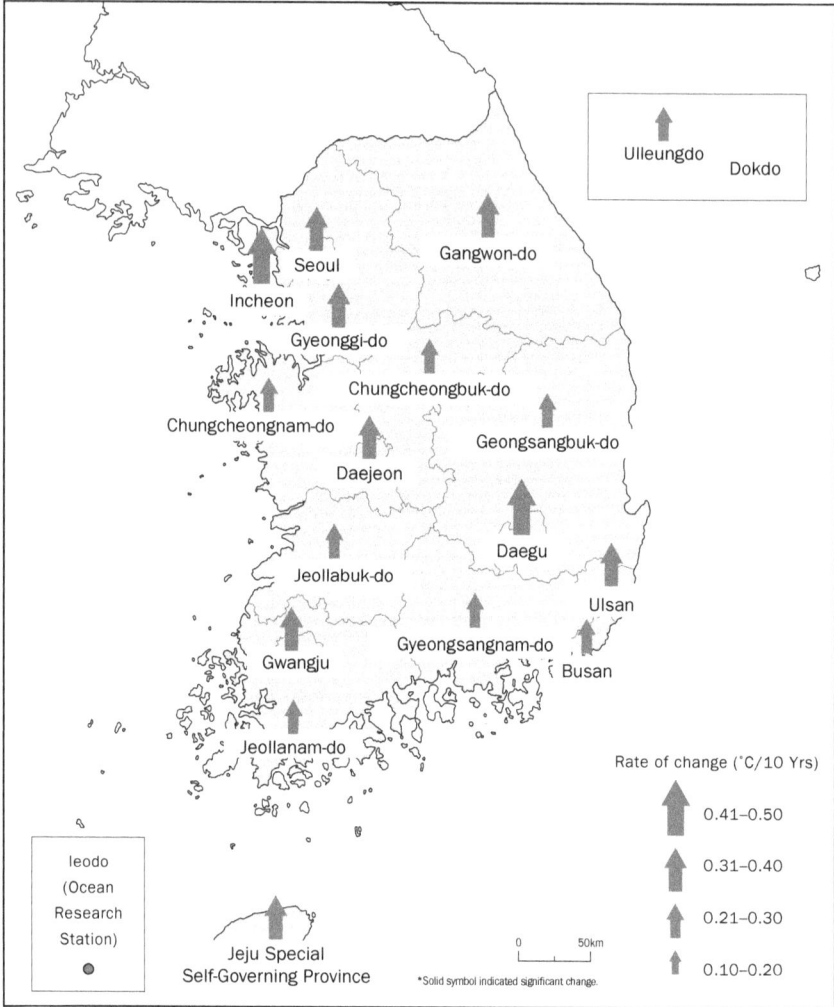

FIGURE GI.6. Rate of change in annual mean air temperature (1973–2010). *Source: The National Atlas of Korea II,* http://nationalatlas.ngii.go.kr/pages /page_735.php#prettyPhoto.

to support agriculture. Precipitation is rarely under 75 cm per year and often more than 100 cm per year. Although South Korea is less vulnerable to typhoons than neighboring countries, one to three typhoons can be expected each year. Typhoons usually pass over South Korea in late summer, especially in August, and bring torrential rains and flooding. In the winter, the winds are northeasterly and the monsoonal precipitation bands move back to the south, and intense precipitation occurs over southern China and Taiwan.

With significant interannual variability of the East Asian monsoon, and given the relationship between the intensity of summer monsoon and rainfall amounts, droughts and deluge frequently occur across the peninsula, sometimes resulting in disastrous floods. During the mid-1990s, North Korea suffered intense massive floods that caused extensive death and disaster and deeply affected the political, social, and economic dimensions of the country (as discussed by Ewa Eriksson Fortier and Suzy Kim in chapter 5). In the summer of 2013, torrential rainfall in North Korea again led to massive floods. Tens of thousands were left homeless and more than ten thousand hectares were inundated with floodwater.[9]

Bodies of Water

The Korean peninsula is surrounded by the Yellow Sea and the East Sea (Sea of Japan). Twenty-six major rivers flow throughout the Korean peninsula, including the Yalu, Han, and Nakdong Rivers (figure GI.7). The Yalu and Tumen Rivers have historically demarcated the border between China and Korea and have been an important point of cross-cultural, economic, and political exchange between Korea and neighboring countries (a point raised by Joseph Seeley in chapter 2). Except for glacier-formed lakes, the majority of lakes in North and South Korea have been formed from the establishment of dams and reservoirs. South Korea has more than 17,491 dams, weirs, and reservoirs. Some of the most prominent are shown in figure GI.7.

The aquatic culture in and surrounding the peninsula is rich and diverse. The temperature of the ocean currents surrounding the peninsula play a major role in determining the types of fish species in the water—a process directly influenced by global warming trends (see figure GI.8). Ranging from cold-sea to warm-sea species, the main types of fish and seafood caught in the waters around South Korea include mackerel, squid, blue crab, anchovy, and hairtail and yellow corvina.[10] The central-western seaboard of the peninsula is rich in fish life, making it a highly disputed area of fishing among North Korea, South Korea, and China.

Land and Soil

The peninsula is nearly six hundred miles long; its entire landmass stands around 84,565 square miles (figure GI.9). Seventy percent of the Korean peninsula is covered with mountains. Some of the major mountain ranges include the Taebaek, Nangmin, and Hamgyong mountain ranges. The highest mountain on the peninsula is Mount Paektu, located in North Korea. Hallasan, located on Jeju Island

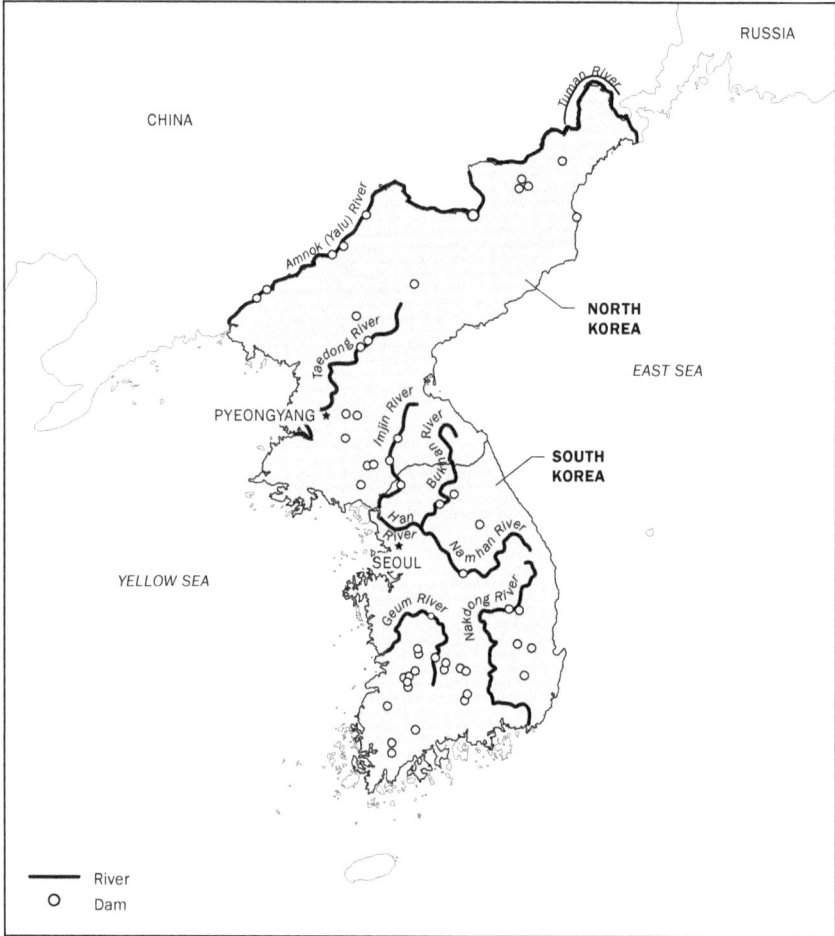

FIGURE GI.7.   Major rivers and dams on the Korean peninsula (2022). Image by Leah Nichols and Marc Los Huertos.

(the southernmost point of the country), is the tallest mountain in South Korea. As a volcanic island, Jeju has long held diverse ecosystems that have been shaped by its relatively warm climate (as Jeongsu Shin makes clear in her analysis of its distinctive woodlands, known as *gotjawal*, in chapter 9).

Forest stock is more dense in South Korea, while the amount of forest land is larger in North Korea. The peninsula supports three types of forest areas: (1) subboreal forest in the north, with species such as fir, birch, and larch; (2) cooltemperate forest in the center, with species such as oak, ash, and pine; and (3) warm-temperate forest in the south that includes species such as oak (as John

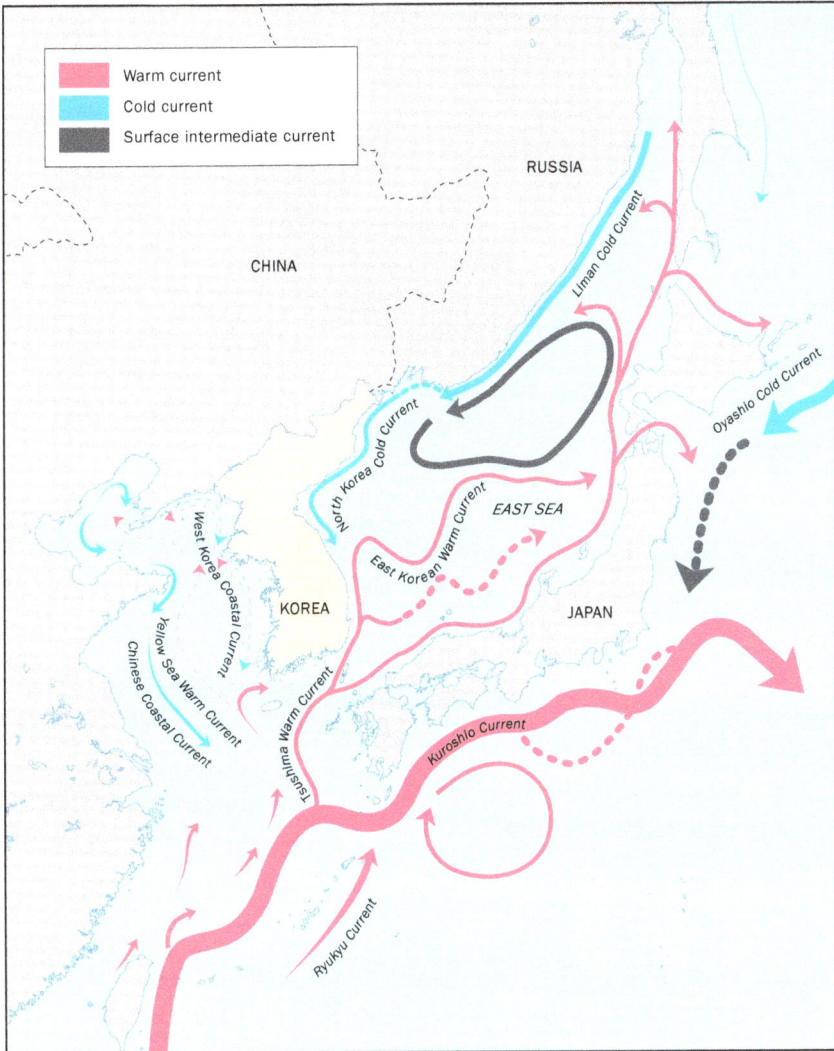

FIGURE GI.8.   Ocean currents around the Korean peninsula. *Source: The National Atlas of Korea II*, http://nationalatlas.ngii.go.kr/pages/page_747.php.

Lee reveals in chapter 1, pine trees in particular have had a special place in the premodern and modern environmental history of Korea).

These forest areas have produced three distinct ecoregions on the Korean peninsula: (1) the Manchurian Mixed Forests ecoregion, which covers the northern part of the peninsula and parts of China and the Russian Far East and whose climate is conditioned by factors from interior Asia; (2) the Central Korean Deciduous

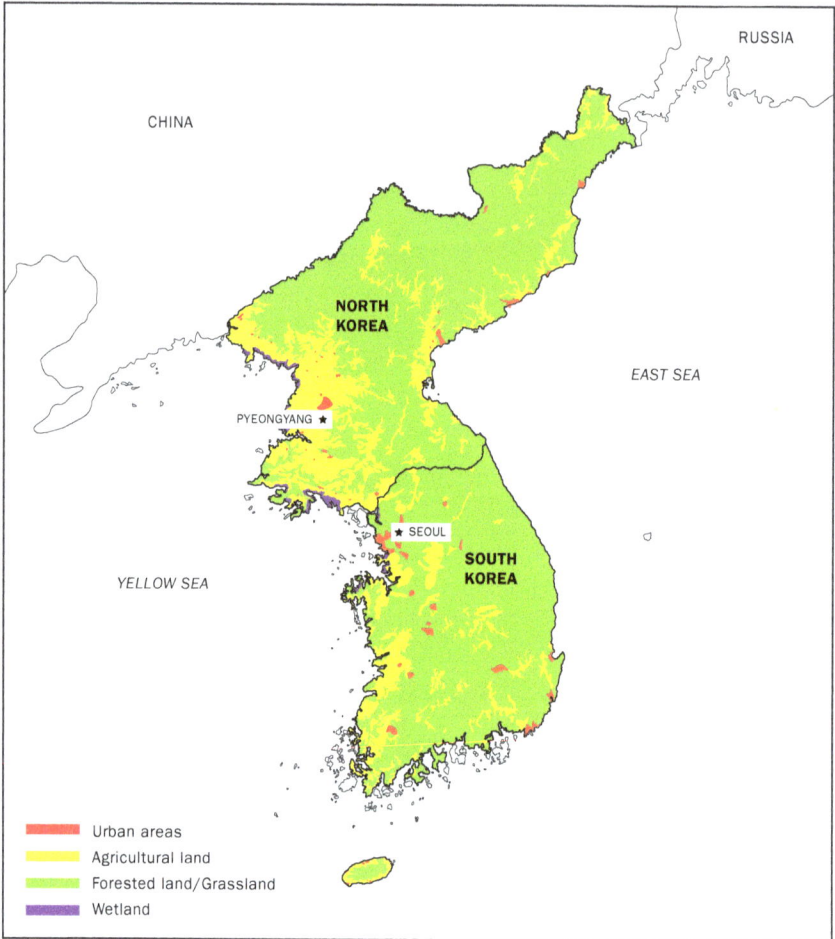

FIGURE GI.9.   Land usage on the Korean peninsula (2022). Image by Leah Nichols and Marc Los Huertos.

Forests ecoregion, which occupies most of the peninsula and is less vulnerable to typhoons; and (3) the Warm-Temperate Evergreen Broadleaf Forests ecoregion, which extends from the southern coast to islands in the south, including Jeju Island.[11] According to one 2015 government survey, more than 45,295 plant and animal species inhabit South Korea. Insects represent the largest proportion, followed by invertebrates, birds, and plants.[12] Among birds, the red-crowned crane has stood out as a valued and revered animal in Korean culture. Symbolizing peace, harmony, and long life, cranes have flourished in areas next to the DMZ (figure GI.10).

A large number of cranes, in particular, can be found in mudflats in South Korea. The mudflats or tidal flats (*getbol*) along South Korea's western and south-

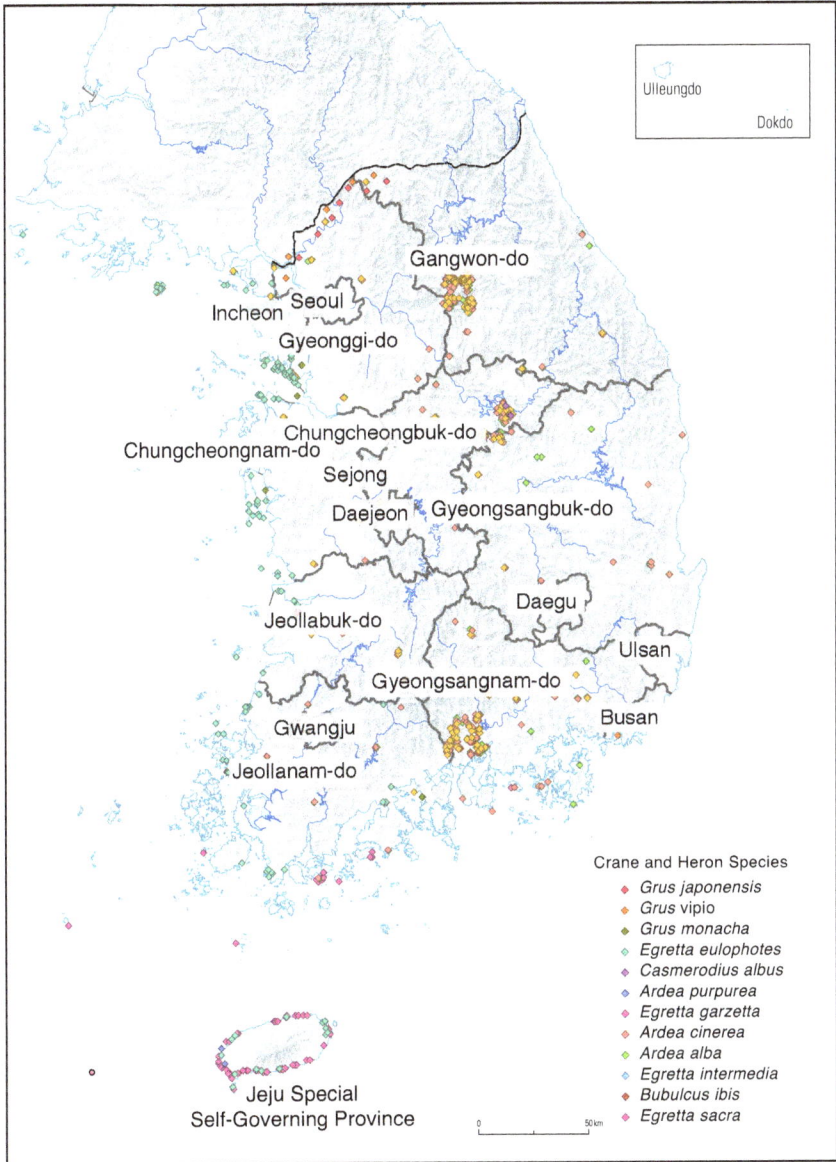

FIGURE GI.10. Distribution of crane and heron species in South Korea.
Source: The National Atlas of Korea II, http://nationalatlas.ngii.go.kr/pages
/page_708.php.

ern coast stand out for their dynamic geological features and biodiversity, especially when it is revealed during low tides. As a "coastal wetland that form[s] when mud is deposited by tides or rivers,"[13] the mudflats measure nearly 2,500 square kilometers and feature a rich, diverse ecosystem. By one estimate, these sites host no less than "2,150 species of flora and fauna, including 22 globally threatened or near-threatened species." Among the endemic fauna are mud octopuses (*Octopus minor*), deposit feeders like Japanese mud crabs (*Macrophthalmus japonica*), and fiddler crabs (*Uca lactea*), in addition to the 118 migratory bird species for which this area provides critical habitat.[14] Owing to this biodiversity, 1,284 square meters of South Korea's mudflats have been designated as UNESCO World Heritage sites.

Because of its mountainous terrain, only one-fifth of the peninsula can be used for agricultural cultivation. Some of the soil types in South Korea include inceptisol, entisol, ultisol, alfisol, andisol, mollisol, and histisol. Nearly 74 percent of land in South Korea carries inceptisol soil. Over two-thirds of the peninsula is composed of granite gneiss, which is a metamorphic rock. Consequently, according to experts in plant and soil science, "since the mineral composition is often similar to granite and weathering rates are slow, gneiss tends to lead to acidic, poorly developed soils."[15] Acidic soils are widely distributed throughout the peninsula. The high relief of the land caused by the mountainous nature of the country, along with heavy precipitation, impacts the state of soil on the peninsula. In particular, erosion has been a major factor behind the disruption of soil. The organic matter of the soil has been declining since the early twentieth century. Between 1936 and the 1960s, soil organic matter fell from 3.3 percent to 2.6 percent in Korea (the soil organic matter of productive agricultural soil ranges between 3 and 6 percent). Soil deficiencies led to the growing use of chemical fertilizers for modern agricultural endeavors starting in the 1920s. The application of chemical fertilizer and pesticides dramatically increased in South and North Korea starting in the 1960s, which has spurred a drive to reverse the chemicalization of soil in South Korea through organic agriculture (discussed in more detail by Yonjae Paik in chapter 8). Still, whether by means of organic or chemical fertilizers, land in North and South Korea continually requires an external stimulus to maintain the fertility of soil and to make the land productive for agricultural cultivation, which increases costs. In South Korea, this issue has particularly led to drives to purchase land outside the country to produce feed for livestock in order to meet the demand for beef by consumers—an insatiable process of consumption that, as the essays in part 3 suggest, hold profound economic and cultural implications for the country.

The biodiversity on the Korean peninsula is rich and complex, with its variety of species and its textured and layered landscape that includes wetlands, water bodies, forests, and mountains. Its mountainous terrain and lush forests, in particular, give the peninsula its distinctive qualities in comparison to areas outside of North and South Korea. The peninsula's nonhuman features, of course, have never been immune to changes and transformations, as the discussions in this book make clear. Biological, geological, chemical, and climatic forces have shaped and reshaped land, water, and air over time, to say nothing of the politics surrounding them. The pace, degree, and scale of these influences and the changes produced from them have always depended on the geo- and biophysical makeup of the peninsula. Yet, nonhuman forces alone have not been the main agents of continuity or change in the environment. Humans and their built systems have also indelibly constituted and transformed the environment, as well as shaped the way the environment is represented through anthropocentric constructed narratives. Environmental change, as such, should be viewed as a process of dynamic interaction between human and nonhuman forces—a "dance" between nature and humankind that has configured both landscapes and people's lives. At different points of history, it has been delicate, forceful, or erratic. The chapters that follow capture these dances through intimate profiles of particular configurations of spaces, sites, and species. They engage in their own form of narrative construction to explore how the forces of nature, broadly defined, have collectively shaped and reshaped worlds on the Korean peninsula.

Part 1
IMPERIAL
INTERVENTIONS

David Fedman

Situated on the far eastern edge of the Eurasian steppe, Korea has long occupied an interstitial position in northeast Asia. With more than five thousand miles of coastline, roughly 3,500 islets, and a rich seafaring tradition, Korea is also firmly enmeshed in the economic and political currents of the Pacific Rim. The peninsula, as such, has historically formed a key node in the circulation of, among other things, ideas, peoples, and materials across the Asia-Pacific. Korea's borders and governing institutions may have changed over time, but the broader currents of circulation have remained a fact of life in the peninsula, shaping everything from flora to fauna, religion to diplomacy.

If the peninsula's place at a crossroads of Asia has linked it to these broader currents, it has also exposed Korea to foreign incursions. One such invasion—the subject of chapter 1—began in 1231, when the Mongol empire launched a series of military campaigns against the Koryŏ dynastic kingdom (912–1392). This destruction in many respects paled in comparison to that wrought during the Imjin War, a conflict precipitated by the Japanese warlord Toyotomi Hideyoshi's ruinous invasion of Korea in the closing years of the sixteenth century. Four centuries later, Japanese soldiers, settlers, and traders returned to Korea, this time under the banner of high imperialism. After years of jockeying with French, British, Chinese, American, and Russian interests for influence over Korea's markets and politics, the Japanese eventually cemented their control, establishing a protectorate in 1905 before annexing Korea in 1910. Liberation from Japanese rule in August 1945 only revealed for many Koreans that they would be swapping out one occupying force for two new ones—the Soviets in the north and the Americans in the south. So began the national division of Korea, setting the stage for a calamitous war that would carve into the landscape legacies still visible today.

Each in their own way, these foreign occupations left a lasting impression on Korean environments. They were, for one thing, highly destructive and disruptive takeovers, clearing the way for large-scale interventions in the landscape and environmental governance. Warfare profoundly altered Korea's environments, but so too did reconstruction. Imperial administrations and military governments introduced a host of land-use policies, regulations, and techniques. Some were geared toward facilitating land expropriation and resource extraction. Others were meant to stamp the Korean landscape in the mold of foreign environments by transplanting botanical specimen and agricultural practices from abroad. Even in their absence, these military incursions left a legacy on the land. The seemingly ever-present threat of invasion instilled in Korea's military and political leadership a rightful concern with national defense—a reality that, as John S. Lee shows in chapter 1, held sway over natural resource conservation across generations.

Foreign efforts to remake and rule over Korea's environments were more than simply utilitarian. As both chapters in part 1 make clear, they were also tied to broader efforts to control communities, impose order, and uphold imperial hierarchies of power. Whether by leveraging new technologies or appealing to their own traditions of environmental stewardship, occupying administrations drew on discourses of civilization and progress to lend credence to their claims of enlightened rule. At the same time, they used the levers of environmental policy— new laws, institutions, and surveillance systems—to tighten their grasp over agrarian life and rural society. In enclosing woodlands, establishing ranches, and constructing dams, imperial administrations sought to not only harness the productive power of the land but also reorganize society. In this sense, foreign interventions in Korea's landscape should also be understood as ideological enterprises linked to broader efforts to assimilate subjects and inculcate imperial fealty. Indeed, as much as these occupations introduced new materials to Korea—nonnative trees, say, or new types of fish—they also promoted new ideas about environmental rule that outlived most imperial institutions.

Such efforts, of course, did not always go as planned. It was one thing to temporarily prop up an occupying force; it was another altogether to implement sweeping environmental reforms long term. Plants and animals that traveled alongside settlers and scientists sometimes fared poorly or ran amok. With new connections to the region and the world came new nodes for the diffusion of pathogens, viruses, and other portmanteau biota. Weather events and natural disasters conspired against the edicts of warlords and the blueprints of engineers. Peasants, moreover, often pushed back. Far from case studies in all-powerful imperial agents unilaterally imposing their agenda, efforts to remake Korean environments were marked at every turn by both *negotiation* and *contingency*. The Sup'ung Dam is an instructive case in point. There, as Joseph Seeley shows in chapter 2, monumental visions of industry collided with complex realities on the ground, giving rise to a project of riparian improvement that transformed far more than the energy infrastructure of the region.

Once lodged in the soil, let loose into pastures, or promulgated into law, these imperial interventions took on new life, accruing additional layers of significance, meaning, and utility over centuries. All the more reason, then, to look deep into Korea's preindustrial past to understand the processes underlying the ideological and material construction of Korean nature. Behind nationalistic claims to a seemingly timeless and distinctive Korean nature lie traces of a far more complex and interesting transnational history of imperialism, one that etched a unique signature in the landscape. The next two chapters illuminate key episodes of this transnational history, adding new depth to our understanding of the very nature of what Ann Stoler has called "imperial debris." They show us how to recover traces of imperialism from the historical record and what Korea's place between empires meant for the natural world.

1

A STATE OF RANCHES AND FORESTS

The Environmental Legacy of the Mongol
Empire in Korea

John S. Lee

In 1270, the Mongols attacked a last group of holdouts huddled in Korea's south-western islands. The struggle, known as the Sambyŏlch'o Rebellion, concluded with the Koryŏ dynasty (918–1392) firmly under the thumb of the Mongol Yuan empire (1271–1368).[1] The invaders then set their eyes on the Japanese archipelago. In preparation for ill-fated expeditions in 1274 and 1281, the Mongols corralled horses and ranches to supply their cavalry and felled swaths of timber to build the necessary ships. The majority of these resource drives ran through the southwest of the Korean peninsula, across the coasts of present-day Chŏlla Province and particularly into the three thousand islands that dot Korea's southern and western waters.

In this chapter, I argue that the Yuan pattern of resource utilization in southwest Korea, namely their extensive ranching and forestry practices, left a significant institutional and environmental legacy. The ranches (목장 牧場) that they established in the southwest did not die with the Yuan; rather, the ranches were continuously managed and even expanded under the Chosŏn dynasty (1392–1910). The Mongolian horses that the Yuan imported into the peninsula mixed with native Korean strains to produce the Jeju horse, mainstay of Chosŏn transportation and cavalry. The same pine stands sourced by the Mongols for their fleets would be subsequently protected by early Chosŏn bureaucrats. Even when some southwestern ranches fell into disuse in the seventeenth century, the old pastures transitioned into pine stands, providing the timber-hungry late Chosŏn government with another source of state forests.

The common materiality of horses and pines invites a broader, world-historical perspective into Korea's history and environment. Historical studies by Pekka

Hämäläinen, Peter Mitchell, Greg Bankoff, Sandra Swart, and Pamela Crossley have highlighted, in rich fashion, the role of the horse in the transformation of settlement patterns, ecologies, and modalities of social structuration and resource extraction across the preindustrial world.[2] A growing body of scholarship has also examined the role of the horse in the making of Eurasian steppe empires.[3] A study of Mongol environmental legacies in a northeast Asian littoral can diversify our understandings of the relationships among horses, humans, and a broad nexus of institutional and environmental change.[4]

The intersection of empire and environment that I mark here is not one of mere resource extraction and native response. Nor is it one of overwhelming biological expansion by a foreign body.[5] The fitting metaphor is that of the palimpsest, the medieval texts that scribes would erase and write over while leaving the original work detectable to a careful observer. Likewise, a long historical view of southwestern Korea between the thirteenth and seventeenth centuries reveals a palimpsest of shifting populations, new species, and old ideas. Foreign invasion, material extraction, new imports, and more expansive institutions—the paraphernalia of empire—were catalysts in a long process, initial imprints in the landscape that successors would write over but not completely erase. The making of an agrarian bureaucracy in Chosŏn Korea occurred over landscapes shaped by Mongol ranches and equine cultures.

In preindustrial Korea, the impact of the Mongol conquests is best understood through a centuries-long perspective that focuses not on the initial burst of imperial contact but rather on the gradual shifts in sylvan and equine ecologies and institutions that become visible in the *longue durée*. The Mongols did not convert Korea to a pastoral society; nor did they overthrow the indigenous elite. Their impact was transformative in the long term, in the pastures and pines that sustained fleets centuries after the Mongols departed and in the powerful bureaucratic institutions that corralled sylvan and equine resources and ensconced the centrality of the state in Korean lives, both human and nonhuman.

Yuan Ranches and the Making of the Jeju Horse

Archaeology traces domesticated horses to the earliest states on the Korean peninsula. Like almost all northeast Asian horse breeds, Korean horses split from the Przewalski's horse (*Equus ferus przewalskii*) between 120,000 and 240,000 years ago. The resultant Korean horse used in the Three Kingdoms and Unified Silla period was similar to the famed Mongolian breed: short, stocky, and tolerant of cold, with no need for horseshoes.[6]

The Koryŏ dynasty arose through military conquest and continued to require horses for military campaigns against Jurchens in the north and for internal pacification within the peninsula. The early Koryŏ state recognized Jeju Island, referred to in premodern times as T'amna (탐라 耽羅), as a prime source of horses. The volcanic isle's rocky lava forms render many areas unfit for agriculture but quite suitable for pastures and forests (a topic taken up more fully by Jeongsu Shin in chapter 8).[7] Regular requisitions of Jeju horses date back to 1025, and legal stipulations regarding the proper care of Jeju horses can be found as early as 1071.[8] Horses were fed different crops and portions based on fourteen different grades, with warhorses receiving the most portions.[9] Thus, even before the Mongols arrived, statist management of horses was already in place.

What the Mongols did was dramatically intensify the process of horse management on the southern islands. After completing the conquest of southern Korea in the 1270s, the Mongols established an extensive set of ranches on Jeju Island, staffed by 1,700 troops. Across the southern coastal regions of Koryŏ, the Yuan also established various myriarchies (만호부 萬戶府), military districts that headquartered troops and administered surrounding areas.[10] In this initial Yuan resource drive into Korea's south, Jeju was the centerpiece. The Yuan dynasty treated Jeju Island as a separate administrative zone, the country of T'amna (탐라국 耽羅國), distinct from the rest of Koryŏ.[11] Most importantly, the island was listed as one of fourteen "imperial ranch districts" (牧區) established by the Yuan throughout their empire.[12]

The Mongols instituted eight main ranches across the western and eastern ends of Jeju Island and imported Mongolian horses to fill the pastures. The first recorded imports are 160 Mongolian horses that arrived on Jeju in 1276.[13] They quickly interbred with native Korean strains. Cavalry steeds were the early priority. Jeju and other southern islands such as Hŭksan were seen as convenient bases for attacking the Southern Song dynasty and the Japanese archipelago.

Even after the failure of the Japanese invasions, the Mongols continued to expand ranches on Jeju Island. Donkeys, mules, oxen, pigs, even deer, dogs, and falcons were added as managed stocks.[14] Most of all, the horse population continued to grow. Thanks to steady Mongol imports and strict protections, Jeju held between twenty thousand and thirty thousand horses by 1373.[15] The by-product was the Jeju horse, a mix of Mongolian and Korean strains—an offspring of empire (figure 1.1).

Imperial impositions affect both inflows and outflows of resources, and horses were no different. The Yuan demanded numerous types of tribute from their Koryŏ vassals, including horses, and the Mongols could also freely extract livestock from their Jeju ranches. In 1287, the Yuan established a livestock administration office to manage the requisition of horses.[16] Six years later, in 1293, Jeju

FIGURE 1.1.   The Jeju horse. *Source*: Wikimedia Commons, Cheju mayuksŏng t'im, https://commons.wikimedia.org/wiki/File:Jeju_horse_(mother_and_daugh ter).jpg. Creative Commons License (CC-BY-SA-4.0).

islanders presented the Yuan court with a tribute of four hundred horses.[17] Throughout the 1290s, the Yuan court continued to send officials to assess Jeju horse stocks and take them back to northern China.[18] Koryŏ royalty also participated in the exchanges. For instance, in 1296, King Ch'ungnyŏl (1236–1308) sent a wedding gift of eighty-one white horses to the Yuan emperor.[19] The number eighty-one was particular noteworthy; the number nine and its multiples possessed special religious significance among the Mongols.[20]

By the mid-fourteenth century, the Yuan empire was falling apart, and the Mongols were on the retreat from the Korean peninsula. Their horses, however, stayed on Jeju. The late Koryŏ government continued to maintain a Livestock Management Office (司僕寺), and the Chosŏn government used the office to administer the Jeju ranches and even expand state-controlled pastures throughout the southern islands.

Moreover, the Yuan's successor, the Ming dynasty (1368–1644), continued to request the Jeju horse as part of the revamped tribute system. When Chosŏn King T'aejong (r. 1401–1418) sent a herd of Jeju horses to the Ming Yongle emperor (r. 1402–1424), Yongle supposedly exclaimed, "These are heavenly horses [天馬]! Truly, your king loves me."[21] According to Chosŏn official Hŏ Kyun (1569–1618), the Ming emperor was so impressed by the Jeju mounts that he ordered the composition, "Ode to the Heavenly Horse" (天馬歌).[22] Even after the Yuan fell, horses from Jeju would continue to stream into northern China, as part of an exchange and as a breed forged by a previous empire.

Mongol Fleets, Divine Winds, and Koryŏ Pines

The Yuan impact on Korean environments was not limited to horses and pastures. Southwestern Korea is also part of a rich coastal forest zone ideal for timbering and shipbuilding. The Mongols, with their characteristic alacrity, recognized the area's potential. Even before they had fully crushed the Sambyŏlch'o holdouts, Mongol generals ordered significant amounts of timber to be extracted from Jeju and other southern islands such as Hŭksan. In 1272, the vassalized Koryŏ government established a Warship and Army Supply Supervisory Bureau to aid Mongol preparations for invading Japan. In turn, the Mongols ordered 1,500 ships built in 1279 and another 3,000 built in 1281 in shipyards across China, Manchuria, and Korea.[23] They demanded nine hundred ships from Koryŏ alone in 1274 and another nine hundred in 1280. Much of the shipbuilding timber came from Haenam and Pyŏnsan in Chŏlla Province—precisely the same areas that would later supply the Chosŏn dynasty for centuries with high-quality timber.[24]

Both the 1274 and 1281 invasions met untimely ends due to fierce Japanese resistance and propitious typhoons. Parts of the Yuan fleets have been left to posterity thanks to the efforts of nautical archaeology. One such archaeologist, Randall Sasaki, has analyzed the timber remains of sunken Yuan vessels discovered off the coast of Kyushu in the early 1980s. His research attests that most of the sunken vessels, particularly the larger warships, originated from eastern China. Korean-made vessels, distinctive for their wide, flat bottoms and heavy use of pine and wooden joinery, were not numerous at the Kyushu site. Sasaki's argument corroborates evidence that Korean warships did not suffer casualties commensurate to those of larger Chinese vessels made of camphor and fir species from the Yangzi River delta.[25]

The Mongol reliance on Chinese timber for larger warships partly confirms a trend toward pine dominance in Koryŏ-era Korean forests. The most common Korean pines, *Pinus densiflora* and *Pinus thunbergii*, are shade-intolerant, secondary-growth species that prosper after deciduous competitors have been reduced. Historical surveys of construction material conducted by Pak Wŏn'gyu and Yi Kwanghŭi indicate that oak was the prevailing material during ancient times and the Three Kingdoms era (57 BCE–668 CE), constituting 94 percent and 57 percent, respectively, of surveyed sites. In contrast, pine composed

6 percent of surveyed Three Kingdoms–era edifices. Then suddenly, in the Koryŏ era, pine took on 71 percent of surveyed construction material, a dominance that only intensified in the early to mid-Chosŏn (73 percent) and late Chosŏn eras (88 percent).[26]

Why did pine suddenly become so prominent in the Koryŏ era? Korean forest historians tend to blame the Mongol invasions. According to this argument, the decades of warfare between 1231 and 1273 decimated much of the Korean landscape. Fast-growing succession species such as pine then prospered in the Mongols' deadly wake.[27] Considering the immense number of people killed and towns destroyed during the Mongol invasions, there may have been barren areas where pine succession transpired. However, war tends to fog evidence about where, when, or whether such ecological devastation occurred. Post-invasion Yuan policies, such as the imperial ranches and shipbuilding, I argue, had a far more lasting, well-documented impact on Korean environments.

Cultural predilections further solidified pine's dominance. Protection of trees, particularly pines, was central to early Koryŏ geomantic beliefs that tied terrestrial management to political legitimacy and cosmic order.[28] When a major insect infestation afflicted pine trees around Kaesŏng in 1102, the state ordered Buddhist monks to exorcise the pests by chanting the Flower Garland Sutra for five days. Afterward, the government dispatched soldiers to remove the pests.[29] The capital, Kaesŏng, was even alternatively called Songdo (松都), the City of Pines.[30] Accordingly, it is plausible that a combination of climate, culture, invasions, and Yuan policies significantly shifted the content of Korean forests between 918 and 1388 toward pine. By the mid-fourteenth century, as the Mongols retreated from the Korean peninsula, Koryŏ elites were privileging the ubiquitous, easily workable pine over all other trees, which they collectively dismissed as "miscellaneous" (잡목 雜木). For instance, the poem "Woodcutting Youth" (초동 樵童) by Yi Saek (1328–1396) narrates the labor of a young woodcutter logging copious pine stands around Kaesŏng amid "not a single miscellaneous tree."[31] In later centuries, Chosŏn policies would forbid the cutting of pine across hundreds of state forests across the peninsula while still permitting the removal of miscellaneous trees. Ongoing ecological transitions, perhaps accelerated by the Mongol invasions, elevated the pine to the top of Korea's institutional and ecological hierarchy into the late fourteenth century and beyond, with significant consequences for the rest of Korean history.

Meanwhile, with Yuan power waning, King Kongmin (1330–1374, r. 1351–1374) tried to reassert central control over resources, including woodland areas. In 1356, Kongmin complained that "groups of disloyal officials are arbitrarily seizing forests and marshes and exacting copious revenues from them. [Consequently], state expenditures [국용 國用] wane by the day, and the people's lives and incomes wither. Henceforth, forests [산림 山林] will be placed under the authority of the Construction Directorate [繕工寺] . . . to loosen restrictions [on their use] and lighten exactions."[32] Unfortunately for Kongmin and the Koryŏ dynasty, it would take a new regime to reassert full bureaucratic control over the peninsula's forests. The Chosŏn dynasty would unleash a new wave of institutions aimed at corralling ranches and pine forests for state use.

Ranches and Forests in a Post-Mongol State

The Chosŏn dynasty can be considered a post-Mongol successor state in the same vein as the Ming (1368–1644), Timurids (1370–1507), and Muscovy (1283–1547).[33] Chosŏn's founder, Yi Sŏnggye (1335–1408), was the son of a military officer who had served the Mongols in the northern border region. Key officials such as Chŏng Tojŏn (1342–1398) and Kwŏn Kŭn (1352–1409) were pupils of the aforementioned Yi Saek, a man who, like his father Yi Kok (1298–1351), had passed civil examinations in Yuan China and returned to Koryŏ soaked in the intellectual ferment of Dadu. And of course, along the southern coasts and islands, the descendants of Mongolian horses roamed across pastures amid rows of verdant pines.

Following the Mongol example, the Chosŏn government quickly instituted new regulations to secure coastal pine forests for the shipyards. As early as 1407, the Chosŏn government promulgated orders to all magistrates throughout the country to plant pine trees for naval timber. A court memorial from that year noted that "recently, pine tree stands have been almost exhausted" because of the demands of warship construction. The report recommended that felling and fires be banned in "all forests where pine trees could feasibly grow."[34]

The Koreans were motivated by the rising threat of maritime raiders, known in records as the Waegu (왜구 倭寇), from the Japanese archipelago. By the turn of the fifteenth century, the island of Tsushima, nestled in the Korea Strait between southern Korea and western Japan, had achieved notoriety as a pirate den. The island's mountainous terrain hampered conventional agriculture while its geographic position eased coastal raiding. Even after Korean governments launched two expeditions to subdue Tsushima in 1389 and 1396, the islanders did not cease their raids.[35] In 1418, a series of famines struck Tsushima, prompting an intrepid group to sail out and attack Ming China. Along the way, the islanders ransacked the southern Chŏlla coast and destroyed numerous Chosŏn warships in Ch'ungch'ŏng Province.[36]

In response, a frustrated Chosŏn government planned its largest campaign against Tsushima to date. In the summer of 1419, a Chosŏn armada of 226 warships and 17,885 troops stormed into the Korea Strait and attacked Tsushima; during a month-long campaign, Chosŏn soldiers burned 2,007 houses, destroyed 124 ships, and beheaded 123 raiders.[37] Then, wary of the coming typhoon season, Koreans left the island in late July while threatening to attack again in the autumn if the islanders did not stop their raids.[38] The ruling Sō clan of Tsushima, in response, agreed to rein in their raiders in exchange for limited trading privileges in southern Korean ports.[39]

Using the same bases and resources as did the Mongols, the Chosŏn state temporarily crushed the Waegu threat. The pressing need for warships, moreover, locked the Chosŏn government into further dependence on the coastal pine forests. Over the course of the 1420s and 1430s, the Chosŏn government cordoned off hundreds of pine forests as Restricted Forests (금산 禁山) for state use. Pine timber from these state forests were to be reserved for warship, government edifice, and coffin construction.[40]

Simultaneously, southern ranches also expanded under the new regime. In 1407, the same year Chosŏn launched its first major forest regulations, the government also assigned forty-eight officials to manage the eight ranches across Jeju and made plans to expand the number of horses.[41] Horses were designated not only for cavalry but also for post stations and the Ming tribute system. Similar provisions were made throughout the 1420s and 1430s to expand ranches across the southern islands.[42] The government managed and expanded ranches using the Livestock Management Office from the Koryŏ era, placing it under the authority of the Board of Military Affairs (兵曹). Additionally, military officials such as deputy cavalry commanders and deputy naval commanders were put in charge of dozens of designated ranch areas.[43] Beneath the new wave of bureaucratic personnel were thousands of corvée herders (목자 牧子) who actually managed the ranches.[44] Intense designation of bureaucratic personnel to ranches fit the early Chosŏn pattern of government expansion, an expansion that delved not only into pastures and forests but also into land reclamation, military mobilization, and even social behavior and burial rites.

Interestingly, there was significant overlap between areas assigned as state ranches and as state forests. For instance, in 1454, the Board of Military Affairs ordered the expansion of ranches into the Haenam region of Chŏlla Province. Noting that the prospects for wet-paddy cultivation were poor in the area, the government ordered local naval personnel to cordon off parts of the region for ranching.[45] Haenam also happened to be home to six Restricted Forests.[46] The great majority of Chosŏn state forests in the south covered the same island and coastal regions where the state also established ranches. In the early fifteenth century, the Chosŏn government issued further regulations that restricted logging and banned slash-and-burn agriculture (화전 火田) within state ranches.[47]

Ecological transitions further entwined horse ranches and pine forests in south-western Korea. The domestic horse is a browser that prefers a mixed diet of grass, shrubs, flowering plants, and young trees. Horses will feed on young deciduous trees; however, they avoid most conifers, including pine.[48] The great white pine stands of New England are a by-product of the heavy grazing regime that proliferated in eastern North America during the early nineteenth century.[49] Decades of grazing lead to elimination of hardwoods and leave open, weaker seedbeds in which the shade-intolerant pine prospers. Thus, one can add a Mongol legacy—the Jeju horse and the wide institutionalization of ranches—to the causes of intense pine proliferation that so influenced Chosŏn-era policies and environments.[50]

The transition of ranches to "pasture pine" intensified in the seventeenth century. After the Imjin War (1592–1598), the Chosŏn government placed increasing emphasis on warships and gunpowder weaponry at the expense of cavalry. Wartime refugees and population growth in the southwest further threatened the old pasture zones. In 1635, an official from the Livestock Management Office complained that only forty-six out of the 119 state ranches were actually raising horses. Most had become overrun with wartime refugees reclaiming them into paddy land.[51] Since arable land and timber could potentially replenish a state depleted by war, the Chosŏn government accordingly encouraged land reclamation for agriculture and the expansion of state forest zones.[52] As one Chosŏn official put in 1680: "In one year, one reclaimed field could recoup the value of several horses. Why not move the horses and let people come into the islands to farm?"[53]

The number of horses on state ranches precipitously declined in the latter half of the Chosŏn dynasty, falling from an estimated forty thousand animals in 1470 to half that number in 1678.[54] Quality of stock also diminished. By the early nineteenth century, the scholar-official Chŏng Yagyong (1762–1836) was describing "so-called military horses" as "only as big as donkeys . . . and as small as rats," their bodies "infected with rashes and boils" from neglect and poor breeding.[55] In contrast, state forests and pines only increased in number and significance. In 1448, there were 291 state forests in Chosŏn Korea; by 1808, that number had expanded to 678 sites. The majority of the new forests were established in the Naktong River basin in Kyŏngsang Province and the island and coastal zones of southwestern Korea.[56]

Equine and Sylvan Legacies in the *Longue Durée*

Though the place of horses in Korean life declined, the environmental legacies of the Mongols were still visible in the twentieth century. In the 1930s, German geographer Hermann Lautensach observed that "no other part of Korea is as rich in pasture land as Jeju Island, and animal husbandry is accordingly nowhere more important. Particularly in winter one sees here large herds of ponies, cattle, and goats, a completely unaccustomed sight on the peninsula. . . . Jeju Island is by far the foremost horse raising area in Korea, with 70 percent of the total stock."[57] Meanwhile, just across the sea, he noted that the southwestern islands, what Lautensach called the "southern coast borderland," contained rich secondary forests "composed almost exclusively of pines."[58]

What I have presented here is a preindustrial case of long-term institutional and environmental change initiated by a foreign empire and broadened under a post-Mongol successor state on the Korean peninsula. This particular intersection of empire and environment was not one of mere imposition and drastic change—this was no Columbian exchange. The Mongol legacy can be seen in the Jeju horses, the southern pines, and the continuous, intensifying statist attempts between the thirteenth and seventeenth centuries aimed at shaping land and personnel for the sake of livestock and trees. The Chosŏn state influenced environments already shaped by Yuan policies. Pines and horses were corralled into institutional pathways paved by Yuan predecessors. In the twentieth century, colonial Japanese scientific management and its descendants would be laid over landscapes shaped by Chosŏn institutions, extending a palimpsest that requires a historian's treatment to unravel.

Finally, one must consider the view from the southwest and the islands. What was the Mongol-Koryŏ-Chosŏn transition from the perspective of the Jeju islander, the Haenam fisherman, or the Pyŏnsan woodcutter? I end here with a proposal to reconsider processes of state formation on the Korean peninsula. Conventional narratives regarding Chosŏn Korea focus on Confucianization and the rise of a Sinitic high culture, particularly the development of the *yangban* crescent that cuts from Seoul through the southern rice basket in Chŏlla and Kyŏngsang Provinces. There, a core elite dominated society for centuries through the maintenance of kinship networks, ascriptive status, and landed assets.[59]

In the southwestern borderlands, however, a dominant paradigm between the thirteenth and nineteenth centuries was not just Confucianization but also administrative expansion and environmental change. Alongside the *yangban* crescent and its role in the making of Chosŏn society, one must include the equine and sylvan crescents that curved through the western and southern coasts. It was there, in the islands in the southwest and among their pastures and forests, where the ambitions of Mongol generals and Chosŏn bureaucrats unleashed the long-term transformation of ecologies and institutions. There, the state transcended eras. Whether the ruler was Mongol, Koryŏ, or Chosŏn mattered less than the interplay between policies and processes on the ground, the changes in the land that drew government institutions into everyday life. For the people, flora, and fauna of southwestern Korea, the state was an organizing vehicle, a builder and restrictor of spaces, a collector and distributor of resources—a state of ranches and forests.

2

DAMMED FISH

Piscatorial Developmentalism and the Remaking of the Yalu River

Joseph Seeley

Between 1937 and 1940, Japanese colonial officials displaced approximately seventy thousand Chinese and Korean farmers along the Yalu River to make way for a massive new hydroelectric project. The Sup'ung Dam, second largest in the world at the time of its completion, was created to supply electricity for major industrial projects in Korea and Manchuria, two strategically vital realms of Japanese imperial governance. Sensing that it would be a "waste" not to utilize the massive reservoir created by the dam, colonial officials soon brought new tenants to the now-submerged spaces farmers formerly occupied.[1] These were millions of fish, whose scaly bodies were intended to fill the caloric needs of a growing Japanese empire in what was called the "world's number one fish hatchery."[2]

Japanese dam construction violently transformed the ecology and politics of the Sino-Korean border at the Yalu River. Drawing on sources in Japanese, Chinese, and Korean, this chapter shows how colonial dam construction led to a reimagining and reengineering of the river's fish ecologies that would outlast Japan's colonial rule and shape the postcolonial histories of North Korea and China. For centuries the Yalu formed a contentious northern boundary of the Korean peninsula. What fishing did take place in the river was limited in scale and racked by cross-border conflicts over riparian access. This changed with the Japanese takeover of Manchuria in 1931 and the outbreak of the Second Sino-Japanese War in 1937. Wartime exigencies drove Japanese colonial regimes in Korea and Manchukuo, previously divided over the question of fishing rights, to agree on plans to develop the Sup'ung Reservoir into a site for large-scale freshwater aquaculture. At the same time these plans were being drawn up, construction of the Sup'ung Dam was negatively affecting the Yalu's downstream fisheries. The complex legacies of this intervention in the Yalu's underwater ecologies remained after Japan's defeat in World War II. Even as postcolonial regimes in China and North Korea disavowed the legacies of the Japanese occupation, they shared with their predecessors a developmental logic that valued the aquacultural potential of the Sup'ung Reservoir over now-diminished native fisheries downstream. This cooperative, cross-border commitment to technologically intensive and interventionist forms of reservoir aquaculture over the conservation of preexisting fish populations, which I call "piscatorial developmentalism," has clear roots in Korea's colonial history and the attempt of Japan's wartime state to extract caloric as well as hydroelectric energy from the river.

The case of the Sup'ung Reservoir fishery offers a unique case study for understanding the environmental legacies of Japanese colonial rule in Korea and Northeast Asia more broadly. The ramifications of Japanese colonial rule for the peninsula's human history have been hotly debated, but only recently have scholars begun to turn their attention to the environmental consequences of the same period. Along with scientific forestry and other aspects of the colonial state's environmental policy, freshwater aquaculture was part of a similar imperial project to remake the productive capabilities of the landscape by harnessing "modern" scientific expertise and technology.[3] Previous historians have analyzed Yalu dam construction largely in terms of its human consequences, demonstrating how the Sup'ung Dam served as yet another tool of exploitative colonial power.[4] This chapter builds on these studies while also peering under the river's surface to highlight the impact of the dam's construction on the Yalu's fisheries. A focus on piscatorial developmentalism allows us to consider fish and their dynamic ecologies as important actants in the story of Korean state-led developmentalism and its colonial antecedents. As the case of the Sup'ung Reservoir shows, this project would have long-lasting consequences for the postcolonial environmental histories of the Democratic People's Republic of Korea (DPRK) and People's Republic of China (PRC), irrevocably changing the Yalu environment in ways that continue to shape the development of countries on both sides of the river border.

The Yalu as Contested Piscatorial Periphery

The Yalu River (Chinese: Yalu Jiang; Korean: Amnokkang 압록강; Japanese: Ōryokkō) originates 2,500 meters above sea level at its headwaters on Mount Paektu on the Sino-North Korean border before flowing approximately 803 kilometers (499 miles) westward into the Yellow Sea. It is the longest river on the

Korean peninsula and one of the major rivers of northeast Asia. The river has served as a political boundary between Korea and northeastern China for centuries. It is also home to more than seventy fish species, which have long ignored such artificial distinctions between human states.[5]

Local human populations had been fishing in the Yalu for millennia, but the boundary-crossing habits of their quarry did not attract protracted controversy until the early twentieth century, when fishing rights became a source of diplomatic dispute between Qing-dynasty China and a newly emergent Japanese empire. Japan's presence in the Yalu region was the result of successive military victories in the First Sino-Japanese War (1894–1895) and Russo-Japanese War (1904–1905). After the creation of a Japanese protectorate over Korea in 1905, the aggressive policing of Japanese and Korean fishing rights in the Yalu became another method of weakening China's sovereignty along the Sino-Korean border. While Sino-Japanese conflicts over marine fisheries have received greater scholarly attention, the case of the Yalu shows that Japan's piscatorial colonialism also extended into the riparian arteries of its growing continental empire.[6] After the creation of new "fishing districts" in April 1909, the protectorate regime began patrolling the lower Yalu and making plans to "threaten" Chinese fishermen operating in the region.[7] It also launched vigorous protests against Chinese authorities who attempted to "illegally" collect taxes from Korean fishermen.[8] These measures, in combination with the use of newer fishing net technology by Korean and Japanese fishermen, effectively pushed out a once-dominant Chinese presence from the river. In locales as distant as Shanghai, distraught Chinese journalists reported that Japan was "seizing" access rights to the Yalu from Chinese fishermen.[9]

Despite its geopolitical significance, Yalu fishing during this period remained a small-scale local industry. The primary fishing grounds of the Yalu contested by the two opposing sides was an eight-*li* (roughly thirty-kilometer) stretch near the river's mouth at the Yellow Sea. Until the creation of the Sup'ung Reservoir decades later, it was the only commercially viable fishery on the entire eight-hundred-kilometer-long river. The fishery products of greatest economic importance were shrimp and icefish.[10] Icefish, a thin, translucent fish native to freshwater environments throughout East and Southeast Asia, were considered by observers to be a particularly notable "specialty product" of the river.[11] Yalu icefish were valued for their size, which was larger than their counterparts in other parts of the Japanese empire. They were also harvested in greatest numbers during the early spring, when they traveled upstream to spawn, which lent them the moniker "cherry blossom icefish."[12] During this time, coastal fishermen would congregate in the river, with period accounts reporting that the springtime fishing boats were "as thick as a forest."[13] Yet in terms of overall economic value, the impact of this fishing was limited: in 1936, for example, the icefish harvest, at 54,623 yen, formed only 2.4 percent of the total value of fish harvested in surrounding North Pyŏngan Province, as marine fish species continued to be the primary focus of fishermen in the region.[14]

The seeming commercial insignificance of Yalu fisheries was one factor that encouraged the river's selection as a site of hydroelectric development. Beginning in 1921, eleven years after Japan fully annexed Korea as a colony, the Government-General of Korea's Communications Bureau began a multiyear survey of the maximum and normal streamflows of Korean rivers. This information would be used to construct the high dams necessary to supply electricity for regional industrialization and urbanization.[15] When engineers surveyed the Yalu, they noted the presence of a "few" full-time fishermen near the river's mouth, but otherwise stated that fisheries "would pose no obstacle to the selection of future hydroelectric sites."[16] In an effort to make the flowing river "legible" to engineers planning hydroelectric development, surveyors wrote the Yalu's underwater denizens completely out of their charts and equations.[17] The attitudes of hydropower proponents would have noticeable consequences for the river's fisheries.[18]

Sup'ung Dam Construction and the Beginnings of Yalu Fisheries Development

By the 1930s, Japan's imperial presence in Asia was expanding. Japanese forces invaded northeast China in 1931 and, a year later, declared the creation of Manchukuo, a Japanese puppet state. With territory on both sides of the Yalu now under Japanese control, colonial officials launched an intensive industrialization program to make Korea and northeast China key "supply bases" for further expansion into continental Asia.[19] This required massive inputs of energy, of which hydropower seemed to be an obvious source.

Construction began in 1937 on the Sup'ung Dam (see figure 2.1), the first of seven projected dams on the Yalu, and soon after its effects were rippling out below the river's surface. In June 1938, major newspapers in Korea reported an unusual decrease in the annual springtime icefish harvest. Whereas the annual icefish catch typically yielded between 25,000–30,000 *kan* (or roughly 93,000–112,000 kilograms) of fish, as of late May 1938, fishermen had harvested only 4,000 *kan*, a fraction of the yearly average. The culprit for this "dramatic decline," newspapers reported, was the cement that flowed into the river from the dam construction site as well as railroad projects farther upstream.[20]

As contemporary observers worryingly noted, the decline of icefish harvests from Yalu River pollution was far from an isolated phenomenon. As a result of

FIGURE 2.1. Photograph of the Sup'ung Dam. *Source:* Wikimedia Commons, https://upload.wikimedia.org/wikipedia/commons/6/68/SupongDamAug2010 -2.jpg.

rapid industrialization in 1930s Korea and Manchuria, freshwater fish populations throughout the region were suffering from the unfiltered flow of industrial waste into major rivers. In an act of emerging environmental consciousness as well as anticolonial protest, editorialists in the Korean nationalist newspaper *Tonga ilbo* (동아일보) called for efforts to protect the Yalu icefish and other river fish populations. "The protection of Korea's special fishery products is not only an economic question, but also a vital issue of preserving unique local specialties and Korea's arts and culture," the newspaper argued.[21] In February 1939, the Government-General of Korea's Bureau of Agriculture and Industry promised to launch a survey of industrial pollution's effects on fish populations, which would also assess the potential installation and operation of waste filtration systems.[22] There is little indication, however, that such studies had any practical effect on colonial policy. Historian Katō Keiki notes that regulations on industrial pollution in colonial Korea and other parts of the Japanese empire were practically nonexistent, and that repeated calls by Korean observers to implement regulations similar to those that existed in the Japanese metropole were disregarded in the name of wartime exigencies.[23] As a result, fish populations in the Yalu and other colonial rivers suffered, along with humans, the negative consequences of unregulated industrial development and wartime mobilization.

At the same time the Yalu's icefish fishery was suffering from the effects of dam construction, however, hydroelectric development also sparked an unprecedented surge of interest in creating new fisheries farther upstream. Prior to the 1930s, very few scientific surveys of the Yalu's fish populations had been undertaken.[24] This relative disinterest in the Yalu's underwater resources reflected a greater focus by fishery scientists on more profitable coastal fisheries as well as difficulties stemming from the contested border politics of the Yalu.[25] But in 1938, the central Fisheries Experiment Station of the Government-General of Korea, located in the coastal city of Pusan, sent a team of technicians to conduct the first comprehensive survey of the Yalu's fish populations and assess potential paths for further fisheries development.[26] Among those dispatched to survey the Yalu was Chŏng Mun-gi, an ethnically Korean fisheries technician employed by the Pusan Fisheries Experiment Station. Although the vast majority of his colleagues were Japanese, Chŏng's prominent role on the Yalu survey team demonstrates that the ecological reengineering of the Yalu from 1937 to 1945 cannot be explained under the simple rubric of "Japanese expertise," as Aaron S. Moore has argued regarding Sup'ung Dam construction.[27]

In addition to systematically recording all the fish species in the river, another goal of the survey team was to assess the negative effects of Sup'ung Dam construction on preexisting fisheries and devise means to potentially mitigate this damage. As the team's leaders reported in the Korean-language *Tonga ilbo*, dam construction posed a significant "obstacle" to fisheries that had long been an important supplementary source of nutrition and income for local farmers.[28] Confronted with a massive concrete barrier that would cut off access for migrating fish from different parts of the river, technicians raised the possibility of constructing a fish ladder or "fish path" (Japanese: *gyodō*; Korean: *ŏdo* 어도) to help fish swim over the dam.[29] But projected maintenance costs had caused engineers from the Japanese-owned South Manchuria Railway Company to deem a Sup'ung Dam fish ladder "unnecessary" in an earlier 1937 report, recommending instead that reparations be made to local fishermen if the need arose.[30]

In addition to conducting taxonomic surveys and considering solutions for dam-related obstacles to fish migration, the Yalu survey team also proposed plans for increasing the river's fish yields. These proposals centered on using aquaculture to create a large-scale freshwater fishery in the Sup'ung Reservoir, which, upon completion, would be the largest man-made lake in Asia.[31] By constructing fish hatcheries and periodically releasing large amounts of fish eggs and juvenile fish into the lake, colonial Korean officials ambitiously predicted that the value of the Yalu's annual fish yield could be increased to 3–4 million yen from its previous value of only 60,000–70,000 yen.[32] Not to be outdone by their counterparts on the Korean side of the Yalu, in 1939 officials from Andong Province in the Japanese puppet state of Manchukuo also dispatched a team of fisheries experts to independently survey fish populations in the upper Yalu and its tributaries.[33]

While official rhetoric stressed "Korean-Manchurian unity" when it came to joint river development projects like the Sup'ung Dam, debates over Yalu fisheries exposed the limits of this "unity" at the border. The Japanese takeover of Manchuria in 1931 did little to dissipate conflicts over fishing rights between the Manchurian and Korean sides of the Yalu. A 1935 study commissioned by the South Manchurian Railway Company complained about colonial Korean officials' "monopolistic" policing of access to the lower Yalu fishery.[34] Throughout the 1930s and into the early 1940s, repeated failed attempts were made to reach a compromise on the issue. And just when a consensus between both parties finally seemed to be reached, in September 1940, talks collapsed again, caused by what one Korean newspaper called the "changing attitudes" of Manchukuo officials and the concerted pleas of Korean and Japanese fishermen "willing to die" before they yielded their three-decades-long control of the lower Yalu's icefish fishery.[35] Officials in Manchukuo and colonial Korea also disagreed over how to best use the reservoir that would be created by the Sup'ung Dam. This lack of consensus led to the suggestion that both sides either independently develop the reservoir as an aquacultural and scenic site or delegate the task to a newly created quasi-governmental corporation.[36]

Despite continued disagreements about fisheries development, the shared commitment of Manchukuo and Korean officials to Sup'ung Dam construction was already producing noticeable effects on the Yalu's social and natural ecology. As previously mentioned, icefish harvests in the lower Yalu declined appreciably in 1938, just after dam construction had begun.[37] These harvests stabilized by 1939–1940, though the threat of industrial pollution on local fish populations remained.[38] For approximately seventy thousand Korean and Manchurian farmers in the slated path of the Sup'ung Reservoir, the situation was bleaker. Whereas Korean and Manchukuo officials bureaucratically bickered on various points of Yalu development, in the name of cheap electric energy they were remarkably efficient at creating mechanisms to displace these populations in the reservoir's path. As Aaron S. Moore documents, the quasi-governmental Yalu River Hydropower Company purchased mass amounts of land from farmers, often at undervalued prices. When farmers protested such underhanded tactics, company officials then appealed to colonial law and the powerful arm of local police to enforce their actions. Forcibly displaced from their riverside homes, these farmers were relocated to colonization projects in northern Manchuria. As one journalist wrote sympathetically of these villagers' plight, "For those villagers forced to leave behind their beloved hometowns, land, familiar mountains and rivers, and their friends and family . . . can you really expect them to understand the policy of 'constructing a New Asia'? For them it is simply the greatest disaster of their lives."[39]

As the Sup'ung Dam project was uprooting human communities along the river, new plans were being made for the flooded spaces they would leave behind. Building on successive years of negotiation and fish population surveys, a group of forty colonial Korean and Manchukuo fisheries officials convened in July 1941 to discuss the future of Yalu fisheries, especially plans for the Sup'ung Reservoir. The shared imperial loyalties of these attendees allowed them to eventually overcome their divisions and reach a consensus on the future of the reservoir fishery. After discussion, both sides agreed to the plan suggested by the Government-General of Korea, which included the provisions that each government would separately build and administer fish hatcheries that would periodically release fish into the reservoir, and that these respective hatcheries would be distinguished by specific types of fish raised. Many of the fish species were not native to the Yalu River ecosystem. Indeed, while earlier surveys had been conducted to assess the potential of farming particularly "delicious" native fish on a commercial scale, the grand ambitions of fisheries planners favored the introduction of nonnative species that had already been successfully farmed in other parts of the empire. The colonial Korean hatchery would focus on raising salmon and pond loach, while the Manchukuo hatchery would raise eels and various types of carp.[40] The total budget was set at one million yen for what one newspaper heralded in hyperbolic terms as "the world's number-one freshwater hatchery."[41]

Fisheries officials participated in a process of ecological reengineering that mirrored patterns of biological displacement and introduction taking place throughout the Japanese empire. Poor farmers from Korea moved to rural Manchuria to work newly reclaimed land as agricultural colonists, while at the same time thousands of laborers were forcibly displaced from rural areas in Korea to work in Japanese factories and mines.[42] While these human populations were relocated to meet imperial ambitions, other organisms were undergoing a similar process of mobilization. As William Tsutsui documents, wartime mobilization meant the active reclamation of marginal lands, the encouragement of monocultural rice production in colonies such as Korea and Taiwan, and the large-scale extraction of timber resources from all corners of the empire.[43] In this milieu of biological mobilization, aquaculture and the transplanting of fish into new aquatic habitats formed an integral, if hitherto less-studied, part of imperial planning. As wartime exigencies meant an increasingly desperate scramble for fish protein, coastal ecosystems, lakes, rivers, ponds, irrigation canals, and rice paddies throughout the empire became home to fish species such as salmon, carp, and sweetfish, in an effort to shore up imperial food security.[44]

The Yalu and its biological populations were mobilized to provide caloric as well as hydroelectric energy for an increasingly resource-hungry Japanese empire.

In October 1943, fishery technicians moved thirty million sweetfish eggs from an aquacultural facility in the nearby Ch'ŏngch'ŏn River to the Sup'ung Reservoir. The results were "encouraging," officials reported, and thus provided the basis for additional aquacultural experiments in the reservoir the next year.[45] In February 1944 a team of technicians from the Pusan Fisheries Experiment Station further planted fifty million wakasagi (*Hypomesus nipponensis*) eggs in the reservoir.[46] By this time, Japanese strategic ambitions in the Pacific were taking a turn for the worse, giving further urgency to plans to turn the reservoir into a thriving new fishery. Wartime scarcity meant that more ambitious plans for the reservoir had to be scaled back. In 1944, for example, the budget for fisheries officials on the Korean side of the Yalu was only 209,217 yen, the bulk of which was supplied by the Yalu River Hydropower Company.[47] Yet despite budgetary limits, officials continued with their efforts to turn the Sup'ung Reservoir into the largest freshwater fishery in the region until Japan's defeat in World War II and the collapse of its continental empire in 1945.

Piscatorial Developmentalism and the Postcolonial Yalu

How did local colonized populations react to efforts to create the "world's number-one fish hatchery"? As the case of the decimated 1938 icefish harvest demonstrates, the effects of hydroelectric development posed potential threats to local fishing economies along the river.[48] Yet for those in closer proximity to the Sup'ung Dam, written testimony provides evidence of positive reactions to the fishing opportunities created by hydroelectric development as well. Reflecting on his youth on the Yalu's riverbanks, former resident Kim Tae-sin recalls, "I caught a large amount of fish in the Yalu. . . . Below the dam eels trying to ascend upriver would mingle in huge numbers. . . . There was also a lot of fish in the Sup'ung Reservoir."[49]

The fish planted in the Sup'ung Reservoir would outlast, at least briefly, the Japanese imperial presence in the region, though it was ultimately the technocratic legacies of piscatorial developmentalism that proved most resilient. Japan's defeat in World War II resulted in their total retreat from the Yalu region. In the resulting political upheaval, local fishermen took to using dynamite to stun fish and harvest them in large numbers.[50] Another former resident, Pak Sŏngnam, recalled, "In the Sup'ung Reservoir the fish were so plentiful you could catch them with your bare hands."[51] Such plenty would be fleeting, however, as the use of dynamite to catch fish and the disruptive effects of dam construction, which altered the river's temperature and flow, eventually took their toll. The widely destructive effects of the Korean War (1950–1953) also wreaked havoc on the reservoir's fish populations. Among the many stories that emerged from the conflict was that of hungry soldiers using hand grenades to extract fish from the Yalu River.[52] By the early 1960s, surveys conducted by Chinese and North Korean fisheries technicians noted that the numbers of "economically valuable" fish had declined precipitously.[53] The solution to this decline, these technicians suggested, was scientific aquaculture, demonstrating how quickly the methods and logic of piscatorial developmentalism were emulated by industrializing and equally resource-hungry postcolonial states on the Yalu River.

In 1959, fisheries technicians from the Democratic People's Republic of Korea (North Korea) and the People's Republic of China signed the first of many agreements on joint development of the Sup'ung Reservoir fishery.[54] In subsequent decades, fish yields from the reservoir would increase dramatically as China became the world's top country for fish farming and a leading proponent of what has since been termed the Blue Revolution, an aquacultural answer to the more well-known Green Revolution.[55] But, in a deliberate twist, early Japanese efforts to develop the aquacultural potential of the Yalu were purposefully forgotten. Eager to minimize possible continuities with the actions of Japanese imperialists in the region, a Chinese report on Sup'ung Reservoir aquaculture stated that "during the first period in the reservoir's history from 1943 to 1960 only primitive forms of fishing were carried out, while no measures whatsoever were taken to increase fish production."[56]

PRC and DPRK media alike portrayed Yalu fishery development as part of a broader effort to reclaim the river from its colonial past. A 1963 article in the PRC mouthpiece *People's Daily* contrasted the painful history of displacement caused by colonial dam construction with postcolonial development of the reservoir's resources, claiming that the former "lake of tears" was now an "inexhaustible treasure trove."[57] Meanwhile in 1963 the North Korean journal *Chosŏn susan* 조선수산 (Korean fisheries) proclaimed that reservoir fish yields were increasing thanks to the "brilliantly implemented" plans made by fisheries technicians. By 1965, another North Korean periodical boasted that "over 10,000 tons of fish" were being harvested annually from the reservoir built "with the sweat and blood of the Korean people."[58] Postcolonial regimes differentiated between colonial and postcolonial Yalu development, but both eras shared an emphasis on transborder exploitation of the Sup'ung Reservoir fishery.

The survival of the logic of piscatorial developmentalism into the postcolonial era would have dramatic effects on the Yalu's fish populations. Colonial dam construction altered Yalu water temperatures and the velocity of the river's current, a development that favored some fish species while harming others. The most severe ecological consequences of industrial development along the Yalu would be seen later in the twentieth century. Although icefish harvests in the lower Yalu stabilized by 1939–1940 following their initial precipitous drop in 1938, in succeeding decades the construction of three additional dams and increased industrial pollution, especially after the 1970s, caused native icefish populations in the river to nearly disappear.[59]

As the river's icefish fishery became more poisoned and unproductive, however, the scale and profitability of reservoir aquaculture increased exponentially, growing from an annual harvest of forty-seven tons in 1961 to three thousand tons by 1989.[60] In terms of purely utilitarian value, China's Blue Revolution, manifested at Sup'ung and in lakes and reservoirs throughout the country, has successfully lowered the cost of fish throughout the country and has been instrumental in shoring up the country's food security. Although rampant industrial pollution continues to affect the Yalu estuary near the twin border cities of Dandong and Sinŭiju, today the upstream Sup'ung Reservoir is touted as an "unpolluted" aquatic treasure trove that produces copious amounts of valuable fish. A 2018 special broadcast from the local Liaoning provincial station boasted how fish grown in Sup'ung, "Asia's largest net cage fish farming facility," were exported to South Korea as well as provinces all over China.[61]

In contemporary North Korea, Sup'ung aquaculture is also promoted as a means of securing essential food supplies for the resource-pressed state. Economic sanctions imposed on North Korea in retaliation for its pursuit of nuclear arms has spurred the regime to look to the country's rivers and lakes as a critical domestic source of protein. In 2017, the same year that the US government began pursuing a policy of "maximum pressure" toward North Korea and pushing the international community to implement further sanctions against the regime, North Korean media outlets published multiple articles promoting fish farming throughout the country. Such articles typically led with a quote from Supreme Leader Kim Jong-un, proclaiming the need to "not only farm fish in fish ponds," but also in "rivers and lakes."[62] By the end of the year, the *Rodong sinmun* 로동신문 (Workers' daily), official mouthpiece of the regime, proclaimed that 270 new mobile fish farming cages had been installed in lakes, rivers, and reservoirs throughout the country, including a thousand square meters of new cages in the Sup'ung Reservoir, and that overall output has supposedly doubled in the same period.[63] Just as Japan's wartime anxieties prompted a newly attentive gaze toward the piscatorial potential of the Sup'ung Reservoir, a seemingly hostile international climate around present-day North Korea has prompted the regime to more feverishly exploit the Yalu's aquacultural resources.

Environmental historians are often critical of dam construction's negative consequences for preexisting fish populations,[64] and the case of the Yalu certainly provides reason for caution as well. Although certain varieties of icefish are farmed in the Sup'ung Reservoir today, along with other fish species, the "cherry blossom" icefish that once congregated seasonally in the lower Yalu estuary now survive only in much reduced numbers. At the same time, the attraction of piscatorial developmentalism for ensuring reliably scalable quantities of fish for developing countries, much like the thousands of tons of fish now harvested from the Sup'ung Reservoir annually, seems sure. As people not just in Korea but all over the world grapple with the material and ethical implications of piscatorial developmentalism, an understanding of its imperial origins in Northeast Asia and its complex, ongoing consequences for the region's past, present, and future is essential.

Part 2
CRISIS AND RESPONSE

Eleana J. Kim

Building on our investigation of Korean environments and imperial relations from part 1, part 2 offers a deeper examination of the relationship between state power and environments. Indeed, the ability of states to maintain political legitimacy is closely tied to their ability to harness and access natural resources—to ensure the basic necessities for food, fuel, and shelter. When the supply of natural resources diminishes, whether from ecological changes or overexploitation, the material basis of economic life and social stability also comes under threat.

Given Korea's shifting status across several centuries as a tributary state, occupied colony, and divided Cold War nation, an environmental perspective can offer new insights into seemingly settled histories of war and militarization, as well as industrial development and urbanization. For instance, we can ask questions about how large-scale climatic shifts such as the Pacific Decadal Oscillation (PDO), a climatic pattern similar to the better-known El Niño, affected Korean fisheries during World War II and contributed to the weakening of the Japanese empire during a crucial phase in the total war effort. Or, as Sooa Im McCormick does in chapter 3, we could consider how the long-term consequences of the Little Ice Age, the period of climatic cooling between the fourteenth and nineteenth centuries, commonly associated only with Europe and North America, also affected the Korean peninsula. McCormick shows how the environmental changes induced by this cooling touched the very materiality of Chosŏn society, affecting everything from silks to ceramics.

When considering the period following the Asia-Pacific War, the relationship between states and environmental crisis appears to be inseparable from war and industrialization. The partition of the peninsula in August 1945 imposed a Cold War bipolar order onto the newly liberated Korean nation and set the two states on course for a bloody fratricidal war that has yet to be formally concluded. This division and the subsequent establishment of the DPRK in the north and the ROK in the south also cemented two different political and economic systems, which lay the ideological bedrock for inter-Korean enmity that has endured beyond the end of the Cold War.

The Soviet-style central state planning of North Korea focused its efforts on industrialization, expanding on the infrastructure built by the Japanese, particularly the mining of heavy metals and ores as well as manufacturing, processing, and chemical production plants. Before the national division, agricultural production had been concentrated in southern Korea, given its warmer climate and wider expanses of arable land. Following the war, therefore, South Korea lacked the North Korea's technical and infrastructural advantages. The DPRK boasted a more prosperous economy and higher standard of living until the end of the 1960s, when South Korea's state-driven industrialization efforts began to close the economic gap.

Even as the Cold War competition between the two states revolved around economic and industrial development, the environmental costs of the ROK's rapid development, particularly under President Park Chung-hee, did not go unnoticed by the DPRK. State publications like *Korean Nature*, published by the DPRK's Association for Nature Conservation, featured editorials such as one titled "Slaughter and Destruction without Gunshot," which echoed the antistate slogans of South Korea's nascent antipollution activists: "Today environmental pollution is highlighted as a grave social problem in capitalist countries, particularly as the gravest issue in south Korea, a cancer to the globe."[1] In contrast to the South Korean state's disregard for the toxic effects of industrialization, the DPRK, as Ewa Eriksson Fortier and Suzy Kim describe in chapter 5, articulated a commitment to environmental conservation and climate change as early as the 1970s. *Korean Nature* celebrated Kim Il Sung's environmental policies through articles such as "Korea, the People's Paradise Turning Ever More Fertile and Scenic."[2] Tellingly, however, the article betrays a high modernist approach to the environment—it is accompanied by a photograph of the Migok plain of Sariwŏn city (also the site of a major coal mine), with irrigated and industrialized agricultural fields as far as the camera-lens eye can see.

The warring nations' fortunes had swung dramatically by the 1970s, and with rates of GDP growth doubling and tripling under the authoritarian dictatorships of Park Chung-hee and Chun Doo-hwan, South Korea was approvingly dubbed by Western observers a Little Tiger economy. As a generation of critical scholarship in Korean studies has emphasized, the embrace of capitalist growth came with many costs—to workers' rights, women's liberation, children's welfare, and activists' futures—but also to sustainable ecologies. Indeed, on both sides of the DMZ, rapid industrialization and the effects of unending militarization contributed to the slow violence of environmental toxicity. In the south, unfettered development not only polluted the air and the soil but also produced unprecedented volumes of waste. In chapter 4, Hyojin Pak describes the material detritus collected at the site of Nanjido, Seoul's largest landfill, a social and ecological palimpsest recording the many layers of South Korea's compressed modernity. Over a few short decades it was converted from a riverine island into a "reclaimed" massive landfill, which later became the site of the 2002 World Cup stadium before being converted back into a green space, reflecting the efficiency with which the South Korean state has buried its socially and environmentally toxic pasts under an eco-friendly veneer, no less developmentalist in design.

In the DPRK, despite the state's stated commitments to environmental sustainability, decades of state planning policies prioritizing industrial agricultural production have resulted in soil degradation and deforestation at massive scale. With the fall of the Soviet Union in 1991, the DPRK lost its main source of petroleum, used for both fuel and fertilizers, and the mass immiseration and starvation of the North Korean people began. The conditions that McCormick describes in chapter 3 as taking place in late-seventeenth-century Korea were to return to North Korea in the 1990s, when a period of alternating floods and droughts led to widespread famine. An untold number—from hundreds of thousands to millions—of people died after scouring the land for any scrap of edible matter. International food aid began to enter the country in the early 1990s, yet a host of economic constraints, including the US-led sanctions regime, has impeded the goal of food security. Moreover, as Fortier and Kim describe in chapter 5, despite the diversification of some agricultural production, the north continues to be highly vulnerable to climate change disasters.

Today, many crises and disasters are facing Koreans on both sides of the DMZ, including COVID-19, epidemics like African swine flu affecting farm animals, the increasing prevalence of malaria, and flooding events dislodging landmines into civilian areas. This is to say nothing of extreme weather events related to climate change—more frequent and intense typhoons, longer periods of drought, colder winters, hotter summers, and rising sea levels. Addressing each of these will require decisive state action, yet despite the inclusion of cross-border concerns like infectious disease epidemics and environmental security in the Pyongyang Joint Declaration (signed by ROK President Moon Jae-in and DPRK leader

Kim Jong-un in September 2018), inter-Korean cooperation has been stalled. In the absence of peace and cooperation on the peninsula, future environmental disasters will likely lack the coordinated response required, and other solutions to mitigate the effects of the climate crisis on the lives of everyday people in Korea will be urgently needed.

3

THE POLITICS OF FRUGALITY

Environmental Crisis and Artistic Production
in Eighteenth-Century Korea

Sooa Im McCormick

Under the spell of scholarly reappraisal about late Chosŏn-period Korea, eighteenth-century Korea is generally perceived as "an age of peace and prosperity," governed by two sagacious monarchs: Yŏngjo and Chŏngjo.[1] Yet, while such roseate portraits of a golden age of the Chosŏn dynasty rightly highlight the emergence of a new faith in Korea's own history and culture, they often overlook deep-seated problems that beset Korea at that time.[2] One such problem, which has only recently come under the scrutiny of Korean scholars, was the occurrence of climatic oddities and their consequences for public health, economics, and politics. As Kim Tŏk-chin has shown, climate oddities were the direct cause of two different famines, both devastating: the first in the year of Kyŏngsin (1670–1671) and the second in the year of Ŭlpyŏng (1695–1696), which ended up wiping out between 23 to 33 percent of the Korean population.[3] Widespread natural disasters did not stop, but rather prevailed, threatening economic sustainability during the era, spanning the reigns of the Yŏngjo (r. 1724–1776) and Chŏngjo (r. 1777–1800).

In step with the recent wave of interest in the intersection of environmental studies and history, this essay examines the politics of frugality and its strong mark on the visual and material culture of eighteenth-century Korea. I will propose that the "modest," "austere," and "restrained" aspects of eighteenth-century Korean art were not driven simply by the Chosŏn ruling house's loyal adherent to neo-Confucian principles,[4] but rather were shaped by the state's response to climatic oddities, ecological changes, and the economic crises they precipitated.

From Summer Snow to Cannibalism

During the latter half of the seventeenth century, Korea experienced an unpredictable fluctuation of severely dry and cold spells leading to famines and epidemics. The environmental implications of these climatic changes were profound, as the following account from the time makes clear:

> In the summer of 1755, due to the three months of heavy rain, ears of rice rotted, and cotton flowers did not bloom. Thus, a very lean year was predicted. In some places like Pyongyang, day after day, floods were leaving many people homeless and some even dead. However, the government officials and *yangban* landowners paid no attention to this disaster and indulged in drinking.[5]

Numerous historians have remarked on the widespread social and political disorder and catastrophic climatic changes that troubled populations across the globe in the seventeenth century. The Little Ice Age, a term referring to an extended period of below-normal temperatures from the late fourteenth to the mid-nineteenth centuries, has been generally accepted as the main cause of these crises. Some scholars such as William Atwell have gone so far as to suggest that the Little Ice Age hastened the collapse of the Ming dynasty.[6]

Environmental historians generally agree that the effects of the Little Ice Age were felt most acutely in Korea toward the end of the seventeenth century.[7] In 1697, when famine was at its peak, King Sukjong (r. 1674–1720) had to make a desperate appeal to Qing Emperor Kangxi (r. 1661–1722) for food aid. At that time, thirty thousand sacks of rice were sent from the Qing court, ten thousand of which were immediately distributed.[8]

Compared to the second half of the seventeenth century, the situation in eighteenth-century Korea had improved slightly, but harsh weather, epidemics, high mortality rates, malnutrition, and the collapse of community were part of ordinary life.[9] Numerous daily logs compiled in royal archives such as the *Veritable Records* testify to unseasonable weather patterns throughout the century.[10] One such example, dated to 1709, attests that a layer of ice as thick as paper formed in the East Sea in the middle of August.[11] Recent bio-historical studies have demonstrated that lowered sea temperatures caused herring to form large shoals around the coasts of the Korean peninsula. At the time, the Chinese nicknamed the herring "Chosŏn fish."[12]

Never having fully recovered from the deadly famines at the end of the seventeenth century, the population growth rate remained exceedingly low, while the number of homeless approached its peak.[13] The harsh climate also drove starving people to commit savage crimes, such as cannibalism. The term *yin-*

sangsik (人相食), that is, "eating each other," frequently appeared in official records until the end of the eighteenth century.[14]

Yet, despite these conditions, scholarly representations of eighteenth-century Korea as "an age of peace and prosperity" prevail. This is especially true in the field of Korean art history.[15] Korean paintings that deal with genre scenes, collectively called *sŏkhwa* (속화), bucolic imagery of men tilling fields and women turning their spinning wheels, have been generally interpreted as "truthful" or "candid" documentation of Korea prospering under right-minded monarchs during the eighteenth century (figure 3.1).[16]

FIGURE 3.1. *Threshing*, attributed to Kim Hong-do (1745–after 1806), from the *Danwon Album*, late 1700s, Chosŏn dynasty (1392–1910). Album leaf; ink and light color on paper. *Source:* National Museum of Korea. Image Courtesy of National Museum of Korea, Deoksu 4917.

FIGURE 3.2.   Porcelain jar, 1700s, Chosŏn dynasty, Cleveland Museum of Art.
Source: Image courtesy of Cleveland Museum of Art 1983.28.

Such a perspective also looms large in the existing narrativization of Chosŏn-period ceramics and their visual features. The Metropolitan Museum of Art's 2001 publication, for example, affirmed that "in the late 14th century, with the adoption of Neo-Confucianism by the Chosŏn dynasty as the new state ideology and dominant social philosophy, the artistic tastes of the elite shifted dramatically in favor of simpler and more austere objects" (figure 3.2).[17] Kyŏng-suk Kang perhaps best captured this outlook when she wrote in her 2012 study that "Korean white porcelain demonstrates the Neo-Confucian principles, reaching its artistic apex in the 18th century."[18] The National Museum of Korea adhered to a similar logic when, in its 2015 exhibition catalogue, it described eighteenth-century prohibitions against the use of cobalt blue as an expression of the state's faithful adherence to neo-Confucian principles.[19]

These narratives, however, do not sufficiently explain why a large number of flamboyant types of blue-and-white porcelains were produced in fifteenth- and sixteenth-century Korea under the patronage of the same neo-Confucian Chosŏn state for royal consumption.[20] Such a simplistic view that singles out the metaphysics of neo-Confucianism in explaining modest, restrained, and austere aspects of eighteenth-century Korean visual and material culture, and even characterizes such aesthetic aspects as if they were part of the Korean cultural DNA, belies a complex correlation between ecology and economy.

Sumptuary Laws

Like other cultures, ruling houses in premodern East Asia exercised sumptuary laws, which aimed to restrain or regulate production and rein in overconsumption as a means of differentiating rulers' privileged authority.[21] The founder of the Ming dynasty in China, the Hongwu Emperor (r. 1368–1398), for instance, issued various edicts that regulated the size of tombs and the use of utensils, as highlighted in the following official legal code, called the *Statutes of the Great Ming*:

> Dukes, Marquises and officials of the First and Second Ranks might have wine pots and wine cups of gold, and for the rest use silver. Officials of the Third and Fifth Ranks might have pots of silver and wine cups of gold, while those of the Sixth to Ninth Ranks might have pots and cups of silver, for the rest making use of porcelain or lacquer.[22]

Hongwu's sumptuary laws, however, did not apply to the emperor himself or his inner circle, but were rather geared toward establishing strict hierarchical distinctions across social classes, a political necessity in the nascent Ming empire.

Eighteenth-century Chosŏn Korean rulers, by contrast, applied strict sumptuary laws on themselves more than anyone else. Such self-imposed sumptuary laws were deployed as a means to compel compliance by the ancient paradigm of Resonance between Heaven and People (天人感應). To realize a harmonious cosmos and to ensure heavenly blessings, rulers were supposed to act like moralistic sages who modeled Confucian ethics—filial piety, frugality, benevolence, and so forth.

The late seventeenth-century Chosŏn ruling house's discretion to consume expensive materials was exercised with great restraint because the state constantly suffered from serious budget deficits caused by successive tax relief programs for the victims of natural disasters, famines, and epidemics.[23] Dragon jars, for example, vessels reserved only for the king and crown prince, had to be painted in the more economical iron oxide rather than the expensive cobalt blue (figure 3.3). In some cases, pieces of paper bearing drawings of dragons in blue ink were glued onto the surfaces of white porcelain vases. Called faux-dragon jars, these cheaper alternative versions of blue-and-white porcelain jars furnished the tables of royal ceremonial feasts during the late seventeenth century.[24]

FIGURE 3.3. Jar with dragon and clouds design, late 1600s, Chosŏn dynasty, Cleveland Museum of Art. *Source*: Image Courtesy of Cleveland Museum of Art Leonard C. Hanna, Jr. Fund 1986.69.

Beginning in the second half of the eighteenth century, the royal house's self-imposed sumptuary laws became systematically implemented. In 1720, King Yŏngjo pointed to a frugal lifestyle as the only solution to control the state's shrinking budget, with rapidly growing expenditures.[25] To signal the royal court's status as a paragon of frugality, he appointed Pak Mun–su (1691–1756),[26] a court official well-known for his financial acumen, to publish various books that would lay the groundwork for the royal court to implement the strict sumptuary measures: *Rules and Regulation of the Board of Taxation* 度支定例 (1749), *Rules and Regulation of State Weddings* 國婚定例 (1749), and *Rules and Regulation of the Department of Weaving* 尙方定例 (1750). These new protocols aimed to cut unnecessary court expenditures by compelling the use of cheaper resources and the reuse of existing materials.[27]

Unfortunately, such self-imposed sumptuary laws did not produce satisfactory results in resolving the state's chronic budget deficit.[28] Nonetheless, they remained central to eighteenth-century Korean politics and soon became coupled with the program of fashioning the king's political persona as a "moralistic sage."

In fact, Yŏngjo and Chŏngjo successfully magnified their moralistic sagacity in the eyes of the public, and their political opponents. Their frugal lifestyles served as a powerful tool to justify their kingly authority and political decisions amid deepening ecological and economic calamities.[29]

Within and Beyond Neo-Confucian Principles

In their analyses of Korean white porcelain, leading Korean ceramic specialists such as Chŏng Yang-mo have proposed that "the newly found confidence in Korean cultural tradition in the 18th century was expressed in the style of white porcelains."[30] Kang Kyŏng-suk goes further to suggest that "Korean white porcelain reached its distinctive artistic climax in the 18th century." Kang, however, is puzzled as to why flamboyant copper-red glazed porcelains became popular in the period, a time in which Confucian ideals of austerity were widely promoted.[31] Kang's observation, which sharply contradicts the mainstream narrativization of eighteenth-century ceramic wares, expands the context beyond neo-Confucian aesthetics, challenging prevailing notions of Chosŏn-period art's inherent love for "modest" and "humble" materiality.[32]

After the devastating Imjin War (1592–1598), the quality of Korean blue-and-white porcelains drastically declined. Yet, Yŏngjo and Chŏngjo's sumptuary laws made it even harder for ceramic artists to conduct any experiments for technical advancement. In anticipation of widespread consumption of cobalt blue, thanks to its lowered price, Yŏngjo in 1754 issued a royal decree banning the use of cobalt blue except for decorating dragon jars.[33] His successor Chŏngjo continued the same more or less negative attitude toward luxury porcelain wares. In addition to continuing the ban on cobalt blue, he also prohibited the potters of the state kilns from using saggar, an essential device for the manufacture of multicolored, underglazed porcelain vessels.[34]

To date, many scholars have pointed to rulers' adherence to neo-Confucian principles or to their eccentric personal disdain of luxury to explain the decline of late Chosŏn blue-and-white porcelains. I argue, by contrast, that eighteenth-century sumptuary laws implemented in response to deteriorating ecological conditions were the primary cause.

Three natural ingredients are essential to making ceramic works: kaolin clay, firewood, and fresh water. Securing a steady supply of the first two ingredients had become extremely difficult in Korea by the eighteenth century. The highest quality of clay suitable for porcelain making came from Pongsan in Hwanghae Province, Sŏnch'ŏn in P'yŏngan Province, and Yang'gu in Kangwŏn Province.

The local governors resisted the central government's demands for kaolin clay on behalf of the villagers. In one account in the *Veritable Records* dated to 1714, the governor of Yang'gu pleaded to stop the central government's constant request for white clay.[35] Another account recorded in the *Veritable Records* reveals that Chŏngjo was empathetic about the laborious process of obtaining high-quality clay; he even identified the government's efforts to source high-quality porcelain works as a serious burden on the poverty-stricken public's livelihood.[36]

To make matters more difficult, finding and securing a steady supply of fuelwood for the kilns was no easy task in a time of fierce competition over forest resources. Scholars like Chung Jung-nam have made a convincing case about the correlation between the widespread usage of the underfloor heating system known as *ondol* in eighteenth-century residential buildings and extremely cold winter conditions during the Little Ice Age. According to Chung, the widespread use of underfloor heating systems, from the top to the bottom of Chosŏn society, compounded fuel demands, thereby accelerating deforestation.[37]

A wide range of written accounts from the late eighteenth century testifies to the scarcity and rising cost of firewood. Ch'ae Chae-kong (1720–1799), for example, complained that the cost of firewood, which previously was only 8–9 *nyang*, had risen to 30–40 *nyang*. About the dearth of trees, Chŏng Yak-chŏn (1758–1816) later lamented that "even if a rich person died in the countryside, it would take at least ten days to find sufficient wood in order to build a coffin."[38] The Chosŏn government's tax policies only exacerbated deforestation. By granting tax exemptions to those who converted unused land or mountainsides into arable land, they incentivized the burning and clearing of forests.[39] Even famous scenic spots such as pine forests in Samilp'o were not spared from fire-field cultivation.[40]

The extreme shortage of firewood was no small obstacle for ceramic production and the state-run kiln system. During the seventeenth century, state kilns were established in five locations: Tanbeol-ri, Sangrim-ri, Sŏngdong-ri, Songjŏng-ri, and Yusa-ri. Later, during the eighteenth century, they were relocated to Keumsa-ri. Yŏngjo, however, found the existing system of moving the state kilns every ten years too costly and fiscally unsustainable.[41] In 1752, Yŏngjo decided to build the state kilns permanently in Punwon-ri, instead of moving them around to the vicinity of a forested area. To secure the supply of firewood, boats that carried firewood through the Uchŏng River had to pay taxes.[42]

Though few contemporary scholars have linked the scarcity of firewood to the decline in the overall quality of late Chosŏn ceramics, a number of elite commentators in the early nineteenth century made just this association. Those who visited Beijing, for instance, where they observed highly sophisticated porcelain works, minced no words about the problems in the existing state kiln system back in Korea. Pak Che-ga (1750–1805) expressed his embarrassment about the rustic qualities of Chosŏn ceramics due to the outdated techniques in comparison to Chinese examples.[43] Yi Hui-kyŏng (1745–after 1805), after visiting Beijing five times as part of an annual tributary entourage, was similarly unsparing in his assessment of the outdated Chosŏn state-run kiln system.[44] Such commentary speaks not only to the frustrations of scholar officials but also to why contemporary scholars need to move beyond assessments that simply pair the humble materiality of eighteenth-century white porcelains with the ideal of neo-Confucian aesthetics.

No Patterned Silk and No Weaving Looms

In eighteenth-century Korea, both agriculture and sericulture were daunting enterprises. Through thousands of years of selective breeding, the silkworm has become one of the most important domesticated insects. As silkworms are cold-blooded animals, temperature has a direct effect on their physiological activities, growth in particular.[45] Temperature fluctuations across the Little Ice Age consequently posed a host of challenges for the growth of silkworms and, by extension, for sericulture as a whole.

Even the mulberry tree, an arboreal type known for its adaptability to a wide range of temperatures and soils, struggled to grow under these conditions. Many reports convey how sudden snow and heavy frost could destroy mulberry saplings. Some local governors reported to the central government about the people's general unwillingness to tend to silkworms.[46]

The royal house nonetheless remained deeply invested in the king's performance of state rituals related to both agriculture and sericulture. In 1767, Queen Chŏngsun (1745–1805) performed a whole set of sericulture ceremonies, while Yŏngjo himself conducted the plowing ceremony. At that time, the king proudly announced that *he* was the one who restored this ancient ceremony, which had been forgotten for hundreds of years.[47]

In light of such fervent promotion of sericulture, it seems unlikely that eighteenth-century Korean rulers objected to silk products simply because of their luxurious nature. Many official records reveal that Yŏngjo was extremely concerned about the origin of silk products, making a clear distinction between plain gauze as locally produced silk and patterned damask as an imported luxury.[48] He repeatedly underscored the need to make wider use of gauze in the royal court and prohibited court officials from wearing Chinese patterned damask.[49]

While scholars have long attributed Chosŏn austerity measures to the king's eccentric contempt of luxury, an alternative explanation lies in the state's chronic budget deficit, caused by frequently exercised tax relief programs for natural disaster victims, food aid, and unbalanced trade with China. In such dire circumstances, sumptuary laws were among the few available remedies. One cannot separate Yŏngjo's disdainful attitude toward patterned silk from regular reports of wasteful and extravagant consumption of Chinese luxury goods.[50]

To underscore the gravity of his prohibition on Chinese silks, Yŏngjo had several merchants who purchased patterned silk in Beijing arrested and punished by death. Yi Myŏng-chik, for example, was arrested for having procured Chinese silks in Beijing.[51] The king's harsh ban on Chinese silks was well known to Qing textile merchants, as the following passage from the *Veritable Records* makes clear:

> The sumptuary law recently announced is the one that elucidates the king's divine virtue. It provides an opportunity to restore the custom and behavior of the state, but also to inform the world. . . . Zheng Shi-tai was so surprised to hear this new law and had to tell his contracted weavers to pause production. He remarked, "your king is truly divine and virtuous, but from now on we will have no way to make a living."[52]

In 1756, Yŏngjo made one final blow to the silk workshop in the royal court, then already in peril. He had all looms in the royal court dismantled, effectively grinding the production of patterned silk to a halt.[53] Later, in an effort to ban the local production of patterned silk, even privately owned looms were ordered to be destroyed.[54]

Korean textile art historian Sim Yŏn-ok laments that a series of sumptuary laws, which had been initiated by Yŏngjo, inhibited technological advancement in the field of textile arts.[55] According to her research, by the early twentieth century consumers of high-quality patterned silk had to rely mostly on imported textiles.[56] To illustrate this point, Sim compared the three surviving examples of the wedding ceremony robe (翟衣)—those housed at the National Palace Museum, the Seoul Museum of History, and the Museum of Kyung Hee University—to a few silk samples in the collection of Kawashima Textile Museum in Japan. The comparison revealed that the silk used for the empress's ritual robes from the National Palace Museum and the Museum of Kyung Hee University is identical to the Japanese silk made in the Kyoto-based Kawashima Company. Ironically, Queen Myŏngsŏng, the last Queen of the Chosŏn dynasty who strove to assert independence from Japan's growing political and economic influence, had to rely on high-quality silk imported from Japan because the techniques of weaving refined patterned silk had been completely lost by the early twentieth century.

In contrast to preceding centuries, in which it had been beset by successive foreign invasions, eighteenth-century Korea deserves the title of Pax Coreana, thanks to its relative political stability. One might also describe it as the glorious epoch of Korean art and culture, since the Chosŏn state recognized itself as the forefront of Confucian civilization in the region, bringing forth great artists and artworks. Nevertheless, a rich body of evidence gleaned from both written sources and climate proxy data strongly suggests that the state, even under the rule of so-called sagacious monarchs, was struggling in the face of the ecological calamity and economic insecurity ushered in by the effects of the Little Ice Age.

The splendor of eighteenth-century Korea and its art does not reside in its material richness, but in its dearth. Prolonged climatic oddities and economic crises gave Yŏngjo and Chŏngjo no other choice but to redefine the neo-Confucian ethics of consumption, which long remained as an abstract metaphysical concept practiced in every sector of Chosŏn society. The simple, austere, and modest traits that distinguish eighteenth-century Korean visual and material culture thus reflects the politics of frugality. Far from evidence of an inherent penchant for neo-Confucian aesthetics imprinted into Korea's national culture, these qualities reflect a long history of human resilience and adaptability in the face of environmental change.

4

BETWEEN MEMORY AND AMNESIA

Seoul's Nanjido Landfill, 1978–1993

Hyojin Pak

Nanjido, best known as the site of the stadium for the 2002 World Cup, is often praised as a successful landfill reclamation case. A Seoul landfill between 1978 and 1993, Nanjido was transformed from an "island of triple abundance (삼다 도)" (i.e., dust, odors, and flies) into an ecological park. While Nanjido was material testimony to the "rapid growth that overlooked environmental degradation," it was also home to thousands of waste pickers and a venue for various illicit businesses related to the disposal process.[1] All these aspects—waste piled outdoors, ramshackle shanties, gangs blackmailing garbage haulers in a city-run landfill—ran counter to official efforts to cast Seoul as a modern, developed city.

Nanjido began operation when the country was still under a military dictatorship and had few disposal regulations, and when its waste was mostly ashes. Developing rapidly, Seoul needed to locate undesirable but integral facilities (e.g., landfills and sewage treatment facilities) on the urban periphery. It also needed to accommodate its growing urban population and labor force. In hindsight, Nanjido offered both. Tucked away from the city, Nanjido hid the city's waste as well as its shanties and urban poor. After fifteen years of operation, Nanjido—and its ninety-two million cubic meters of waste—shifted into a different social and political environment. Unlike under the dictatorship, post-landfill planning for Nanjido involved not only the city but also local environmental governance bodies and civil society. The construction of the post-landfill park, however, still proceeded in a top-down, bureaucratic way, which caused conflicts over its use as late as 2008.

The reclaimed landfill and the redeveloped Sang-am dong area feature an ecological park, a World Cup stadium, large-scale apartment complexes, and a business district that houses major broadcasting stations. Nothing illuminates its past. Scholars have shown a similar pattern of erasure, portraying Nanjido as an exceptional, extralegal space, describing either "an internal colony"[2] or a particular "Nanjido culture"[3]—approaches that prevent us from seeing Nanjido in light of the broader structural conditions of Korean society. This amnesia reflects the characteristics of waste and landfill: waste signals a desire to forget, and a landfill, as its container, is a space dedicated to oblivion.[4] If a landfill is "a place that organizes and frames things *as* waste," as Gay Hawkins writes, waste and landfill have the power to reveal what was refused and rejected, what was meant to be excluded and extinguished, and what is designed to be remembered or forgotten.[5] Indeed, landfill preserves history by encasing the material remnants of the city.[6] With this memorial capacity, a landfill can reveal what we choose to remember and how we see this landscape. Grappling with the two seemingly contradictory traits—memory and amnesia—in this chapter we seek to reconcile this duality through understanding Nanjido. Rather than sidelining waste as a static object of management, I turn to material and metaphorical waste to examine how waste provided a means for life, labor, and politics, only to be discarded after Nanjido's reclamation.

Nanjido: The Site

Nanjido was once one of the islands of Saet Stream (Saetkang), a branch of the Han River, on the outskirts of Seoul (figure 4.1). Before the landfill, Nanjido was well known for its nature and its pastoral landscape, and provided a picnic and retreat site for Seoulites.

What changed Nanjido's fate was the 1978 inception of the landfill. After the construction of a breakwater in January 1977, which reclaimed 2.9 million square meters (878,280 *pyŏng*) of land, the city designated Nanjido as a landfill.[7] Dumping started by filling the lowlands until it reached ground level, a method known as trench landfilling.[8] Nanjido first received waste from Seoul's six districts and became Seoul's primary landfill by 1982. As early as 1983, 70 percent of the available landfill space was filled. Both the city and the Office of the Environment (OOE, Hwankyŏngch'ŏng) sought to develop future disposal plans, particularly a new landfill site in the metropolitan area. In the mid-1980s, with Nanjido approaching full capacity, the city considered two options: constructing an incineration-based waste treatment plant,[9] or turning Nanjido into a sanitary landfill using a mounding landfill method.[10] With the failure of the waste treatment plant,[11] and the delay in selecting a new landfill site,[12] the city opted for mounding landfilling. Despite the recommendations for sanitary landfilling,

FIGURE 4.1.   The Nanjido landfill, Seoul. Image by Hyojin Pak.

Nanjido continued as an open dump for mixed refuse (figure 4.2).[13] At the time of its closure, Nanjido had two garbage hills and a former quarry with landfill mounds more than ninety meters above sea level.

The range of waste deposited at Nanjido covered all aspects of city life. In the late 1970s, with more than 80 percent of the city's waste made up of coal briquette ashes from household heating, the city's attention shifted more toward recycling ash than toward a sanitary landfill.[14] However, patterns of waste generation quickly changed: Seoul's per capita waste generation almost doubled, from 1.36 kg in 1970 to 2.5 kg in 1980, and the material composition of the waste showed a sharp decline in ash and a steady increase in combustible waste.[15] Although Nanjido was a

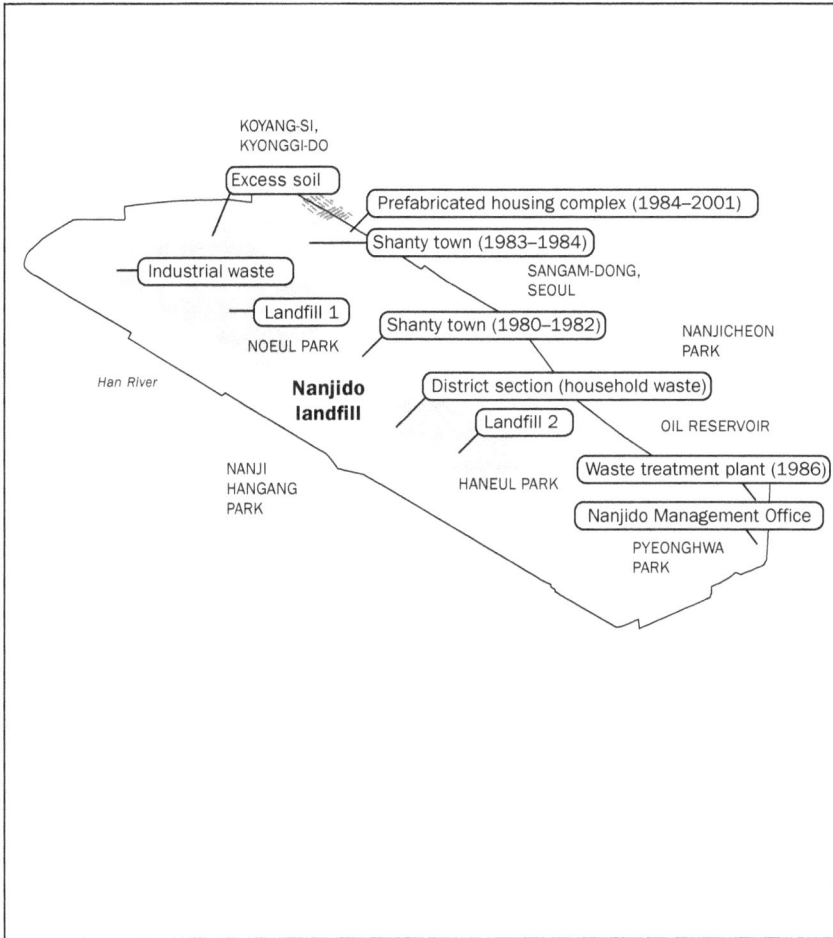

KOYANG-SI,
KYONGGI-DO

Excess soil

Prefabricated housing complex (1984–2001)

Shanty town (1983–1984)

SANGAM-DONG,
SEOUL

Industrial waste

Landfill 1

NOEUL PARK

Shanty town (1980–1982)

NANJICHEON
PARK

Han River

**Nanjido
landfill**

District section (household waste)

Landfill 2

OIL RESERVOIR

NANJI
HANGANG
PARK

HANEUL PARK

Waste treatment plant (1986)

Nanjido Management Office

PYEONGHWA
PARK

FIGURE 4.2. An overview of the Nanjido landfill/World Cup Park. Image by Hyojin Pak.

household waste disposal site, all kinds of waste ended up there: construction debris and excess soil from the city's housing and infrastructure (subway) projects; postproduction waste from small- and medium-sized factories in Seoul and the metropolitan area; and sludge from the city's sewage treatment facility. As shown in figure 4.2, different streams of waste—household, industrial, and construction, for example—occupied different areas in the landfill, which were organized and maintained by different types of workers. It is to this form of labor organization I now turn.

The Organization of Labor

At Nanjido's inception, a team in the cleaning division of the Map'o district office oversaw landfill operations.[16] The city's lack of managerial and operational capacity opened up possibilities for informal workers. Indeed, its day-to-day operations were run by a mix of city workers, a range of waste pickers who recycled waste, and other workers who dealt with construction waste and excess soil and were known to be part of organized crime groups.[17] What essentially emerged was a hybridized labor organization in which city workers, informal waste pickers, and illicit businesses worked alongside each other under a clear division of labor in different sections of the landfill.

This labor organization shaped the power dynamics among workers. City workers were divided into two groups. White-collar administrators and engineers governed the overall planning of the landfill, while blue-collar workers (bulldozer operators, incoming waste inspectors, security guards, and field superintendents) oversaw day-to-day operations at dumpsites. The two groups, however, had conflicting interests over landfill operations, such as illegal dumping. Alluding to potential corruption, office workers reported that they kept crackdown schedules confidential from blue-collar workers.

Waste pickers were divided into first-line (앞벌이) and second-line (뒷벌이) pickers, working either in district or private truck sections. In the district section (구청차 구역), where the city's municipal waste collection trucks unloaded their waste, first-line pickers organized themselves according to Seoul's administrative divisions. Each district formed a team with a district crew leader (총무), registered members (대원), and self-determined regulations. District teams had limited positions, which required a permit fee: the number of crews were proportional to the amount of waste, whereas the permit fee was proportional to the profitability of the waste. Second-line positions did not require a fee. They worked after the first-line pickers, following the back of the bulldozer that flattened the dump surface and rummaging residual waste; second-line pickers also ran more risk of being hit by a bulldozer.[18] Waste pickers managed their dumpsites and organized the collection and sale of waste materials without the city's intervention. Waste pickers collected recyclable material from incoming unseparated waste, sorted it, and sold it to intermediary buyers who came to the landfill every ten days.

In the private section (개인차 구역), where private garbage haulers unloaded their waste, each subcontracted hauler was allocated a dumpsite. Each site was run by a waste picker who "bought" or "rented" the truck, working on their own or with day laborers. Private haulers carried waste from apartment complexes, commercial buildings, marketplaces, and US Army bases. The more profitable the waste, the more expensive the permit fee. An association of private garbage haulers, the Korea Environment Refuse Association (KERF), dispatched its workers to Nanjido to oversee the private section.[19]

Waste pickers organized their labor according to their access to waste, which was hierarchical and competitive. Each district team competed to gain better dumpsite locations. First-line pickers defended their rights against second-line pickers. Second-line pickers, while occupying the lowest position, defended their territory against newcomers. Despite the competition and the entry barriers, there was a degree of mobility, either within waste picker positions or outside of landfill waste work, such as providing goods and services for landfill dwellers or venturing into the informal waste economy.[20]

Despite this diverse range of workers, there was no overarching control. In the district section, blue-collar workers oversaw both dumpsites and informal waste pickers. Other city workers, especially white-collar workers, had little contact with waste pickers. In the private truck section and the soil truck section, both of which were left to their own devices, landfill administrators tended to work with the heads of the groups when the need arose, such as for dumping yard adjustments or dumpsite relocations. Both geographical distances and labor organization ensured that informal workers, unless they worked in the same section, did not interact much with each other.

At the outset, it might have seemed that landfill engineers planned and allocated the dumping areas. Within the confines of the allocated space, waste pickers competed over better access to incoming trucks and garbage pits, each occupying a different position according to their skills, networks, and resources. The spatial arrangement of the dumping sections—the district truck, the private truck, the soil truck—reflected the different types of labor undertaken at Nanjido and their social relations.

The Multiple Uses and Forces of Waste

A landfill is a place where discarded things, once familiar, can take on new and unexpected uses. Faced with a surge of waste, Nanjido workers found ingenious uses for it. For waste pickers, Nanjido enabled new forms of reusing and recycling, and refuse itself was used to build their lives there. If one was resourceful, the landfill offered ample sources of building materials from construction sites, as well as household appliances. Wooden beams and metal rods stood as pillars; plywood, cardboard, plastic tarps, or felted fabric from construction sites built up walls and roofs; discarded linoleum flooring created a livable surface; opaque vinyl films opened a window; wooden and metal crates, discarded drum cans, and metal pipes set up an impromptu kitchenette, either at the dumpsite or at home, using the methane gas leached from the dump as a heat source. Scavenging and reusing were not just a matter of subsistence or thrift: they created value from otherwise valueless items and formed the material bases of the waste pickers' lives, not as commodities, but as materials that could be reworked, repurposed, and refurbished into the necessities of life.

Necessity begat invention, and improvisatory uses of trash were typical among waste pickers. The incoming garbage—a combination of coal briquette ash, excess soil, and demolition debris—became covering material, forming the surface of the dumping area.[21] This process, called "daily cover" in sanitary landfilling practice, was undertaken mostly by waste pickers. One district crew leader recalled how his team crews went all the way down to the Yanghwajin Foreign Missionary Cemetery on the riverside expressway, five kilometers to the east from the dumpsite.[22] Waste pickers were on the lookout for flatbed trucks with side panels, which tended to haul less soil than dump trucks. There, they could also inspect which truck carried "good construction waste": refuse that had little moisture. Crews then hitched a ride on the truck to induce the drivers to come to their dumpsite: they covered the dumpsite surface with bricks, rubble, and construction debris, often with bare hands. Only after waste pickers had evenly arranged covering materials did the city's bulldozer operator go over to the dumpsite to flatten the surface.

The instrumentalization of waste, as a covering material and as pavement, kept landfill operation costs low for the city but shifted risk to waste pickers and truck drivers. The mixture of garbage and soil shrank over time; the waste's decomposition created sinkholes; and the combination of rainwater, leachate, and garbage tended to collapse. These waste-slides eroded the landfill slopes,[23] and they also took the lives of waste pickers.[24] Rain-filled roads became morasses of mud, filled with landfill runoff that stranded or tipped trucks. Most dangerous, the waste-paved ground surface damaged vehicles. Nails and wires punctured or coiled around tires and in brakes; debris would jam or wind around wheels, chassis, and engines, to be noticed by drivers only after leaving the dumpsite. Garbage truck drivers recalled handling breakdowns and maintenance immediately on their own, out-of-pocket, to avoid a potential garbage crisis in the city.[25]

Beyond postconsumption household waste, Nanjido also received various types of industrial waste, the risks of which fell disproportionately on waste pickers. The danger of sludge pits was one example; created both by the city and by illegal dumping, they posed an acute threat to waste pickers. Not infrequently, a waste picker, while attempting to grab recyclables—something as mundane as a yogurt bottle—would slip into a sludge pit.[26] While they would invariably be rescued, the trauma lingered. There were other hazards as well, such as chemical or medical waste: needles pricked feet, hydrochloric acid burned skin. This open dumping of mixed waste increased the likelihood of injuries and other health consequences.

Waste pickers did not always tolerate the city's neglect of the landfill's operation. While Nanjido had long been used as a disposal site for nonhazardous industrial waste, the disposal of sewage-plant sludge roused waste pickers to collective action. The stench from the sludge prevented them from working, and industrial waste, supposedly restricted to Landfill 1 (figure 4.2), was encroaching on the municipal waste section (Landfill 2), exposing them to hazardous materials.[27] In June 1988, two hundred waste pickers occupied the landfill access road, demanding the separation of industrial from municipal waste. Although the Map'o district office agreed to their demand, waste pickers took further action three weeks later. In July 1988, all of Nanjido's 3,500 waste pickers petitioned the Map'o district office to demand a ban on industrial waste disposal in Nanjido.[28] Nonetheless, while the city and the OOE were looking into alternatives, the disposal of industrial waste continued in Nanjido.

At Nanjido, waste served as not only a means of work and life, but as an accessible, inexpensive, and effective tool for exercising power. Office workers reported that organized crime groups would intimidate or harass them. One means of intimidation was to dump waste at the landfill management office: such acts inverted the power relationship and the hierarchy between city workers and illicit gangs, explicitly associating city workers with "waste."[29] The degrading force of waste became a strategy the gangs used to advance their goals, whether for securing more dumping space or more convenient dumpling locations, or illegally profiting from the public landfill.

Some city workers also strategically used waste to improve their labor conditions and thereby the city's landfill operations. In November 1989, when a heavy downpour blocked landfill access, a municipal garbage truck driver attempted to enter the landfill via a route used exclusively for the soil truck section. For this, he was beaten by members of a gang. Out of solidarity and long-standing frustration, five hundred truck drivers went on strike, blocking landfill access and dumping garbage onto the road. Collectively dumping more than two thousand tons of waste, they "parked" their trucks on the riverside expressway, forming a convoy more than two kilometers long.[30]

In this replacement of orderly practice (disposal of waste in the landfill) with a disorderly one (dumping of waste on the roads), we are reminded of Mary Douglas's seminal theory of "dirt as matter out of place."[31] Indeed, the strike inadvertently revealed how waste threatened the existing system of order. Compared to other city workers' reasonable but unheeded demands, waste dumping was an effective political strategy for bringing immediate reaction. Negotiations

proceeded expeditiously, and the results came out the next day: increased budgets, improved infrastructure, and the move of the landfill administration into
a separate office with more decision-making power.[32] Waste dumping here was
not just a reaction to the violent incident. It was also a means of revealing the
city's neglect and of appealing for a more orderly disposal process, using the disgust and discomfort that waste provoked.[33]

Nanjido, intrinsically connected to waste, saw its attendant symbolic power
appropriated by others, the first being the police. The 1980s saw waves of labor
unrest, with more laborers agitating for unionization and increased labor protections. In breaking strikes, riot police would arrest strikers and abandon them
at Nanjido.[34] Writers from the Literary Association of Puch'ŏn Laborers illustrated this dumping experience in a narrative poem:[35] "[Being] dragged away in
a caged police vehicle like mere baggage / Nanjido dumping ground / We were
dumped there / Even prison cells were not for us / [Being] trampled down as we
are / Wherever it is, for us, it is a prison cell, an execution ground / But [we are]
never trash."[36] In the following stanza, accepting themselves as "us, the laborers, the wheel that runs the world," the speakers refuse the charge that they are
"trash," throwing it back on the sources of their oppression (i.e., foreign aid and
loans, dictatorship, violence, torture, and so on).[37] By criticizing their repressors
as "trash," the poetic subjects—the protesting laborers—reclaimed their position not as victims but as historical agents driving social change.

Members of parliament (MPs) also criticized this practice. In February 1989,
during the plenary session, one MP, Ryu Sŭng-gyu, condemned the harsh policing
of the strikers, particularly the act of "throwing them out in Nanjido."[38] He re-
proached the minister for internal affairs, asking him if the laborers were only
"garbage" to the police. As the minister justified the incident as "separating and
dispersing the workers," another MP, (Roh Moo-hyun), who became the president
of South Korea in 2002, yelled from his seat, "Are these people trash, so much so
that the police discarded them in Nanjido?"[39] By dumping labor protestors, activists, and dissidents in Nanjido, the police exploited the symbolic association of
waste.[40] Insulting and dismissing their actions were effective means of control,
and Nanjido delivered the workings of police power extremely effectively.

The Nanjido landfill was officially closed in March 1993, but temporarily re-
opened in 1995. Seoul's Samp'ung Department Store, a then-five-year-old building
marking the era of affluence and consumerism, collapsed on June 29 of that year.[41]
Immediately after, the city shipped the debris from the collapse site to several locations, but it soon designated Nanjido as the main disposal site. Only Nanjido could
accommodate the mess of the collapse, be safely sealed off both temporarily (the
unloading period) and permanently, and allow for future investigation. Landfill 1,

where industrial and construction waste were deposited (now Noŭl Park) received the debris. During a month of evacuation, thirty-four thousand tons of debris were disposed across fifty thousand square meters (15,000 *pyŏng*). A series of belated investigations at the demand of bereaved families revealed 142 human remains amid the rubble, turning Nanjido into "the second Samp'ung site." Of the 502 people who died in the disaster, more than one hundred still remained missing.[42] Nanjido had become a burial site for Samp'ung victims.

The rise and demise of Nanjido was a collective process of producing material waste, discarding the material remnants of human life, and forgetting both the landfill's contents and the labor that built it. Nanjido allowed Seoulites to cherish the fruits of the country's unprecedented economic growth, its unfettered production and consumption, without having to attend to its environmental consequences. Waste pickers who perished in Nanjido, workers who were discarded after protests, and Samp'ung victims interred there all epitomized the unseen consequences of the country's accelerated, if short-sighted, development. Despite their symbolic meaning and moral implications, none altered the way Nanjido was restored and remembered. After the closure, two landfill mounds and their mass volume of waste stood as visual evidence of the processes that had both dictated the lives of waste pickers and transformed the landscape—if only to be revitalized after the stabilization.

Reclaiming Landfill, Reclaiming Memory

When Nanjido was closed in March 1993, the landfill became situated in a different context both domestically and internationally. Korea had democratized and local self-government began in 1995. Civil society was expanding, especially environmental movements, whose participation in various governing bodies culminated in the institutionalization of environmental issues and more stringent regulation.[43] The country also engaged with global environmental governance, such as implementing Agenda 21 and establishing the Green Seoul Citizens Committee (GSCC, Noksaek Sŏul simin wiwŏnhoe) in 1996.[44]

The direction of post-landfill planning came from South Korea's cohosting the 2002 FIFA World Cup and the construction of the main stadium in the Nanjido (Sang-am dong) area. Despite the initial debates on commercial land development, two things affected the city's decision: ground stability (which needed postclosure monitoring) and promoting the "environmentally friendly" FIFA through ecological restoration of Nanjido.[45] Yet, its highly centralized process conflicted with both civil society and the GSCC, especially regarding golf course construction at the Landfill 1 site, which nearly brought to a halt a then-nascent environmental governing body.[46] Ultimately, disputes over the entrance fee, rather than environmental concerns, led to the closure of the golf course.[47]

The accumulation of waste, as well as the array of human labor invested in the years of the landfilling process, allow us to see Nanjido as a repository for the consequences of Seoul's urbanization and development. Yet, through stabilization and reclamation, Nanjido also distances itself from its past: its appearance transformed into different land uses, most notably an ecological park. This new landscape evokes neither the force of waste that turned the once flourishing land into ruin, nor the people who lived, worked, or, in some cases, perished in the landfill. Once a home for peasants and the urban poor, a convenient urban periphery for disposal and sewage treatment facilities, the World Cup Park and its neighboring area now serve middle-class Seoulites and their needs, leaving the mountains of waste and shanties behind in history. However, Nanjido rarely revives these memories. Ironically, but perhaps appropriately, it is the landfill's historical memory itself that is discarded. Without reclaiming this memory, however, the reclamation of the landfill is incomplete.

5

NORTH KOREA CAUGHT BETWEEN DEVELOPMENTALISM AND HUMANITARIANISM

Ewa Eriksson Fortier and Suzy Kim

In November 2017, news flashed around the world about the defection of a North Korean soldier stationed in the Joint Security Area at the Demilitarized Zone (DMZ) separating the two Koreas. Shot during the dramatic crossing, the soldier made headlines for the parasitic worms found in his intestines during surgery, with the surgeon showing off graphic photos of the soldier's conditions, which the doctor had "never seen anything like" before.[1] As humanitarian health workers know, however, this is a common condition in the developing world that can be prevented by access to safe water and sanitation, and treated with drugs or surgery if available, as in postwar Vietnam.[2]

This case underscores the extent to which environmental crises are fraught with politics, both in the way domestic policies are framed within a country and, for North Korea, in how its environment is understood and addressed by international actors from the United Nations to humanitarian organizations. In disregard of doctor-patient confidentiality, the public release of the details of the soldier's health status has been repeatedly used by politicians and pundits alike to highlight the difference in conditions between the two Koreas. However, what is revealed in the tragic story is North Korea's environmental crises. The condition of the soldier connects three basic issues in the environmental history of the Democratic People's Republic of Korea (hereafter DPRK, or North Korea): (1) the direct impact of the Korean War on its environment; (2) the indirect impact of ongoing conflict on its capacity to handle these environmental problems; and finally (3) the severe constraints on humanitarian organizations in addressing environmental factors of the health crises in North Korea.[3]

The soldier's post along the DMZ is a direct result and continuing legacy of the Korean War (1950–1953). Not only was he shot to prevent his crossing one of the most heavily militarized borders in the world, but upon full medical examination, his health condition reportedly included hepatitis, pneumonia, and malnutrition. However, as the *Guardian* reported, "Parasitic worms were also common in South Korea between 40 and 50 years ago . . . but disappeared as economic conditions improved."[4] Indeed, exposed to similar parasites in their own lifetimes, older South Koreans still continue to regularly ingest antiparasitic drugs.

Until the 1970s, the North Korean government had been able to supply farmers with chemical fertilizers, but in the face of increasing economic hardship in subsequent decades, animal and human waste had to be used to secure food production. In the 1990s, following the dissolution of the Socialist Bloc and thus the end of trade and oil subsidies, there was a devastating flood, which led to a severe famine, known in North Korea as the Arduous March. Humanitarian groups responded to North Korea's request for aid, but met with challenges as the country came under repeated sanctions.[5] According to the International Federation of Red Cross and Red Crescent Societies (IFRC), "an estimated 10.3 million people [in the DPRK] suffer from food insecurity, under-nutrition and a lack of access to basic services" caused by recurrent natural hazards that, in 2018, included "a heatwave, a dry spell, a typhoon, floods and landslides" and a broad sanctions regime that has limited state access to such basic medical supplies as "vaccines, antiviral medicines, rapid testing kits, personal protective equipment for health workers and hand sanitizer."[6] Even as the condition of the soldier illustrates what can happen when supplies of fertilizer and provisions of clean water and sanitation facilities are discontinued, these most basic forms of aid can be constrained by politicized differentiations between humanitarian and development aid based on separate funding sources.

As argued by sociologist Chong-Ae Yu, North Korea's predicaments are symptomatic of industrial agricultural production, in general, and are difficult to resolve through strict separation between humanitarian and development programs. From its founding in 1948 until the early 1980s, North Korea had met its food needs. To compensate for its short growing season and the fact that only 18 percent of its land is arable, the state developed a decentralized system of cooperative farms, aided by centralized investments in rural electrification, irrigation, mechanization, agrochemicals, and hybrid seeds.[7] Dependence on coal and hydropower plants, however, accelerated negative impacts on the environment, exacerbated by greater weather anomalies. Overreliance on chemical fertilizers resulted in soil acidification and thus decreasing yields. As previous plots produced less, more marginal lands and forests were cleared for production, leading to deforestation and soil erosion, worsened by foraging, directly contributing to more severe flooding. And still, facing these compounding problems, increasing sanctions since 2006 severely hamper North Korea's ability to import new seeds and technology. In light of this history, and the national goal of self-reliance, North Korea has prioritized development support over humanitarian aid to resuscitate the agricultural industry in the long term, especially as the most severe famine period came to an end. Needless to say, disruption of financial links and the added restrictions on oil and fuel imports, as well as metal and other necessities in the series of UN sanctions since 2017, negatively impact the humanitarian *and* environmental conditions in North Korea.[8]

North Korea's environment has thus been shaped by the common twentieth-century drive for industrial development in the form of state-led developmentalism with an emphasis on domestic heavy industries as opposed to imports and consumer goods. Like South Korea in the same period, this approach was a prime feature of North Korea's economic policy between the 1960s and 1980s until the disasters and subsequent famine of the 1990s, when it had to supplement its developmentalism with humanitarian aid. One of the key arguments of this chapter in situating North Korea *between* developmentalism and humanitarianism is to demonstrate how inadequate these paradigms of economic growth and international assistance are in the face of environmental crises, which require long-term solutions rather than short-term development goals and humanitarian funding. Despite recent reports of shifts toward greater commitment to science and technology, these goals have long been emphasized in North Korean official policy; whether an alternative beyond developmentalism and humanitarianism can be found remains to be seen, but this chapter's focus on community responses to environmental crises highlights the importance of localized indigenous knowledges born of experience.

Linking the humanitarian situation in North Korea as directly related to the environment, we combine the history of North Korea's approach to the environment with the operational experience of humanitarian work at the village level. We first examine the development of North Korean assessments about the environment, starting in the late 1970s, that linked climate change to impacts on food production, resulting in the passage of the Environmental Protection Law in 1986, even as industrial developmentalism remained the paradigm. In the second half of the chapter, we discuss the evolution and scope of the Integrated Community Development Programme (ICDP) implemented by cooperative farms since the 2000s providing local resources and extensive labor at the village (*ri*) level through the DPRK Red Cross, technically and financially supported by the IFRC and individual long-term partner national Red Cross societies.[9] In the context of macro-level analyses of domestic policies and international regulatory regimes, we focus on the micro-level effects and strategies based on fieldwork, linking contemporary practices to the history of environmental policy as recorded in North Korean publications since the 1970s.

As a collaborative effort that combines historical research with humanitarian fieldwork, we make use of in-country operational experience (during the 2006–2009 period, on behalf of the IFRC, as well as the Swedish Red Cross in 2016) and historical analysis of North Korean sources from the 1970s to the 2010s with particular attention to the official Korean Workers' Party newspaper, *Rodong sinmun*, on issues of environmental protection and climate change in the face of persistent food insecurities.[10] Climate change has increased the frequency of disasters and community exposure to the effects of deforestation, landslides, extreme weather, and more frequent and devastating floods, with debilitating consequences on food production.[11] North Korea is one of the places most vulnerable to climate change, not only geographically (as are parts of Africa), but also politically, because of the international sanctions regime. As a result, North Korea has little recourse. When access to resources to improve production, like fertilizers, irrigation equipment, and technologies, are restricted, even minute changes in weather patterns result in outsized impacts on food production and population sustainability.

Environmental Conditions, Climate Change, and Food Security

Information about the total land area in the DPRK varies somewhat depending on the source, but it is estimated to be around 123,000 km^2. Of this, less than 20 percent is arable land and roughly 75 to 80 percent is mountainous, with forest cover between 50,310 km^2 (41.78 percent, World Bank) and 89,273 km^2 (73 percent, MoLEP).[12] The western and southern areas of the country consist of lowland plains with arable land, while the northeast is mountainous with smaller plains along the rivers and the coast. The main roads are paved, but more remote areas have dirt or gravel roads, which are slippery during rain and sometimes impassable because of snow during the winter. According to the DPRK Ministry of Land and Environment Protection (MoLEP), the area of arable land is 18,390 km^2, most of which is used in dry field farming (10,050 km^2), followed by paddy fields (5,740 km^2).[13] Orchards cover about 1,440 km^2 and mulberry farms about 850 km^2. Although the amount of arable land in the DPRK is too limited to allow for full self-sufficiency in production of food, this is still the goal. Domestic food production, defined as a national security issue, is the major responsibility of cooperative farms at the village level. The Food and Agricultural Organization (FAO) reports that the rural economy is characterized mostly by the operation of cooperative farms, with a smaller number of state farms.[14] According to the Central Bureau of Statistics,

FIGURE 5.1. Women farmers watering fields. Courtesy of Swedish Red Cross.

there are 707 state farms employing 802,000 farmers, and 2,513 cooperative farms with 2.54 million farmers, only a small number of whom receive international support to improve the sustainability of their production.[15] Some of the most disaster-prone communities receive support from the DPRK Red Cross assisted by international Red Cross partners.[16]

At the *ri* level, cooperative farms consist of 2,500–4,000 people divided into 1,000–1,500 households, although the population can vary from one thousand to ten thousand people. A *ri* level cooperative farm may comprise one or several villages. Some are traditional villages where families have lived over many generations for several hundred years; others are rather recently established, during the 1960s and later. The environment is unique to each location, and the living conditions are different. Cooperative farm activities are led by a manager, male or female, supported by a cooperative farm management team. Female cooperative farm managers have a reputation of being effective (see figure 5.1). People are divided into a number of work teams depending on the size of the community. For example, Samsŏng Ri in Hongwŏn County, in South Hamgyŏng Province, with a population of 3,850 people (1,152 households) has nine work teams, of which six focus on agriculture (rice, maize, beans, potatoes) and three cultivate fruits (apples, pear, peach, plums) and mushrooms, and raise livestock (cows, goats, pigs, fish). Each family has an individual home with a kitchen garden of sixteen *p'yŏng* (52.8m^2), where they grow vegetables for their own consumption (cabbage, radish, eggplant, tomatoes, chili, and the like) and breed small livestock for food and sale (pigs, ducks, chickens, dogs, rabbits). Kitchen gardens are very important sources of food for people, sometimes providing as much food as the rations under the Public Distribution System.

Cooperative farms face myriad challenges, the most dangerous of which stem from the Korean War. The conflict subjected North Korea to a sustained US bombing campaign that leveled the country, leaving environmental hazards in the ground.[17] Many unexploded ordnance (UXO) still remain, and North Korean authorities report that there have been more than 16,215 victims of explosive remnants since the end of the war.[18] Farmers are frequent victims of these exploding devices, particularly as the mines move during natural disasters such as floods and landslides. The International Committee of the Red Cross (ICRC) provides training to the police authorities in their removal and disposal. As a result of these legacies of the war, as well as ongoing environmental concerns most directly related to food production, the DPRK government has placed high priority on environmental protection and has adopted a range of environmental laws.[19]

One of the earliest references to climate change (기후변화, *kihu pyŏnhwa*) in *Rodong sinmun* began with an article in March 1979 that reported on the grave concern expressed by world meteorologists about abnormal weather conditions, warning that climate change would only become more severe in the future.[20] Connections between climate change, energy needs, economic conditions, and food provisions were difficult to ignore as the situation grew worse from shortages to outright famine in the 1990s. Climate change, to be sure, has been used to obscure government responsibility for food shortages and other ecological problems. Such political uses notwithstanding, the topic of climate change has gained traction in North Korean reporting as developing countries worldwide have faced food crises and famine conditions in record numbers, especially in the Asia Pacific region.[21] Africa was the focus of famine news in the 1980s, but references to food problems dropped out of view as North Korea dealt with its own famine in the 1990s.[22] Signaled in earlier reporting, however, food shortages and famine throughout most of the world were attributed to climate issues such as a cold front (한냉전선, *hannaeng chŏnsŏn*), heat wave (대열파, *taeyŏlp'a*), severe drought (왕가물, *wang kamul*), cold frost and severe cold (찬서리와 강추위, *ch'an sŏri wa kang ch'uwi*), typhoons (태풍, *t'aep'ung*), and heavy rain (무더기비, *mudŏgibi*) "that haven't been seen in hundreds of years, sweeping across the continents and devastating farmlands and causing misery with hunger and desperate famine for hundreds of millions of people."[23] Reporting that production of grains was at its lowest since World War II, articles published in the 1970s began to express serious concern for declining production and growing food shortages worldwide.[24]

Referring to efforts in the developing world to solve its food problem as an important element in overcoming its colonial legacies of underdevelopment and dependency, *Rodong sinmun* argued that "people who are economically dependent on others cannot escape the fate of colonial slaves and cannot do or say what they want."[25] At a time of food crises sweeping across the world, it argued, "imperialists are using the occasion to use food as a weapon to dominate the developing nations and bring them back under their control." However, developing countries can "raise oneself on one's own forces" (자력갱생, *charyŏk kaengsaeng*), it claimed, by irrigation, diversification, and decentralization of rural management through planned development, according to each country's characteristics and given environment. This was North Korea's strategy in dealing with climate change and food problems, developed over the course of the 1970s. This was also the decade when North Korea's Juche ideology of self-reliance was codified in the 1972 Socialist Constitution.

Environmental Protection as National Security

The UN Intergovernmental Panel on Climate Change (IPCC) attributes vulnerability to climate change to three factors: exposure to hazards (such as reduced or increased rainfall); sensitivity to those hazards (such as farming dominated by rain-fed agriculture); and the capacity to adapt to those hazards (for example, whether farmers have the money or skills to grow more drought-resistant crops).[26] According to the IPCC, all three factors apply to the DPRK. By sheer necessity, North Korea has therefore emerged as a "champion in the fight against climate change," ratifying the United Nations Framework Convention on Climate Change (hereafter, UN Convention) in 1994, the Kyoto Protocol in 2005, and the Paris Agreement in 2016.[27] In 2019, the DPRK government established and completed its 2019–2030 national environment protection and disaster risk reduction strategies based on the Sendai Framework for Disaster Risk Reduction.[28] Earlier, on the occasion of World Environment Day in 2008, the *Rodong sinmun* reported on the UN's chosen theme of climate change and energy to foster research on alternative sources of energy, reporting on North Korea's own efforts at protecting the environment through such projects as renewing existing thermal power plants, improving hydroelectric power capacity, promoting wind energy, enlarging forests, introducing advanced farming methods and breeding systems, and using organic fertilizers.[29] The subsequent 2012 report, Democratic People's Republic of Korea: Environment and Climate Change Outlook, submitted by the DPRK in accordance with the UN Convention, elaborated in detail the scientific evidence of the effects of climate change, such as long-term trends in temperature by season and projected change in annual average precipitation, as well as maximum summer temperatures.[30] Adaptation measures, such as better protection against floods, improved organization and connectivity within and between communities, and reinforced adaptive knowledge and capacity, are needed to reduce vulnerability. However, the cost of major infrastructure reinforcement often exceeds national resources, and the current sanctions against the DPRK pose major challenges to the implementation of the UN Convention.

Even before the UN Convention, however, environmental protection (환경보호, *hwan'gyŏng poho*) increasingly became a topic covered by *Rodong sinmun*, especially after the passing of the Environmental Protection Law in April 1986. Comprising fifty-two articles divided into five chapters, the law codified the principles of environmental protection and the formation of government agencies toward this end, delineating their mandate, including procedures for seeking damages.[31] The new legislation institutionalized nature preserves (자연환경보호구, *chayŏn hwan'gyŏng pohogu*) and special protected areas (특별보호구, *t'ŭkbyŏl pohogu*), and tasked local governments with keeping records of local animals and plants and any changes in the environment, including soil, water, and climate. It prohibited damage to the natural environment (including forests, lakes, beaches, and mountains) and protected natural monuments and scenic spots. The law also stipulated the responsibilities of government agencies, factories, and workplaces to prevent pollution by incorporating purification systems to prevent the release of harmful gases, dust, and smoke, and to protect the water system, the seas, ports, rivers, and reservoirs, prohibiting the production and import of banned pesticides or the import of contaminated food products. A nonstanding committee on environmental protection was created as a government body to supplement the responsibility of the agencies related to land management, environmental protection, public health, and radiation management. Any citizen responsible for damaging the environment was held liable for indemnities, while institutions or citizens could also seek damages if harmed by violation of the law. The law sought to guarantee a clean environment for the people, and Article 7 expressly prohibited the development, testing, and use of nuclear and chemical weapons on and near the Korean peninsula as part of its environmental policy.

Leading up to the passage of the law, discussion of the legislation by the Supreme People's Assembly at its Seventh Congress in 1986 was publicized in the *Rodong sinmun* with a full report by Vice President Ri Chong-ok.[32] He emphasized two main points: first, the prevention of pollution to improve people's health by appropriately locating industrial and residential areas in separate zones; and second, the importance of preventing nuclear war.

> At the present time, the issue of environmental protection cannot be separated from the problem of protecting humanity and our environment from the dangers of ruin caused by the provocation of nuclear war by imperialists. . . . The use of nuclear weapons will annihilate all living things, destroying all buildings and facilities, polluting and degrading the natural environment in its entirety, and the aftereffects will continue for a long period of time.

Pointing to the "more than 1,000 nuclear weapons and various chemical weapons" stationed in the US military bases at the time in South Korea, Ri went on to argue that "the Korean peninsula has become the most dangerous zone where nuclear war can burst out at any time."

In 1987, shortly after the passage of the law, special protection zones and nature preserves were newly created or supplemented with weather stations, while key industrial zones added or reinforced detection abilities for environmental pollutants, monitoring weather patterns, forests, and changes in flora and fauna.[33] By doing so, the party newspaper argued, future generations would "inherit a clean and beautiful homeland without pollution." Paradoxically, however, the global search for alternative forms of energy came to focus on nuclear energy. Reporting on its worldwide development as provided by the International Atomic Energy Agency, *Rodong sinmun* reported that, of the thirty-four nuclear reactors under construction worldwide, nineteen were in Asia, and twenty-eight of the thirty-nine newly running reactors were also in Asia.[34] The article went on to argue that, as average national economies had grown 3.5 percent annually between 1990 and 2006, their energy needs had also increased by 3.2 percent. However, as most of these countries relied on fossil fuels, greenhouse gas emissions had also increased, reaching thirty billion tons, or 30 percent of worldwide CO_2 emissions. The article concluded with examples of active development of nuclear reactors in China, India, Iran, and Bangladesh.

Despite the emphasis on nuclear technology as both a threat and a solution to the environment, the everyday reality in North Korea reflects global patterns of the developing world, in which the top causes of infant and childhood mortality are diarrhea and acute respiratory infections caused by lack of access to safe drinking water and adequate sanitation (for almost 40 percent of the population).[35] Cases of pneumonia and tuberculosis are on the rise because of malnourishment and shortage of food, as well as lack of medicines.[36] Calling attention to the close connection between the environment and public health, the party newspaper ran roundtable discussions of those directly working with government units in charge of environmental protection.[37] Citing the vast numbers of those affected by water pollution worldwide—one billion without access to clean water and 2.5 million deaths from waterborne diseases—those at the roundtable emphasized the importance of protecting the soil and water, and preventing the major causes of air pollution, such as sulfur oxides, nitrogen oxides, and carbon dioxide.[38] In addition to such preventive measures, officials advocated the proactive development of new forms of energy, such as solar and wind power, especially with the new international focus on marine energy such as hydroelectric and wave power generation.[39]

Starting in the late 1990s, after the worst of the famine period, increasing references to mass campaigns for reforestation and use of organic pesticides and alternative forms of energy to address environmental damage appeared in *Rodong sinmun*. Laying out the importance of planting trees to protect roads and prevent soil erosion and landslides, several columns in 2002 explained the benefits of acacia trees, which grow well on dry land, preventing soil acidification.[40] Planted along roads, the column argued, the trees can also help with the greenery in cities and prevent air pollution by emitting positive ions that grab dust, up to 10–20 kg of dust per year per tree.[41] This effort was to address the devastating effects of a 1984 policy that cleared a substantial portion of the natural forest for the production of timber, fuel, and food, made worse by massive flooding and landslides, slash-and-burn farming, and foraging during the 1990s famine period, possibly affecting up to two million hectares by 2008.[42]

Since the 1960s, North Korea had relied on a relatively decentralized system of cooperative farms and local initiatives to improve the economy. Households were encouraged to raise livestock and cultivate kitchen gardens for the production of everyday staples. North Korean publications at the time give ample examples of model "socialist builders" raising rabbits, chickens, cows, pigs, silkworms, and honey bees in innovative ways.[43] The 1958 completion of rural collectivization is often blamed for imposing an inefficient centralized system of agricultural production, but farms were again decentralized to the county level by the mid-1960s, consisting of work teams of fifteen to twenty-five people, and had been further broken up into teams of seven to eight people, often relatives and family members, by the mid-1980s.[44] In the face of climate change and greater risk of natural disasters in recent years, similar local initiatives and mobilization can be seen, and one component of this community strategy is the activities supported by the network of the DPRK Red Cross.

DPRK Red Cross and IFRC

The DPRK Red Cross (DPRK RC) was founded in 1946 and is one of 192 active member Red Cross and Red Crescent National Societies of the IFRC. The DPRK RC and its volunteers had already provided emergency assistance and health care during the Korean War, and has since then continued its humanitarian work as an independent auxiliary to the DPRK government, with a lead role in national disaster response, disaster preparedness, and health activities, according to its constitution and 2007 Red Cross Law. Its two hundred sub-branches nationwide engage some twenty thousand volunteers trained in public health, first aid, and disaster response at different levels, as well as project implementation capacity in water and sanitation, disaster preparedness, and, more recently, integrated community development. As designed in the national Red Cross Law, the DPRK RC is a member of the cabinet level Disaster Coordinating Commission, overseeing disaster preparedness and response in major emergencies, as well as represented in provincial level disaster management working groups.[45] The DPRK RC is active across the entire country, with full access to all counties. Annual long-term international support through the IFRC is geographically allocated by the authorities to program areas in South P'yŏngan, North P'yŏngan, South Hamgyŏng, and North Hwanghae Provinces to avoid duplications with other organizations, in addition to emergency relief operations that can cover any province as long as community access is granted.

In the 1960s and 1970s, most cooperative farm households in North Korea had running water in their homes, supplied by pipes made of wood, bamboo, or iron. Today many systems are entirely or partly nonfunctional because of aging installations, lack of financial and material resources for maintenance, difficulties in importing internationally sourced spare parts, and systems destroyed during floods. Remnants of these systems can be seen in homes, with unconnected taps and tiled kitchen water tanks. Lack of access to safe drinking water and sanitation are serious health hazards and cause a range of illnesses, infant mortality, and stunting of children. Some houses have simple wells outside the home, but wells are often contaminated and unsuitable for human or animal consumption. Women commonly walk several kilometers a day to a community water pump to fetch water, or they may need to wash their clothes in streams and rivers, a difficult task during winter when everything is frozen. During the annual kimchi preparations, they wash the cabbage in the rivers. Thus, water and sanitation projects with hygiene promotion (WaSH) has been an important Red Cross activity for twenty years, and from 1999 to 2016, WaSH facilities were delivered to households in more than 220 communities serving more than 780,000 residents, and to more than 147 health institutions.

Communities can apply for support through their local branch of the DPRK Red Cross with detailed information about existing water and sanitation facilities. This includes proposals for improvement with initial design for the water scheme (locations of proposed water sources, pumping stations, reservoirs, pipeline network, and so forth), health data, and test results on the water quality of the current and proposed water sources. Applications are received by the DPRK RC county branches, which conduct a pre-assessment in the communities, together with county government technicians, to verify the feasibility of the proposed work. Subsequently, the DPRK RC and IFRC carry out joint field assessments to identify the final communities and the individual material needs for each community for program implementation. The water supply systems funded by restricted financial resources for emergency humanitarian programs focus mainly on water for household consumption for public health reasons.

Considering the humanitarian context, this may lead to setting higher standards for the amount of water required to be made available by such systems— typically 150 liters per person per day, compared with WHO emergency guidelines that indicate 20 liters per person per day for drinking, basic hygiene, and food preparation. The higher minimum quantity for potable water as a standard reflects an attempt to expand minimal humanitarian program targets to meet some of the needs that would more typically be covered by development aid, such as irrigation for kitchen gardens and water for domestic animals.[46] The international procurement of materials including pipes, pumps, and transformers can take more than six months, which does not include the time taken applying for sanctions exemptions.[47] Steel and cement can be procured nationally with international funding, while the thousands of hours of manual labor needed to implement the project are provided by the community as their own contribution to the project.

Because of the short time frame of emergency projects, spanning six to twelve months, a constant challenge in the project cycle is to secure funding, coordinate international procurement, apply for sanctions exemptions, acquire goods post-order, and transport for the timely arrival of materials so that activities can take place during two short distinct periods of the year: in the spring after the ground has thawed but before the rice planting starts, and in the autumn after the rice harvest but before the ground freezes. The pipes are often laid in the fields, hence the need to avoid the farming seasons without exception.

The DPRK RC has gained a reputation nationally and internationally as a reliable and fast humanitarian actor during times of natural disasters, for larger-scale relief operations supported internationally as well as small-scale support to families left destitute after fires or other calamities. In 1995, the DPRK RC requested international support from members of the IFRC for the first time, following the major flood disaster. An IFRC delegation, established in Pyongyang with some six expatriate and twenty Korean national staff, was maintained in Pyongyang until 2020, when a temporary relocation to Beijing of expatriate staff was necessary because of COVID-19 restrictions. The initial large-scale response focused on distribution of food and nonfood essentials to the affected population.

Over time, the DPRK RC developed annual community-based programs supported by the IFRC, centered on restoration of water supplies to health clinics and households in cooperative farms; distribution of essential drugs and basic medical equipment to more than eight million people in more than two thousand village-level clinics and county-level hospitals; as well as comprehensive disaster preparedness in allocated geographical areas. That broad program contributed to a basic coverage of health- and disaster-related humanitarian needs.

Communities identified by the DPRK RC get support in one or several areas, after a systematic assessment process involving the communities themselves. In particular, the programs focus on disaster-affected communities becoming more aware of their exposure to disaster hazards: learning how they can prepare and organize themselves for future disasters and making structural improvements to minimize the risk of loss of life, homes, and crops during floods or landslides. The local community's own contributions to the programs have been massive and continuous; they provide all labor without financial compensation, and mobilization may involve thousands of villagers to install several kilometers of pipe, plant tree saplings over large areas, or build mitigation structures against floods. For example, during a major measles outbreak in 2007, fifteen thousand Red Cross volunteers assisted the health authorities and UNICEF in two hundred counties to mobilize 10.2 million people for vaccinations during two months.[48]

In 2005, the DPRK government officially informed international organizations, including the IFRC, that the country sought to transition from humanitarian assistance to international cooperation on development and sustainability. The challenge for international organizations was how to finance long-term programs that were more developmental in nature, when funding streams were restricted to short-term (six- to twelve-month) humanitarian budgets for political reasons. Further, on national security grounds, the DPRK could not meet the requirements for banking transparency, external audits of ministry bodies, and strict financial regulations required by development cooperation financing instruments.

Despite these political and funding challenges, in 2012 the DPRK Red Cross started a small pilot project for more integration of community programs toward long-term sustainability, with seed funds from the Norwegian and Swedish governments as well as the German embassy in Pyongyang. The DPRK RC also applied learning from an exchange mission to Nepal, where the Nepal Red Cross carries out similar programs led by the communities themselves. Learning from the pilot project led gradually to a standard program, called the Integrated Community Development Programme (ICDP), with disaster risk management comprising a combination of community-led programs such as disaster preparedness and risk reduction; community-based health and first aid; water, sanitation, and hygiene promotion (WaSH); livelihoods (greenhouses); and reforestation. The

FIGURE 5.2.   Emergency water units. Courtesy of Swedish Red Cross.

positive impact on community resilience against shocks caused by disasters and toward long-term sustainability has been substantially proven by follow-up visits to the communities concerned.

North Korea deals with serious flooding almost every year, causing destruction and loss of lives, homes, and crops. At the same time, drought is common in the spring, coinciding with the rice planting season and affecting sensitive early crops.[49] The disaster preparedness program has a variety of components, including establishment and training of national and provincial Red Cross disaster response teams, which are deployed in time of disasters for evacuations of people and search and rescue, as well as relief distributions and deployment of emergency water treatment units (see figure 5.2). An important part of the preparedness program is to maintain sufficient numbers of pre-stocked "family kits" for immediate dispatch as needed after disasters. Approximately twenty-five thousand such kits, consisting of shelter kits or tarpaulins, quilts, cooking pots, water containers, purification tablets, and hygiene kits are internationally procured in advance, transported to North Korea and safely stored in strategic locations across the country. Even before stricter UN Security Council sanctions were imposed, the international procurement process, from placing an order to delivery, could take a minimum of six months, making pre-stocking in-country the only option for a relevant humanitarian response.

As projects are community led, Community Programme Management Committees are formed by communities, with members selected from a cross section of the community in terms of gender, age, role, and exposure (vulnerability). This encourages active participation of community members, including women, children, persons with disability, and the elderly in identifying the risks, needs, and the capacities to develop community plans. In 2007, the DPRK RC started, as one of several national actors, to pilot community support with vegetable greenhouses, in line with the national five-year plans and policy directions from the government. In addition, small electric food processing machinery such as rice husking machines and equipment to make noodles were provided to further facilitate food preparations and thus improve the food security at the village level. The first generation of greenhouses were small, simple, and low-cost installations, for which the DPRK RC provided resources for procurement of cement, steel, and glass. Over time, the installations became more substantial and technologically modern, for instance, by use of solar panels for electricity.[50] The greenhouses are often managed by disadvantaged women from the community (e.g., women from poorer families, female headed households, women with many children, women with disabilities), after they have been trained, and the increased production of fresh vegetables during longer periods of the year provide a more diverse diet. Groups of vulnerable people in the community are prioritized to receive produce from the greenhouses, brought by volunteers to their homes.

Building on this experience, the DPRK Red Cross, supported by partners from the Swedish, Danish, and Finnish Red Cross and the European Union and in cooperation with the DPRK Academy of Science, launched a Food Security Project in 2016, including international technological exchange and capacity-building. The project plan included the construction of an integrated solar greenhouse with a loop production system that incorporated the breeding of pigs and fish; the methane gas by-product from the livestock was then fed into vegetable production.[51]

After seventy years of protracted conflict in Korea, the situation is critical for people's livelihood and also for the environment, although environmental issues are not North Korea's problems alone. The persistent focus on output in the history of developmentalism and industrial agriculture has depleted the soil throughout the world, even as climate change further accelerates food shortages.[52] Root systems should ideally reach depths below plough level to access water and nutrients with plenty of organic matter, capable of withstanding periods of drought, but depleted soils are proof of an agrarian history of mismanaged land use, foreshadowing a grim future for agriculture and food availability world-wide. Industrial agriculture has largely killed the soil, leaving little microbial activity or organic material such as worms in the soil. The soil in places like North Korea can be, to a large extent, dead, functioning only as a mechanical substrate for plants to stand in to receive chemical nutrients, water, and air. Enormous investments in so-called green manure—nitrogen-fixing crops that are worked into the soil rather than harvested—would be required to support sustainable agriculture. But given the short-term goals *and need* to maximize harvests, North Korea has followed the path of the developing world, with heavy emphasis on monoculture cash crops for short-term returns, further depleting the soil and creating optimal conditions for viruses and parasites.[53]

This chapter has emphasized the social impact of environmental crises and community strategies for dealing with them amid the politics of environmental history as it has unfolded in North Korea. From early warnings of increasing weather anomalies and the adverse impact on food production worldwide to the environmental dangers of weapons of mass destruction, North Korea has followed the debate on environmental crises and their social impact much more closely than one might expect, given its current political standing in the world. In parallel with its nuclear weapons program, North Korea has therefore been an active participant and advocate of the United Nations Framework Convention on Climate Change, voting in 2016 in favor of starting UN negotiations to ban nuclear weapons, although it has yet to sign the new Treaty on the Prohibition of Nuclear Weapons that opened for signatures in 2017.[54]

The inconsistencies reflected in North Korean nuclear policy is symptomatic of the contradictions inherent to nuclear technology, which for under-resourced countries like North Korea can mean both energy and deterrence. Even as nuclear weapons were openly pursued after the fall of the Soviet Bloc, Article 7 of the 1986 Environmental Protection Law banning nuclear weapons was retained through its ensuing amendments and revisions in 1999, 2000, 2005, and 2011, all the way up until 2013, when it was finally deleted on July 24, 2013, by the Supreme People's Assembly.[55] As of 2016, the latest Environmental Protection Law, revised and amended in October 2014, while no longer including the previous ban on nuclear weapons, added significant provisions for recycling (Article 24), water purification (Article 25), development of renewables (Articles 39, 41), and implementation of an environmental protection fund and a pollution emissions tax (Article 50), as well as an annual national survey on environmental conditions (Article 51).[56]

If the current model of development and food production—as well as nuclear technology—is ultimately unsustainable not just for North Korea but globally, then sustained effort and international cooperation are necessary, as demonstrated by North Korea's own efforts to find a path toward "sustainable and re-silient human development."[57] Between the obsolete models of developmentalism and the conventional stopgap measures provided by humanitarianism in the aftermath of developmental failures, the integrated approaches of local first responders like the Red Cross that focus on community development offer a model of sustainability that accounts for our symbiotic relationship with the environment.[58] The IPCC has likewise recognized the value of "agricultural practices that include indigenous and local knowledge" in "overcoming the combined challenges of climate change, food security, biodiversity conservation, and combating desertification and land degradation."[59] In the immediate term, allocation of funding for activities straddling humanitarianism and development are thus crucial in protecting and promoting people's livelihood in an environmentally sustainable way. Meanwhile, it has become clear that science alone cannot address the inherent tensions in short-term economic and security needs that, because of human failures, are often met at the expense of long-term environmental sustainability. In that sense, the lessons of local community responses to environmental crises are as urgent and relevant as ever.

Part 3
PROCESSES OF DISPOSSESSION

Albert L. Park

Environmental destruction appears in different forms, and the industrial food system has been one of the forces most disruptive to nature in the modern era. Intensive crop and livestock production have ripped up landscapes while natural waterways have been torn from their existing context and rerouted to feed thirsty farmlands. The introduction of chemical fertilizers and pesticides have disrupted and degraded soil organic matter at the same time that livestock farms release large volumes of greenhouse gasses such as methane, thereby accelerating global warming. These detrimental effects of food production on the environment arise to no small degree from consumer choices. In their preference for particular foods, consumers play a large role in shaping the market and, by extension, food production. Extensive food cultures lie behind consumer choices, and these cultures valorize food products and dishes—thus establishing hierarchies of food. Food cultures normalize people's food choices in their everyday life. As the chapters in part 3 show, producers and consumers combine to form a potent driver of environmental change, molding patterns of land use to align with the changing tastes and predilections of Korean society.

In the Global North, industrial food systems emphasize the production and consumption of beef. South Korea, in particular, features an extensive beef-eating culture, which has a relatively short history. Before the twentieth century, Koreans mostly employed cattle for work and transportation. Agricultural cultivators relied mainly on cows and bulls for tilling fields. Beef was mostly consumed by the royal family and landed elite. Raising cattle for beef production took off during the Japanese colonial period. At that time, efforts were made to build more livestock farms to breed cattle not only for domestic consumption but also for the export of cattle and beef to neighboring countries. Eating beef became more mainstream only in the 1970s and 1980s, when beef became more affordable. The domestic production of beef grew during that time—a time when eating beef was glamorized as a sign of modern life. Since the early 1990s, the import of inexpensive beef products from the United States and Australia has only increased beef consumption. In fact, South Korea's rate of consumption has outpaced levels in China and Japan. In 2020, according to the OECD, South Korea's per capita consumption of beef was 11.9 kilograms, while China's was 4.2 kilograms and Japan's stood at 7.6 kilograms.

The beef industry in Korea is a multi-billion-dollar enterprise that involves parties inside and outside Korea. In 2020 alone, US companies exported $1.7 billion of beef and beef products to South Korea—making the country the top destination for American beef—while the export value of Australian beef to Korea totaled AD$1.6 billion. In South Korea, producers and wholesalers fuel the beef market as they sell and distribute beef to a variety of outlets, including food markets, grocery stores, butchers, and restaurants. At homes or in restaurants, beef is pervasive on Korean tables. Normally, any gathering, celebration, or important ritual features family and friends sharing beef-based dishes. Its central place in the Korean diet unsurprisingly makes beef into a ready-made symbol with different meanings and purposes. The 2008 Candlelight Protest, for example, turned beef into a signifier of political kowtowing. At that time, people protested President Lee Myung-bak's decision to resume US beef imports despite issues about the safety of imported beef. In terms of nationalism, Koreans praise *hanu*—a breed of cattle that is indigenous to the Korean peninsula and is known for being on par with Japanese wagyu beef—as a symbol of their prestigious food culture. Increasingly, the consumption of beef has come to symbolize virility, strength, and prosperity because narratives of the ideal modern life have promoted beef-eating as a sign of an advanced society.

Beef, in short, holds a central place in Korean society and its industrial food system. It therefore shapes the pathways of nonhuman and human life and the overall environment. In part 3, Anders Riel Muller and Lindsay S. R. Jolivette's chapters help to elucidate the relationships between beef and human and nonhuman processes. Together, they highlight meat production and consumption as processes that not only unsettle and determine landscapes and ecologies but also raise important questions about the treatment of animals and the sometimes invisible costs of the industry. For both authors, meat or, more specifically, beef serves as a vital connection point between human and nonhuman concerns. In particular, the two chapters explore concerns of dispossession through beef and the environmental costs of this process. Whereas Muller's chapter speaks of dispossession as a vehicle for depriving land from non-Koreans outside of the peninsula and shaping the landscapes of South Korea, Jolivette's chapter treats dispossession as a biological process that strips away the humanity of individuals and forces the questioning of what it means to be human. In paying greater heed to acts of land expropriation and ideas of dehumanization, both chapters speak to how beef has unsettled the worlds of humans and animals alike.

Three particular themes structure their approach to the political, cultural, and affective contours of beef and dispossession in South Korea—*destruction, seizing, and systems. Destruction* highlights the role meat and beef have played in the decline of planetary health through the ripping up of lands for livestock production—a process that, as Muller shows, requires that we look beyond the Korean peninsula. Setting her sights on the cultural anxieties that have taken shape around meat consumption, Jolivette considers destruction in a different sense: the imagined decimation of the human race because of the slaughtering of animals and the insatiable consumption of beef. Additionally, both essays touch on the theme of *seizing*—that is, taking hold of resources, foodways, or other bodies in a sudden manner. Their chapters approach seizing by showing how Korean companies have requisitioned land for the production of feed overseas or how Korean films have depicted Korean bodies being taken over by viruses and pathogens and becoming zombies after eating meat. A third theme—*systems*—draws our attention to the various ways that meat production and consumption bind the human and nonhuman worlds together and mediate relationships between the two, whether through markets, culinary practices, or even geopolitics. Taken together, these themes reveal beef to be not just an item for consumption and celebration, but also a vital arena of environmental politics and a source of considerable ecological anxiety.

6

RICE FIELDS, MOUNTAINS, AND THE INVISIBLE MEATIFICATION OF KOREAN AGRICULTURE

Anders Riel Muller (Yeonjun Song)

A trip through the South Korean countryside means passing through landscapes dominated by rice fields and tree-covered mountains. This landscape, and the farmers working the land, represents a kind of national authenticity to many Koreans and stands in contrast to high modernist images of high rises that dominate the urban landscape in South Korea. The countryside evokes a kind of authenticity that positions agricultural producers, the paddy rice landscape, and tree-covered mountains as symbols of Korean national identity and tradition. Of course, such notions are to a large extent imagined. The verdant mountains are mainly the result of reforestation efforts beginning in the 1960s and the current layout of irrigated rice fields owes much to the rural modernization schemes beginning in the 1970s. Irrigated rice fields cover much of the agricultural land area of the southern part of the peninsula within the territory of South Korea. In 2017, more than half of Korea's 1.6 million hectares of agriculturally productive land was used for paddy rice cultivation. The notion that rice is central to Korean culture and identity is thus not only something reproduced through nationalist narratives and food practices, but it also manifest in the physical landscape.[1]

State support of rice production and consumption has been a central pillar of Korean agricultural policy since the 1970s, when the country embarked on a national food self-sufficiency drive reversing two decades of encouragement of Western diets based on mostly US-subsidized food imports.[2] The government of Park Chung-hee implemented a range of agricultural policies to increase domestic agricultural production, initially with a strong emphasis on rice through price-support schemes and agricultural modernization policies focused on new rice varieties, fertilizer production, mechanization, and rural infrastructure.[3] Indeed, as Yonjae Paik reveals in chapter 8, state support for rice production and consumption has been a central pillar of agricultural policy for more than four decades.

In 2013, about a third of the agricultural-sector budget was spent on rice support measures, despite declining rates of consumption.[4] Rice production also remains a major source of income for many of South Korea's approximately one million farm households. On average, the income from rice farming amounted to 63 percent of total farm household income from agricultural activities.[5] Thus, the continued dominance of rice fields in the agricultural landscape reflects the importance of rice at the farm level as well as in agricultural policy. Yet, despite the continued dominance of rice fields in the agricultural landscape, South Korean agriculture has undergone significant changes in the past three decades. The first change is quite visible: the rise of horticulture in poly-tunnel greenhouses since the early 1990s. Greenhouse cultivation has been a major source of new revenue for many of South Korea's small-scale farmers, who still make up the majority of agricultural producers. The controlled environment in greenhouses has enabled longer growing seasons, more effective pest control, and, ultimately, higher yields of especially high-value vegetables, mushrooms, and berries.[6]

But the dominance of rice agriculture conceals major transformations of the Korean agricultural sector over the past three decades. Since the late 1970s, livestock production has risen dramatically, from 249,000 metric tons in 1975 to more than two million metric tons in 2013.[7] That is an eightfold increase in less than forty years, putting South Korea on par with the production numbers of Denmark, a major exporter of meat products in Europe. Meat production has also become the most important source of revenue for the agricultural sector overall.[8] But the expansion of livestock production and transformation of the agricultural sector is barely visible in the landscape. It is useful to compare the cases of Denmark and South Korea, since both countries have roughly the same yearly domestic production of meat, around 2.1 million metric tons. Yet, there are major differences in how this has affected land use in each country. In Denmark, 80 percent of agricultural land (or approximately 3.5 million hectares of farmland) is today used for feed-crop production.[9] By comparison, South Korea produced animal feed on, roughly, only 300,000 hectares of land in 2014 (or roughly 17 percent of total agricultural land).[10]

The difference in land use between Denmark and Korea signifies the extent to which South Korea has expanded livestock production using imported feed crops rather than depending on domestic feed production. Denmark imports approximately 2.1 million tons of soybean products to supplement its domestic production of feed of around thirty million tons, or 7 percent of total feed needs.[11] South

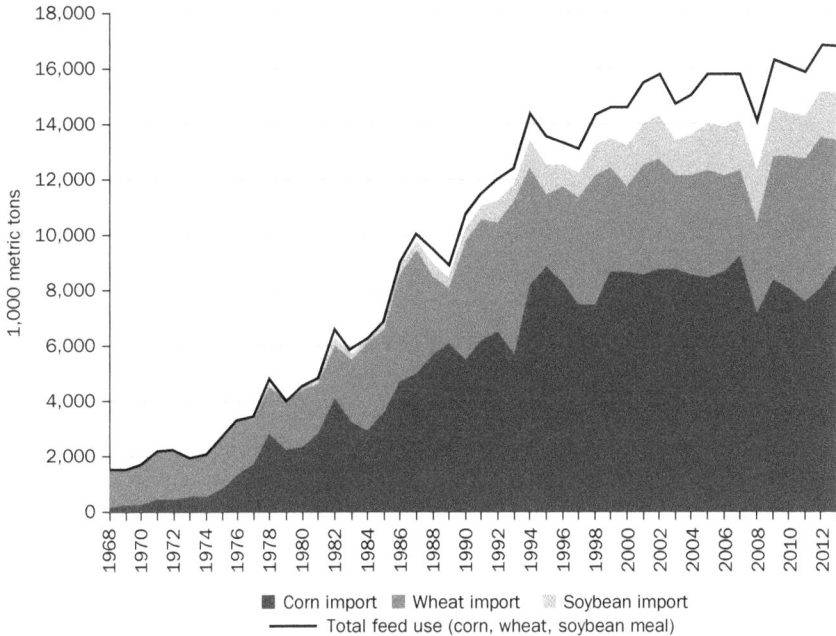

FIGURE 6.1. Imports of corn, wheat, and soybean meal (1000 mt). *Source*: United States Department of Agriculture, Foreign Agricultural Service, Production, Supply and Distribution (online 2014).

Korea imports approximately 76 percent of ingredients for its annual twenty-seven million tons of feed consumption.[12] This makes South Korea not only extremely dependent on feed imports, but also one of the largest grain importers in the world (figure 6.1).

Unlike South Korea, the Danish agricultural landscape has undergone significant changes to feed its growing livestock production in recent decades. Relative large-scale mono-cropped fields of feed grains and roughage today dominate the landscape.[13] One environmental impact of the expansion of feed production is a drastic reduction in biodiversity. The hedgerows between fields that provide shelter and food for wild animals, birds, and insects have become fewer as field sizes have increased. In South Korea, the expansion of animal production has not resulted in significant changes to land use, because of the heavy reliance on imported feed. Despite farm consolidation, the predominant agricultural landscape in South Korea remains that of rice fields intermixed with horticulture and orchards.

This chapter examines how South Korea's biggest agricultural transformation in its modern history occurred without significantly affecting land use and, thereby, agricultural landscapes. How do we conceptualize this externalization of land-use changes in South Korea, and what have been the effects in Korea as well as abroad? To understand how South Korea developed such a significant reliance on import feed for an expanding livestock sector requires studying a particular agricultural policy formation that has been termed a *bifurcation strategy*. McMichael and Kim argue that, in the case of South Korea, the agricultural markets have been characterized by a "subdivision into a heavily protected national circuit of rice, as the basic food staple, and other agro-food circuits involving varying degrees of international commodity relations, such as the livestock complex and processed flour goods."[14]

Building on this work, I here argue that the bifurcation strategy allowed the livestock sector to expand without converting vast tracts of South Korea's agricultural land to pasture and feed grain production. Owing in part to the liberalization of agricultural trade, the environmental effects of livestock production were externalized to territories overseas.[15] Paying careful attention to how bifurcation enables agricultural transformation without major land-use change allows us to complicate academic and political debates that tend to focus on agricultural protection[16] versus free trade policies.[17] There is no doubt that trade liberalization has influenced agriculture in South Korea, often to the detriment of small farmers, but trade liberalization has also enabled *meatification* while maintaining rice agriculture as a principal crop.[18]

To more fully understand South Korea's agri-food politics, then, we must track the meatification of Korean agriculture and diet. Tony Weis argues that "meatification"—that is, rising meat consumption and industrial livestock production—is an inescapable part of the agricultural restructuring of global food systems, especially in Asia.[19] He is echoed by Cindy Schneider, who argues that part of what drives financiers to invest in farmland overseas is the demand for feed grains to meet rapidly growing demand for feed grains from Asian countries such as China and India.[20] This hypothesis nicely captures the situation of South Korea.[21] The rise in meat production plays a major part in the country's declining grain self-sufficiency and the country's incorporation into the transnational and corporate agri-food system, but the historical trajectory for how this came to be in South Korea is more complex and political than what is presented by Weis and Schneider

The South Korean agricultural sector has often been presented as opposed to trade liberalization and a champion of food self-sufficiency.[22] This chapter suggests that the bifurcation policy shows a more ambivalent position toward trade liberalization among South Korean farmers and agricultural industries. While the agricultural sector has been vehemently opposed to trade liberalization of rice and livestock products, it has embraced trade liberalization in other sectors such as the market for feed grains. Though focused mainly on the development of the cattle sector, this analysis reveals dynamics of feed import dependence that bear on the livestock sector writ large.

The Expansion of Livestock Production

Modern commercial livestock production did not occur until the 1970s, when the regime of Park Chung-hee pushed for agricultural modernization and greater food self-sufficiency. Since the late 1950s, South Korea had relied heavily on US food aid and did little to develop the domestic agricultural sector. With waning US aid, the government was forced to either import food or increase domestic production. Consumption patterns also changed. The emerging urban middle class led to higher demand for meat products as a symbol of upward economic mobility.[23] To protect the country's trade balance and limit foreign exchange expenditures, the government instituted restrictions on imports of strategically important agricultural commodities while encouraging domestic production. Commercial meat production in Korea was a direct effect of this state-led food supply policy that intended to meet changing domestic demands and reduced food aid from the United States.[24]

From the mid-1970s, the government heavily encouraged commercial livestock farming through capital injections for new production systems and scientific research. Some sectors became increasingly specialized, unlike the general trend of small-scale multifunctional farms. The Samsung group was a pioneer in the building of large-scale livestock operations. In 1973, Samsung established an intensive, vertically integrated hog breeding and research operation in Kyŏnggi Province.[25] Such was also the case for poultry production, in which large-scale commercial operations also began to address the increasing demand for meat and eggs.[26]

The beef sector developed quite differently. In 1975, 92.5 percent of all cattle was raised on small farms with one or two heads per farm, whereas only 0.9 percent was raised in herd sizes greater than fifty heads.[27] By 1980, almost one million farm households raised cattle, but the average herd size was only 1.4 per household. Of those households, 94 percent raised only one or two head of cattle.[28] Small farmers had a cost advantage because feed produced on-farm such as wild grasses, rice straw, and rice bran were readily available. Large-scale farmers had to rely more on imported feed grains, and these imports were severely restricted by the government.[29] The combination of low capital investments, low labor intensity, and high returns made cattle rearing a very attractive option to many small farmers and was as such incorporated into the existing multifunctional family farm structure.[30]

To provide feed for the livestock sector, the government began to prioritize pastureland development in the late 1970s and early 1980s. Feed production was encouraged through initiatives to reclaim upland areas and research initiatives sought to use idle paddy land for winter forage crops.[31] This led to an increase in pastureland from 57,850 hectares in 1973 to 312,350 hectares in 1981. The number of cattle raised in pastures increased from 139,000 in 1973 to 1,231,000 during that same period.[32] The livestock sector continued to enjoy trade protection during the 1980s and this meant that Korean livestock producers were able to expand production in a relatively protected market free from international competition.[33] The government policy of developing domestic feed production, however, became increasingly difficult to sustain in the 1980s because of pressure from the United States and Australia to open agricultural markets.[34]

In 1980, South Korea faced a severe economic crisis, prompting the Chun Doo-hwan administration to launch an economic liberalization program in return for loans from the International Monetary Fund.[35] South Korea agreed to open up markets for US wheat, tobacco, and feed grains to avoid facing penalties on industrial commodity exports to the United States, the country's biggest export market.[36] The liberalization of feed markets dealt a decisive blow to further expansion of domestic feed production and, in the second half of the 1980s, efforts to develop domestic feed production ended.[37] Imports of feed grains such as corn, wheat, and soybean meal for feed use increased dramatically through the 1980s. In 1980 South Korea imported 4.5 million metric tons of corn, wheat, and soybean meal for feed uses. By 1987, this figure had climbed to ten million metric tons for feed use.[38]

By the early 1980s the contours of the bifurcation policy were thus already visible. South Korea maintained a strong emphasis on national food self-sufficiency for trade balance purposes, but external pressures led the government to allow for limited liberalization of some agricultural commodities. During the Uruguay Round Agreement of Agriculture of the GATT negotiations in the late 1980s, South Korea, under heavy pressure from the United States, agreed to phase out restrictions on remaining agricultural sectors by the 1990s. The outcome was that import quota restrictions on all agricultural commodities, except rice, were lifted and that tariffs would be reduced over a ten-year period. All told, 285 agricultural commodities were scheduled to have import quotas removed over a ten-year period. Items in this group included beef, poultry, pork, and dairy products. Finally, South Korea agreed to reduce subsidies on rice, barley, corn, soybean, and vegetables.[39]

To prepare the agricultural sector for trade liberalization, the Korean government announced a 42 trillion *won* (US$40 billion) agricultural investment and loan program. These programs sought to enhance the competitiveness of the agricultural sector through agricultural modernization and specialization. The program first scheduled to run until 1998 was later extended until 2004 with an additional 45 trillion *won* allocation for agricultural modernization.[40] This new program marked a significant change in Korean agricultural policy, indicating a shift from a productivist-oriented approach to one of structural adjustment.

For cattle producers, structural adjustment meant, among other things, the introduction of quality standards. Until 1992, there was no official quality grading system for beef in Korea; the beef market was quite undifferentiated, and there was little knowledge among the general population of what constituted superior quality. Since the major competition came from US imports, the National Livestock Cooperative Federation responded by introducing a grading system for domestically produced beef that mimicked the US quality system. The quality grading system ranked beef carcasses according to meat yields and meat quality.[41] As in the US grading system, the most important quality criteria was fat marbling, high concentrations of which garnered steep price premiums.[42] The system was implemented nationwide in 1995 and was introduced at the retail level in 1997.[43]

The quality grading system had significant implications for the domestic beef industry. The focus on high fat marbling and white fat color imposed stricter production requirements. Obtaining the optimal level of carcass yield, fat content, fat marbling, and fat color required standardized feeding regimes and knowledge of feed optimization, especially in the final months of the animal's life, when fat marbling enhancement takes place. Central to obtaining the desired meat characteristics (high levels of high intramuscular fat marbling) is the use of soy and corn-rich compound feed. Corn-feeding in the right amounts, especially in the late stages of feeding regimes, is a well-known and widely used practice in the United States, Australia, Canada, and Japan, where fat marbling is also prized.[44]

The grading standards and need for highly specialized compound feed entrenched the need for imported feed grain. While the bifurcation strategy of the early 1980s had protected beef and rice markets from overseas direct competition, trade liberalization and introduction of US grain-fed beef for general consumption prompted Korean cattle producers to shift to compound feed to become competitive in the premium market where profits could be made. Thus, the development of the grading system implemented to help Korean producers adjust to trade liberalization also caused the sector to become increasingly integrated into, especially, the North American and South American industrial grain circuits.[45] From an economic perspective, this was not a major issue because world prices of wheat, corn, and soybean remained low during most of the 1990s and early 2000s. Low world market prices for feed grain thus made it possible for the Korean beef sector to scale up and remain somewhat price competitive, especially vis-à-vis beef from the United States and Australia that still faced import quota restrictions.

The expansion of livestock production is arguably the biggest agricultural transformation in South Korea over the past thirty years. Development and expansion of domestic pastureland to supply feed for the expanding livestock sector was a priority in the late 1970s and early 1980s, in the line with the state's attempt to limit foreign expenditure on agricultural imports. When the government was forced to liberalize parts of the agricultural trade in the early 1980s, the first contours of the bifurcation model was put in place. The bifurcation model was decisive in shaping the contemporary systems of livestock production in South Korea based on imported feed. As trade liberalization was forced on the agricultural sector as part of the Uruguay trade negotiations in the early 1990s, the government attempted to protect the livestock sector by developing quality standards. At the same time, it began to promote the consumption of Korean-produced meat as a patriotic duty, one that brought with it the myriad health benefits of an "indigenous" diet. Needless to say, such claims were fundamentally at odds with the growing dependence on feed from abroad.

Intrasectoral Politics and Bifurcation Policy

One cannot understand the politics behind bifurcation policy without first recognizing the role of agricultural producers in the broader political landscape of South Korean development. Simply put, the crux of agricultural policy formation has been the question of agricultural protectionism versus trade liberalization. The political and academic debates about agricultural protectionism versus trade liberalization have hinged largely on the detrimental effects of trade liberalization for the agricultural sector, on one hand,[46] and the cost-effectiveness of agricultural trade liberalization, on the other.[47] Each side focuses on different aspects of the trade liberalization debate. The first camp is concerned principally with South Korea's ability to maintain agricultural activity in its own right for reasons related to national food self-sufficiency, cultural heritage, and the protection of rural communities. Their critics view agricultural activity as a matter of economic costs and benefits from a broader national economic perspective and have become strong proponents of full trade liberalization. Both sides appear to be right, but at the same time both sides, I argue, also get key points wrong.

As we have seen, the growth of the livestock sector was enabled by the partial liberalization of agricultural trade, by allowing feed imports while concurrently protecting meat markets from outside competition. If the government had continued its policy of food self-sufficiency and agricultural protectionism, the domestic agricultural sector would have had to face some difficult choices about land use. An expansion of livestock based on domestic feed would have required significant land-use changes and a reduction in horticulture and rice production. The predominance of paddy rice cultivation in the Korean landscape would have had to give way for feed-crop production, or at least systems of crop rotation. In either case, the land available for rice and horticulture production would be diminished significantly and, therefore, so would the agricultural landscapes. Thus, in order to understand the trajectory of this phenomenon, we need to also understand the intrasectoral agricultural politics of South Korea in the past decades. Intrasectoral politics refers to the political struggles between different segments of the agricultural sector over agricultural policy formation.[48] For example, the economic interests of rice farmers and livestock farmers may or may not align and as such they may have different policy preferences.

From the late Chosŏn period through Japan's colonial rule in Korea, agriculture on the peninsula was characterized by the concentration of arable landholdings within a small group of elite landowners, who relied heavily on tenants or agricultural laborers. The economic inequalities of this system led to widespread dissatisfaction as well as rebellions against the ruling classes before and during Japanese colonization.[49] Following the dissolution of the Japanese empire and the division of the Korean peninsula, North Korea's regime quickly implemented sweeping land reforms to assuage widespread discontent among the majority who labored as tenant farmers and agricultural workers in an exploitative system exacerbated by Japanese colonial rule. The South Korean state followed suit in the wake of the Korean War in order to appease people's demands.

These land reforms led to a relatively homogeneous small-scale farm agricultural commodity production system, which is still prevalent in South Korea today. Only 8.7 percent of farms are larger than three hectares.[50] This system is defined by its relative homogeneity of agricultural production, with rice, livestock, and horticulture as dominant activities—a "unimodal mini-farm structure," in the words of Larry Burmeister.[51] This unimodal structure has also determined the class identity of farmers in South Korea, at least since the political mobilization of South Korean farmers in the late 1970s and 1980s. The relative homogeneity of farm economic activity across the mini-farm agricultural system, with rice as a major income-generating activity supplemented with either livestock or horticulture for many farmers, played a central role in the political mobilization of farmers.

The multifunctional mini-farm system still dominates South Korean agriculture. Farmers are dependent on multiple streams of agricultural revenue as well as nonfarm income. Any conversion of limited farmland to other uses leads to diminishing income from other agricultural activities. Imported feed allowed the Korean agricultural sector and farmers' organizations to avoid difficult decisions about whether rice or meat production should be given priority on the limited land available. Agricultural policy could maintain rice production as the main agricultural activity in both economic and land-use terms while simultaneously expanding meat production. This explains the ambivalent position that agricultural trade liberalization plays in Korean agricultural policy. To be sure, farmers have vehemently opposed and actively protested attempts to liberalize rice and meat markets with quite some success over the decades. But agricultural trade liberalization also created new economic opportunities that would not have been possible if agricultural self-sufficiency and trade protection policies had continued.

The united front to oppose trade liberalization of rice and livestock sectors[52] is in large part due to political coalitions spanning a range of agricultural subsectors.[53] Rice and livestock producers as well as feed companies were able to muster strong opposition to trade liberalization of rice and meat markets in successive multilateral and bilateral trade negotiations.[54] Liberalization of these sectors would have been detrimental to agricultural producers and feed companies. The liberalization of feed grain imports, on the other hand, supported the economic interests of domestic feed companies, livestock producers, and rice producers as it allowed them to expand livestock operations without converting farmland to feed-crop production. In this sense, the economic interests of rice farmers, livestock producers, and industry were accommodated in the free trade negotiations—or at least a political compromise was reached that balanced the economic interests of dominant agricultural sectors.[55]

Despite some consolidation in the beef cattle sector due to specialization and economies of scale, the vast majority of producers have for the last three decades been relatively small. In 2001, of the total 260,000 cattle farms in South Korea, as many as 256,000 farms had fewer than fifty head of cattle.[56] Most of these were smaller multifunctional farms in which cattle breeding was secondary to rice farming or horticulture. By relying on imported feed, farmers were able to maintain an additional income from cattle without having to convert farmland dedicated to rice or horticulture to feed production. As such, the dependence on imported feed allowed smaller farmers to remain in the cattle sector, but in doing so, they became increasingly enmeshed in global agricultural production systems.

The Consequences of Externalization of Feed Production

The expansion of livestock agriculture in Korea (and concomitant maintenance of rice as the dominant crop in the agricultural landscape) has been one of the effects of the bifurcation policy pursued since the 1980s. Few seem to critically question the fact that South Korea's meat sector relies on roughly four million hectares of farmland overseas—from the US Midwest to Canada, from Australia to Argentina and Brazil.[57] That is an area twice as big as the total area under cultivation in South Korea today.[58] Thus, to view the landscapes that feed the Korean meat sector, we need to move from images of rice fields and mountains to that of large corn and wheat fields on former prairieland in Iowa or Alberta, and soybean fields on what used to be pampas in Argentina or the rainforests of Brazil. It is in these locations that the effects of the meatification of Korean agriculture become fully visible.

The dependence on imported feed continued without much worry until the global food crisis of 2007–2008. As world prices for wheat and corn skyrocketed in those years, Korean livestock producers saw their own production costs soar. The dependence on imported feed suddenly became regarded as a liability rather than an advantage, not because of its negative impacts abroad but rather because international grain production and trade was in the hands of foreign companies. In newspapers and policy papers, experts argued that the problem was that Korean lacked control of overseas grain production and trade. This, these experts argued, led to a situation in which the country's food supply had become dominated by US and Japanese grain trading companies.[59]

These fears fueled the launch of the Overseas Agricultural Development Strategy (OADS), announced by the Lee Myung-bak administration in 2008.[60] To protect national food security, the government announced they would offer low-interest loans and guarantees to Korean companies that were willing to invest in overseas grain production and trade. The strategy had three main objectives: (1) to establish Korean controlled grain-trading companies in key markets such as the United States, Argentina, and Brazil; (2) to encourage investments by Korean nationals in overseas food production and agriculture by leasing and buying farmland mainly in Southeast Asia and Far East Russia; and (3) to explore possibilities for developing domestic feed resources. The last item in this strategy was the most contentious, as it would involve reprioritizing agricultural lands within South Korea, raising difficult questions regarding what crops to prioritize. In the short run, at least, overseas land acquisitions and control of overseas grain procurement production became the key priorities.

At the end of 2014, 149 Korean-owned companies were active in twenty-seven countries, controlling a total of 53,677 hectares of farmland.[61] These figures, while slight, testify to the growing scope of South Korea's expansion abroad. In order to protect the livestock sectors from being at the mercy of foreign corporate interests, South Korean companies were encouraged to establish farming and trading operations overseas. The companies heeding the call of the government ranged from gargantuan corporations such as Samsung and Hyundai to smaller companies and, perhaps most notably, several companies set up by Korean farmers' organizations. The motivation for farmers to invest in overseas farmland was to secure a supply of feed grains at stable prices independent of the world market. OADS thus signaled a significant shift in how South Korea seeks to secure animal feed, by controlling land overseas as well as entering the grain trade. Such a system can only be developed through free trade agreements that allow export and import of feed grains without too many restrictions.

This new strategy had clear impacts on land use in places outside South Korea's territorial borders. One such example was the company Chungnam Overseas Agricultural Corporation (COAC), a joint venture between the Chungnam livestock cooperative and the Chungnam provincial government, which, with the financial and technical assistance of the government, embarked on agricultural investments in Cambodia. To these farmers, OADS was their salvation in times of rising grain prices: "Every cattle farmer had the same concern—there was no future for cattle farms without stable feed supply. The Government's overseas agricultural development project became our new hope."[62]

The company managed to secure 474 hectares of land in the Koh Sla region approximately three hours from the capital Phnom Penh in 2009.[63] Here the farmers constructed milling and drying facilities and started planting corn, which they intended to ship back to Korea. COAC was not the only Korean company growing crops in the Koh Sla region. One study revealed that some of these Korean investments had forced hundreds of local villagers off their land.[64] From personal observation, it is clear that the presence of Korean companies contributed to radically altered land use and landscapes in Koh Sla. The mixture of tropical forest, small-scale subsistence farming, and pastureland has been increasingly replaced by large land concessions for monocrop agriculture intended for export to Korea, among other countries. Other Korean livestock cooperatives (especially those active in Southeast Asia) engaged in similar investments, accelerating dispossession and agricultural transformation overseas.

Overseas agricultural investments continue as livestock producers, along with other agricultural sector producers, keep advocating for trade protection against imported agricultural products at home. A key argument in Korean agricultural policy for continued protection is predicated on the agricultural multifunctionality argument in the Uruguay Agreement that allows for continued protection of agriculture on the grounds that such activity has several positive externalities including environmental protection, balanced economy, and, not least, the protection of cultural heritage.[65] The latter effort includes the continued protection of rice production as a central component of Korean cultural heritage.[66] Yet, as this chapter has shown, the continued dominance of rice fields in the Korean landscape is contingent on the livestock sector's ability to utilize overseas territories for feed production. A cultural landscape still dominated by rice fields is therefore the effect not only of agricultural protection, but also of trade liberalization that has allowed the externalization of feed production overseas.

This chapter examines how the bifurcated agricultural policy pursued from the 1980s enabled the expansion of livestock production in Korea without significant changes to the agricultural landscape in South Korea. Critically, the bifurcation policy protected domestic markets for meat while allowing the expansion of livestock production through imported feed. Whereas the state was willing to liberalize the agricultural sector in order to maintain access to major export markets for industrial goods, the agricultural sector, through political mobilization across subsectors, was able to gain considerable concessions that limited the import of products strategically important to the domestic agricultural sector—most notably rice and meat products. The bifurcation policy essentially became a political compromise that allowed the domestic livestock sector to expand and consolidate itself during the 1980s and 1990s.

Such a compromise also enabled agricultural policy to maintain rice production as the dominant crop by contracting out feed-grain production to overseas territories. Traveling through a Korean agricultural landscape of rice fields intermixed with orchards and horticulture is thus possible because South Korea's livestock sector relies on millions of hectares of industrial scale monoculture overseas. Only by acknowledging the soybean fields of Argentina and Brazil, the cornfields of the US Midwest, or the former tropical forest areas of Cambodia can one truly comprehend how the meatification of South Korean agriculture has altered land use and agricultural landscapes. The massive forest fires that ripped across much of the Amazon basin in the summer of 2019 testify to how the maintenance of a paddy rice landscape in South Korea has destructive effects that ripple well beyond the peninsula.

7

THE ECO-ZOMBIES OF SOUTH KOREAN CINEMA

Consumerism, Carnivores, and Eco-criticism

Lindsay S. R. Jolivette

These days, it is hardly a stretch to say that South Korean food culture is globally most famous for barbeque. "Koreatown" neighborhoods with KBBQ joints on every corner that all manage to stay in business and Korean TV shows that display scene after scene of the attractive main characters eating pork belly together is only the tip of the iceberg. Despite the association between Korea and BBQ, however, heavy reliance on meat as a staple is a relatively new occurrence. The shifts in consumer practices regarding food have taken place in parallel with a multitude of other sociocultural changes in South Korea, and because of the nation's rapid economic and industrial development after the Korean War, the changes in what and how people eat have been dramatic. South Korea was once considered a country of rice, but changes in agricultural policies outlined in chapter 6 caused the consumption of meat and poultry to increase significantly in 1969 and to increase tenfold nationally by 1995, with continued increases into the 2000s.[1] These increases were, and still are, directly linked to the rapid growth of South Korea's GDP (gross domestic product) that began in the 1960s, which granted more people luxury spending power. To meet the growing domestic consumer demand, both animal feed and processed meat products began to be imported in large quantities.[2] These statistics do not exist in a vacuum, however, because food is an integral part of human culture and identity, not just a neutral substance, especially when it comes to meat and contending with the slaughter of other living beings.

South Korea's transformation into a meat-eating nation has not been without its bumps along the way. In addition to socioeconomic examples of carnivorous growing pains—such as the 2008 candlelight vigils protesting the import of American beef—cultural products like film and literature have manifested similar meat-skeptical messaging.[3] In this chapter I focus on the Korean zombie cinema of the mid-2000s and how the genre provides further evidence of sociocultural anxiety caused by the uncomfortable transition into an economy reliant on the commercial meat industry, both domestically and through imports. To do this, I analyze three Korean zombie films, *The Neighbor Zombie*,[4] *Doomsday Book*,[5] and *Zombie School*,[6] all of which were made in the mid-2000s, a period during which the health and safety of the meat industry was becoming an issue of frequent news coverage. Correlatively, not until the early 2000s did zombie films begin to appear in what could be considered significant numbers, suggesting that the terrifying prospect of ingesting contaminated meat was being directly associated with contaminated human bodies in visual media. The three films discussed here raise the question of what it means to be a human in contemporary South Korea amid the tumult of rapid change, especially in terms of what is being ingested. They offer an exploration of sociocultural allegory within a Korean context that speaks to anxieties about food safety, import policy, and the nonhuman, ultimately resulting in an ecological warning about consumer culture that differs from Western zombie films while still maintaining the genre's key question of humanity's future.

Within the context of these larger issues, I argue that *The Neighbor Zombie, Doomsday Book,* and *Zombie School* are manifestations of the anxiety caused by the detrimental ecological effects of the booming commercial meat industry and increased meat consumption. These concerns are expressed within the plots and visual imagery of all three films, and the zombies—in their seemingly mindless state—embody the dangers of passive consumer acceptance of the cultural shift to meat being the major signifier of so-called Korean food. In turn, the desire to consume animal products has led to an acceptance of accompanying health and safety concerns such as contamination and low-quality meat imports that endanger consumers. Far from merely fictional, meat consumption in South Korea brought horrors of its own thanks to multiple health scares in the 2000s that called into question the safety of meat production practices. However, eating meat has become so ingrained in the contemporary culture that to engage with the issue—without addressing it head-on and causing viewers to feel attacked for their everyday diets—requires melding fictional horror with *traces* of reality. Through this amalgamation, these films open a channel for the consideration of eco-critical concerns that are expressed through the potential of an eco-zombie epidemic that threatens the continuation of humanity if the environment is pushed too far toward destruction brought about by society's own negligent consumption.

Being Human in a World of Eco-zombies

Considering the plethora of excellent documentaries and narrative films that discuss environmental degradation directly, one might reasonably ask, why zombies? The distinctness of zombies as a subject is intimately linked to the question of what it means to be a part of human society on planet Earth. In the case of the Korean zombie films discussed here, the connections between human, animal, and nature are of unequivocal importance.[7] The zombies act as an embodiment of these conflicted relationships in a way that accurately addresses the violence and horror of ecological damage with a purposefully fear-inducing intensity that informational documentaries rarely achieve. To create a theoretical framework for this question of the zombie in environmental contexts, I first briefly discuss how the scholars Alexandre Kojève, Akira Lippit, and Sarah Juliet Lauro have conceptualized these categories of human, animal, and nature, before moving on to the analysis of the films themselves.

What defines humanity, and when does this humanity end? Alexandre Kojève wrote that humans revert to a state of animality if they cease to "strive."[8] For one to strive there must be some force of opposition to strive *against*, and it is this will toward overcoming opposition that defines humanity. When considering history through an eco-critical lens, one way humanity has been able to maintain its sense of identity is by striving to differentiate itself from the so-called natural world by creating systems of industrialization and technology. In this striving against "nature," the animal plays an important role as the opposite to the human, and likewise Kojève frames the opposite of humanity as animality. While striving against the animal does offer a system for continued humanity in the Kojèvian sense, this form of striving also simultaneously damages the nonhuman environment and endangers animal life. In a theoretical move that simultaneously confirms Kojève's human/animal duality and highlights that duality's danger, Akira Lippit states that animals must remain in the world to determine, or validate, human existence as separate from nature.[9] Unfortunately, striving often manifests as killing. Although it is not a conscious anxiety, Lippit argues that the growing lack of wild animals and the commodification of animal bodies for meat leads to a "sense of panic for the earth's dwindling resources."[10] This leaves humanity with a double-edged sword; human striving will cease if nature and animals no longer exist, but when this form of striving ceases then so will human subjectivity if another form of striving does not arise. When humanity truly does end, what will come after? As many creative minds have imagined, perhaps it will be zombies.

Zombies are typically thought of as human-derivative supernatural monsters, but scholar Sarah Juliet Lauro has also argued for a conceptualization of eco-zombies that allows for a more expansive meaning.[11] She posits that, in eco-critical contexts, we find zombies that are natural creatures as opposed to supernatural creatures, and those specifically can be thought of as eco-zombies. Rather than being entities comparable to vampires or werewolves, the eco-zombie is a creature of the corporeal world created through "natural" processes, often originating from distinct cases of environmental catastrophe. In this chapter, the framework of the eco-zombie is apt not only because of the connection to environmental damage caused by the meat industry but also because of the historicity the definition provides. The zombies in these films are created from and embody the real ecological concerns of food production and consumption, waste management, and violence against nonhuman bodies taking place in contemporary South Korea.

The idea of an eco-zombie in media acknowledges that there are *ecological* situations as well national disasters (such as COVID-like super viruses) that have the potential to significantly damage *society as a whole*. Lauro further argues that eco-zombies manifest as "eco-punishment" for the wrongs humanity has done to nature.[12] The three films discussed in this chapter portray zombification as a punishment for the violence of the commercial meat industry and mass animal slaughter. The narratives in these films do not relieve their characters of responsibility for their actions of ecological damage and societal misbehavior but, rather, lead to the creation of a zombified subject that must take personal responsibility for their actions against the nonhuman environment in both life and death. To return to Lippit's argument, the degradation of the human subject is a fitting punishment for systematically removing coexistence with animals from society because, without them, humans have nothing to strive against but themselves. The following analysis explores these themes through the imagery and plots of the three films, keeping in mind the historical context that allowed these stories to emerge specifically in 2000s South Korea.

The Neighbor Zombie (2009)

Do humans consume meat responsibly? Or are modern consumers just as animalistic as zombies in their surrender to carnivorous desire? *The Neighbor Zombie*, a production from indie company Kino Mangosteen, poses these questions through speculative consideration of post-zombie life. It tells the full story of a zombie virus outbreak and containment through a series of vignettes that all take place on the same timeline but that follow different characters. From infection to zombification to life post-zombification, each vignette focuses on micro storytelling to show how individuals cope with a zombie pandemic. A consistent theme in the film is the association between zombification and meat. Although it is not meat that *causes* zombification (as it does in *Doomsday Book)*, the zombies in this film are consumed by their desire to eat meat even *before* they fully transform. Partially zombified subjects raid their fridges for animal meat in an attempt to stave off the final stages of zombification and the inevitable craving for human flesh; by having the process of zombification span a desire for both types of meat, the film blurs the line between human and animal bodies and breaks down human conceptions of nonhumans as so distinctly "other." The zombies' inability to control their hunger—even while partially human—not only associates them with animals controlled by internal drives rather than manageable desires but also makes them the embodiment of the modern Korean consumer, who has fought to eat meat even during import and production health scares.

The year before the release of *The Neighbor Zombie*, the Korea FTA changed their agreement with the United States to allow the import of beef from cows that had passed thirty months of age, which was concerning to the general public because the likelihood of cows carrying bovine spongiform encephalopathy (BSE), or mad cow disease, increases with age.[13] This policy change was roundly criticized in media broadcasts, and the subsequent public outcry was far more intense than many expected, especially given the relatively low risk of BSE actually contaminating the meat.[14] Many of the more than one hundred thousand protesters were mothers concerned for the health of their children. At issue was not animal rights or meat processing policy per se, but the government's seeming disinterest in the health of ordinary people.[15] Indeed, negative publicity, risk-averse consumerism, and mistrust toward the United States were all found to be significant factors in the protests. Revealingly, of the protesters who did decrease their beef intake during this scare period, a majority was only trying to reduce the amount of *American* import beef they ate, not the amount of beef overall.[16] Much like the zombies' hunger in *The Neighbor Zombie*, the aversion to meat-eating during the protests was selective—eat animal instead of human, eat Korean beef instead of American beef—and showed little attention to ecological considerations about nonhuman life, domestic industrial slaughter, and the dangers of consumerism in general.

As mentioned, the drive to eat meat in *The Neighbor Zombie* spans human and animal bodies; later in the film, once the outbreak is "controlled," this drive is seen through the eyes of a new social class, "the former zombie"—those that have been cured post-outbreak and struggle with what can best be called a meat addiction. The recovered humans, or post-zombies, are not exactly what would be called normal people. The main character of the post-pandemic vignette, Yong-gŭn, has his life controlled by his desire for meat, even after being "cured," in two main ways: his lingering desire to eat meat (both human and animal) haunts him, and society judges him because he ate human meat in the past. The filming of his story draws the viewer into Yong-gŭn's life and connects us to him by regularly showing his food and apartment through his point of view (POV). He has converted to vegetarianism to try to control his lust for meat, but through his POV we see his plate of rice, *koch'ujang* (red pepper paste, 고추장), and vegetables as he must see them—with distaste. The shot is filtered to wash out the colors of the food and make it look both boring and unappetizing; likewise, the viewer must assume that his dedication to vegetarianism is based purely on willpower, as he holds no appetite for his chosen food. This bland image is juxtaposed with the intensity of his dreams about eating meat, which are portrayed in vibrant color. Yong-gŭn strives against the animalistic urge to eat meat, and by separating himself from the animal (or zombie) side of himself, he seeks to be *more* human. Again, the difference between human meat and animal meat is subverted as Yong-gŭn chooses to forgo all meat products, as if eating animal flesh is akin to eating human flesh, or as if eating an animal is merely one small step away from eating a human.

While he forces himself to eat rice and vegetables to satiate his hunger, Yong-gŭn's attempts to reintegrate into society fail repeatedly. Despite formerly being a successful businessman, his job interviews now consist of questions about his past as a zombie and his desires to eat meat, resulting in one rejection after another. There is a melancholy to the wide shots of him walking through the city, head down, associating both sadness and shame with eating meat in the past. Reading a hiring flyer on an electric pole results in similar disappointment; the advertised job only wants what they refer to as "healthy" candidates—that is, someone untainted by a zombie past. The film's narrative of obsession with healthy living and the connection to meat can easily be read as a reference to the 2008 beef protests. The beef scare created an association between meat and contamination that would also contribute to ongoing movements promoting national foods and well-being in the early 2000s that marked imported foods as less healthy and instead encouraged consumption of domestic organic and non-GMO options as a sign of status as well as health.[17] In correlation with this connection to the protests and health movements, I would argue that although the vegetarian food Yong-gŭn eats is not portrayed as visually delicious, that is not because a life of vegetarianism is meant to be seen as lesser. In fact, its association with Yong-gŭn's strong-willed dedication to overcome his zombie status is what makes him the emotionally poignant character that he is. He will not give in to consumptive desires or live a life of unhealthiness, thereby making vegetarianism the *morally* right choice and far healthier overall.

The portrayal of vegetarian food as simultaneously undesirable and yet morally right raises the question of what it is humans *should* eat. For animals who function on drive and not desire, eating meat is a part of nature, but for humans it is a choice, and doing it excessively without consideration can be considered morally wrong—or even unnatural. This film suggests that mindless consumption of meat is something to be left to animals and zombies, as is highlighted by the post-zombie character's food decisions. Choosing to abstain from his past behavior is what establishes him as truly human again. But what about all of the other post-zombies—or in other words, average consumers—who do not make the choice to go vegetarian and instead continue with a pattern of excessive consumption of both meat and other unneeded items?

Doomsday Book (2011)

How has modern consumerism changed society? Which of these changes are ecologically damaging? And what are the dangers of consuming meat, specifically? *Doomsday Book* is a collection of Korean short films that features one portrayal of a zombie outbreak that occurs because the main character, Yoon Sŏk-u, is negligent in properly disposing of food waste. Subsequently, the processing of that waste sets off a larger chain of events leading to the spread of zombification via Korean barbeque. The story begins with Sŏk-u's family preparing to leave on vacation without him. The family represents the rising middle class of modern South Korea: capable of international travel, owners of a big-screen TV, and disproportionately concerned with their belongings and appearances. After the rest of the family leaves on vacation, Sŏk-u is left to deal with the wasted food and general trash from everything they had recently consumed. The amount of waste the family has created signifies their entrenchment in the materialistic lifestyle, and the fact that food they do not want can just be thrown in the trash signals the distance from South Korea's earlier histories of famine and economic hardship.

The path to zombification begins with the relationship between Sŏk-u and the neighborhood Food Waste Disposal Bin. The mise-en-scène introduction of the waste bin has it centered in the shot, bringing attention to the literal filth running down the container's sides. Material trash and food waste are combined in a pile of slime, shown in a close-up shot to increase the impact of the viscous texture. There is a lack of differentiation between the food consumed and the trash produced from consumerism; everything becomes one primordial substance. The scenes that follow are a montage that serves to connect food waste to animal feed for commercial farms, which in turn creates a connection to a third object: the meat sold to and consumed by the Korean public. After showing the waste container, the shot cuts from a trash truck to a trash processing plant where the food waste is being sorted by masked workers. A dissolve transition merges one image into another, lapsing time and creating a connection between the phases of the waste processing, including multiple close-up shots of the gray, lumpy food waste accompanied by wet, squelching sounds. The purpose of documenting this journey becomes clear as the film hard cuts from the dissolving scenes of waste to a shot of a bag of cattle feed. This true-to-reality portrayal of the recycling system in South Korea turning human food waste into animal feed is essential not only for the plot but also for the larger message of infection via meat consumption.

Besides the concerns for commercial meat cleanliness, one must also consider the environmental impact of the meat industry itself. The amount of waste being generated by consumerism in Korean households has increased significantly in recent decades. To counteract the increase in waste, government policies such as the Pay-As-You-Throw (PAYT) system were implemented, essentially making those who consume more pay more for the processing.[18] Because of the increase in food waste, an unmistakable sign of an economically stable consumerist society, recycling became more prevalent and recycling of food waste for agricultural purposes was implemented. South Korea is one of the few countries, including Japan and the United States, that still repurpose food waste for animal feed—a practice since banned in England, where it is suspected to be connected to foot-and-mouth disease outbreaks in livestock.[19] *Doomsday Book* acknowledges this reality and uses it to highlight not only the abject experience of eating waste-fed animals, but also to emphasize the horror of this process by using it as the cause of zombification.

Much as zombies are creatures that humans view with fear and disgust when faced with their once-human rotting bodies, the idea of rotting food as a substance that humans ingest is also closely tied to disgust and repulsion. The food waste is the rejected part of the consumable object; it is the part that is rotten and the part that causes the "abject" reaction to the idea of taking it back into the self.[20] The terror, in this film's case, is that the separation from the waste is temporary. It is processed and repurposed into animal feed, which is then consumed by the cows and pigs that will then be slaughtered and sold in Korean barbeque restaurants to human patrons. The meat that is eaten has part of the abject food object within it, which allows for a reentry of the waste into the body. As people consume, they waste more, and the more waste that is processed the more the meat becomes infected with it, until meat itself becomes abject and the consumers become filled with waste themselves. Although this connection between disgust and meat consumption can be seen in this zombie film, that connection does not necessarily translate into general consciousness, as meat continues to be a sign of status in Korean consumerist culture, demarcating the spending power to purchase it.

Returning to the film, once the connection between the food waste and cows has been made, the end of the montage is marked by an intense close-up of a gloveless hand mixing a plate of *yuk'oe* (육회)—a combination of raw beef and raw egg served as is. Brightly lit and shot in close-up, the *yuk'oe* arrests the eye with its bloody coloration. The close-ups of food waste and of processed beef are similarly visceral. The textures and sounds are placed prominently in the shots, leaving nothing to the imagination. Afterward, we return to our main character, Sŏk-u, who is enjoying himself on a date, even though the seemingly "pleasant" context of the scene conveys a strong sense of distaste. Close-up camera work of the characters' mouths chewing is employed in excess. Although the two characters are obviously enjoying the food—indicated by their voracious eating speed and groans of pleasure—the spectator knows via the previous montage that this very beef is unclean, contaminated by an unknown taint. This scene foreshadows these characters' zombie fate, as it not only connects them with a type of carnal hunger even before there are any indications that a zombie outbreak is coming, but also because the eating of meat carries forward the disgust previously invoked by the scenes of food waste. This implied meaning is further confirmed by the plot as, ultimately, it is that trip to the barbeque restaurant that turns Sŏk-u, and many others, into zombies because of eating that specific cut of infected beef.

When the audience watches a zombie eating hunks of human flesh, the reaction is not one of shared hunger or craving; it is a reaction of pure revulsion, like what is being evoked by the eating scenes in this film. Herein lies a question that also arises in *The Neighbor Zombie*: Why is eating an animal so different from eating a human? The natural answer to this question, of course, is that eating humans is cannibalism. However, if that is the argument, it is necessary to consider the animal feed processing system in South Korea once again. The animals are given feed made of recycled human food waste, which may contain meat, so while this film obviously questions whether feeding animals waste leads to disease *for* humans, in a way the most unnatural thing about this situation is the way the process forces animals into cannibalism themselves. When viewed from this perspective, the meat industry is itself grotesque and disrupts the natural cycle. It introduces the element of the unnatural into foodways, creating animal cannibalism, which, in the case of *Doomsday Book*, leads to the zombification of humans. Because of the mind-set of striving against nature, however, humans spend as much effort as possible mentally separating themselves from animals, and therefore the consideration of whether animals are being forced into something taboo may never cross a person's mind. Just as the practice of turning food waste into animal feed is rooted in reality, the call to be mindful about consumer habits is a message that should not be ignored in the reality of a rapidly shifting food culture in South Korea.

Zombie School (2014)

Is it *only* stories about humans and human society that can be told through the zombie genre? Or is it possible for eco-zombies to actively include the nonhuman, as Lauro's use of the term suggests? The film *Zombie School* chronicles the experience of three rebellious teens—one girl and two boys—who attend a boarding reform school where extreme acts of violence against animals have occurred. Though the film initially appears to be a typical high school drama, the plot reveals otherwise. After the principal is attacked by a zombie pig, one of the school administrators admits to the students that, to build the school, the farms in the area had been torn down and tens of thousands of pigs were buried alive. This image is analogous not only to the procedures resulting from actual foot-and-mouth outbreaks in South Korea but also to the overall danger development poses to nature. This film departs from the close focus on human interactions with meat and shifts focus to the animals; more than the previous two films, *Zombie School* directly engages with the concept of eco-punishment. In other words, there are consequences for treating animals like disposable objects. Rather than the human characters, the animals drive this story, because it is not their meat that causes zombification but their post-life desire for revenge that gives them the power to come back from the dead. This is the other side of the coin, exposed in the process of striving against the natural world. Although humans may selfishly focus only on cementing their subjectivity, this film considers the direct negative consequences of human society on nature and animals.

The imagery in this film is more typical of traditional Western zombie films, compared with the other Korean examples, because the pigs are shown coming up from underground in the classic rendition of the living dead. Scenes of the pigs coming back to fight the humans are shot through the pigs' POV, illustrated by a red filter placed over the shots that evokes a feeling of blood-tinged eyes filled with rage. The movements of the camera are also erratic, cutting back and forth in a disjointed way that associates it with the uncoordinated way zombies are often seen moving in Western zombie films. However, the viewer never gets a good look at the zombie pigs. We experience them only through their own vision, making it clear that this is *their* story. We are not observing the pigs from the perspective of an outsider, or even as products to be processed and sold, as in *Doomsday Book*. Instead, we here observe the humans from the animal perspective. This focus on rural spaces, and pigs specifically, is significant in the Korean context. Before the 1960s, raising livestock was uncommon in South Korea, even for farmers. If a farm did have a cow, for example, it was used for plowing and other labor, not as a food source.[21] This created a pastoral ideal of farm animals as intimate companions living alongside humans. Although eating meat was not an unknown concept, especially among royalty, the process of raising animals as portrayed in films such as the acclaimed documentary film *Wŏnangsori* (워낭소리), the story of the intimate bond between an old couple and their cow, is still considered a part of the reality of the past, an ideal that is representative of eco-well-being for both environment and animal.[22] The nostalgia for the natural, often considered a call back to simpler times, is part of the increasing concern for healthy living in current times as nature is jeopardized.[23]

Zombie School also connects this issue of animal treatment to the contemporary moment by using real footage from a foot-and-mouth epidemic that occurred in South Korea, blurring the lines between fiction and reality. In 2010, a mass infection of foot-and-mouth disease occurred in Korean commercial livestock. Beginning in November 2010 and lasting until April 2011, this foot-and-mouth epidemic was by far the worst South Korea had ever experienced. Approximately 3.48 million animals—mostly pigs—were culled during the outbreak and the culling method deemed "safest" was live burial, which is mirrored by the plot of the film.[24] Considering the continued increase in pork consumption in the early to mid-2000s, this was a serious concern for both industry and the average consumer. *Zombie School* highlights these issues within the Korean meat industry and extends the problem beyond the meat that will affect the human consumer to the larger issue of how the animals themselves were treated. Evidence of how cruelly the animals were killed is irrefutable, given the video evidence, which means in both reality and film there is legitimation for a fear of eco-punishment. Burying all of those pigs alive was viewed as necessary to protect the meat industry from disease—and, we assume, the public's health by association—but in addition to that, there is also the film's message about developing the countryside and killing or displacing animals in the process. Although a zombie apocalypse is not likely, there is a real question of ramifications for eco-crimes: Will Korea, or Koreans, be punished for being negligent in their care for the country's animals and ecology?

To return to *Zombie School*, once many of the humans have been zombified near the end of the film, a group of students that are still human raid the cafeteria to satiate their hunger. As with the previous films, Korean barbeque makes an appearance. By revealing in dialogue that the food in the scene is coming from the equivalent of the teachers' secret stash, the eating of meat is again associated with people who are well off and have the leisure to consume. With the teachers no longer in the picture, the students cook up as much meat as they want, thereby subverting the hierarchy of privilege. Unfortunately, their feast is interrupted by the zombie horde and the students are ultimately killed. While it is arguable that stopping to rest (and eat) is never a wise choice during a zombie outbreak, the scene of the students eating meat, and their death following immediately after, leads the viewer to make the connection between meat consumption and getting killed. Had the scenes been arranged in a less directly progressive order, that connection may not have been obvious. But here the imagery is closely linked. As the zombification of the staff is already a punishment for the cruelty to animals, the film leaves little doubt that the eating of meat has a similar consequence for the students and implies its own form of eco-punishment. Any form of participation in the slaughter of animals, even for the children who learn to eat meat from the adults around them, is subject to eventual negative consequences.

Considering the rapid increase of meat as a Korean food staple and the continued issues at commercial slaughterhouses, the films discussed here suggest that some blowback is inevitable if the system is not altered. *The Neighbor Zombie* questions the parameters of health and morality, while *Doomsday Book* mirrors the reality of waste processing and *Zombie School* displays extreme disposal of animal bodies to benefit the humans around them. As discussed, the Korea FTA changed their agreement with the United States in 2008 to allow the import of beef from cows that had passed thirty months of age, and in May of that year massive candlelight vigils were held to protest this change in beef import, calling for the government to reconsider for the health of its people.[25] The decision to begin importing meat is a product of the changes in South Korea's economic situation and the increased pressure of globalization on not only business but also food culture. Although the fear publicly expressed in the 2008 beef protests centered on the quality of meat in regard to safety for human consumption, which should be distinguished from concern for the well-being of the animals themselves, I would argue that there is also an underlying concern for how animals are treated in foreign countries in comparison to South Korea. This is related in part to the continued relevance of the pastoral ideal and the possible misconception that Korean meat production in modern capitalist society is still somehow pastoral. The disconnect between the modern, dissociative process of slaughtering animals for meat in factories that remain unseen, and the personal care involved in the antiquated process of raising them yourself, leads to a mistrust of the meat that is coming from factories in other countries. Despite that, however, these films suggest that looking inward toward South Korea's own meat industrial complex reveal deep-seated anxieties about the trajectories of current trends of consumerism, excessive meat production, and environmental degradation in South Korea.

Although these films are in keeping with the convention of using zombies as analogy for social ills, they are not predicting full apocalyptic societal collapse as much as they are critiquing the present society and pinpointing areas that need to change *now*. The Korean zombie—as portrayed in these films—is the individual

Korean: your everyday person who makes decisions about how and what to consume. For this reason, the films are not portraying a future dystopia. They are, rather, addressing issues that can be solved in the present to prevent further damage to the environment. The rate of meat consumption in Korean has continued to increase, but these zombie outbreaks are not portrayed as the end point of history. These zombie films from the mid-2000s captured the sociocultural anxieties of the moment surrounding meat, and current media trends suggest that both zombies and ecological concerns will continue to take on new meaning in the Korean context. Zombie films such as *Train to Busan*[26] and *The Wailing*[27] have gained both domestic and international traction for the genre, but in terms of visualizing ecological issues, films and literature are now engaging more directly with environmental damage and changes in food culture in other genres. Bong Joon-ho's *Okja*[28] is one such example, a film about the meat industry specifically that addresses issues of capitalism as well as animal rights, not to mention many other filmic, textual, and webcomic examples in similar veins. Thus, while *The Neighbor Zombie, Doomsday Book,* and *Zombie School* paint the situation in South Korea as undeniably dire, these films also offer the possibility for ecological redemption post-zombie—if, that is, humanity can cease its striving against nature and strive against overindustrialization instead. The move toward producing more media that addresses the meat industry, and ecological damage in general, suggests a step in the right direction.

Part 4
RECLAIMING LIFE

Eleana J. Kim

Part 3's focus on industrialized meat production foregrounds the consequences of human mastery over other animals and ecologies more broadly. The activists in part 4, rather than asserting domination through slaughter and exploitation, replace mastery with responsibility for other forms of life. In doing so, they look to both the past and future to guide them in their present endeavors to create better relationships between humans and their environments.

A key discourse for understanding contemporary South Korean environmental thought and activism is *saengmyŏng sasang* (생명사상) or life philosophy. It is an invented tradition, derived from Tonghak philosophy (동학; Eastern Learning) of the nineteenth century, which was integrated into discourses of environmental activism in the 1970s and 1980s, at a time when the population explosion and nuclear war were being recognized as worldwide threats to humanity. Those threats were leading people in South Korea and around the world to think about the future of the human race and the planet Earth as our only home.

Saengmyŏng sasang is premised on a non-dualistic holism, in contrast to the state-centric ideologies—whether capitalist or communist—that environmentalists criticized for artificially separating humans from the natural world and thereby facilitating the instrumentalization of nature in the name of narrow anthropocentric interests. *Saengmyŏng sasang* initially drew its cultural legitimacy from Tonghak's founder, Ch'oe Che-u and Ch'oe Si-hyŏng, the movement's second leader, who rejected Western imperialism and advocated radical social transformation. In the 1980s, activist Jang Il-soon and Kim Chi-ha, dissident poet and activist, first introduced *saengmyŏng sasang*, which led to the founding of the

135

organic farming collective Hansalim, discussed by Yonjae Paik in chapter 8. Hansalim emerged in response to the extractive model of agriculture promoted by the state and the international development regime and offered an alternative vision and praxis for fostering ecological relations, extending the notion of care and nurturance to include all living things. Today, Hansalim links rural farmers and urban consumers to build consumer awareness of food systems and the importance of healthy relationships that can form the basis of sustainable ecologies in a highly industrialized, market-driven society.

Since the founding of Hansalim, *saengmyŏng* has become a ubiquitous term in environmental discourses in South Korea, connoting a shared commitment to all life forms, which are viewed as fundamentally interconnected and crucially important to building sustainable futures. This commitment to caring for "life" in all its forms resonates with the biocentric ethos of the deep ecology movement, but *saengmyŏng sasang* is often presented as emerging from a distinctly Korean worldview. This worldview, however, is not universally shared among all Koreans. Although nature appreciation is widely valued and practiced in South Korea, as in other places around the word, urban environmentalists are often at odds with rural communities who might be considered to be the "authentic" stewards of "nature." For instance, as Jeongsu Shin discusses in chapter 9, villagers in Jeju Island rejected the environmentalist project of protecting biodiverse forest landscapes, or *gotjawal*, on the basis of an imagined ancestral past. Nature, as Shin argues, is not only continuously invented, but it is often contested, as landscapes are always influenced by human activities and then interpreted and translated into diverse human frameworks.

Despite these unavoidably difficult negotiations and contestations, *saengmyŏng sasang*, in its conceptualization of "life" and the interdependent relations necessary to foster *saengmyŏng*, promotes inclusiveness when considering the diverse actors and stakeholders whose interests should be considered in any decision-making process about collective futures. This inclusivity is reflected in the call for "ecological democracy" that Nan Kim advocates in chapter 10. While humans debate the benefits and risks of nuclear energy, particularly with respect to the long-term storage of nuclear waste, a broader view of participation and stakeholders will be needed, one that can include nonhumans as well as all future generations of life forms. Indeed, as people in Korea and around the world seek ways to address the climate crisis in its multiscalar effects and unpredictable consequences, reconceptualizing human-nonhuman relations will be crucial to crafting more effective, sustainable, and just solutions.

Hansalim is the best example to date of what a sustained commitment to *saengmyŏng sasang* might yield. Although its project succeeded in building an alternative to the mainstream food industry, critics also point out that it has fallen far short of its radical potential in that it continues to operate within a capitalist system and has thereby failed to achieve the goal of social transformation. Yet, even if the political and social transformations promised by *saengmyŏng sasang* have been small in scale, it is undeniable that the ideas it offers continue to be persuasive. Similar to other decolonial discourses such as *buen vivir* in Latin America or Gaia in cosmopolitical feminist science and technology studies, *saengmyŏng sasang* permits the imagination of other possibilities, ideas that can foster better relations and more sustainable futures by moving away from the Western Enlightenment epistemologies that have led us to our current planetary predicament. In other words, although they might be limited in scale and utopian in substance, these concepts, if nothing else, index the desire for an alternative to the hegemonic system of industrial, militarized capitalism and its biopolitical logics that render whole populations of people disposable and devalue large portions of the earth and its ecologies as economic externalities.

8

COMMUNAL ENVIRONMENTALISM IN THE HISTORY OF THE ORGANIC FARMING MOVEMENT IN SOUTH KOREA

Yonjae Paik

Communal environmentalism refers to a body of thought that extends the reciprocal relationships of communal life to local environments to redress humans' exploitation of nature. In the context of agriculture, it recognizes that methods of land cultivation are determined not only by technological advancement but also by the social structures and underlying ideologies of specific times and places. Hence, it emphasizes the role of communal spaces in realizing reciprocal relationships among humans and between humans and nature. This chapter presents the significance of communal environmentalism in South Korea's organic farming movement and, more specifically, how this movement utilized communal autonomy to overcome the exploitation of farmers and nature within the capitalist nation-state.

Beginning in the 1960s, the government-led Green Revolution made chemical farming the basis of mainstream agriculture in South Korea. The environmental and health problems that arose from intensive chemical farming motivated a group of Protestant farmers to create Chŏngnonghoe (正農會, Association of Righteous Farming) in 1976, marking the beginning of a new farming movement based on organic and communal principles. The movement expanded in the mid-1980s with the creation of Hansalim, an organic cooperative that organized urban consumers into urban-rural communities to support organic farmers. Representing South Korea's organic farming movement, these two groups show how community has been the core value in the organic farmers' search for rural autonomy from the centralized farming system—first created by the state and then liberalized.

Chemical Farming in South Korea

The South Korean government began to actively promote chemical farming as an integral part of its nation-building process in the 1960s. State-led chemical farming was a combination of the Japanese colonial government's rural mobilization and the US-style modern agriculture that became the new standard during the post–Korean War period. In the 1970s, Park Chung-hee's military government combined the Green Revolution (綠色革命, *noksaek hyŏngmyŏng*) with a state-led rural development campaign, the New Village Movement (NVM; *saemaŭl undong*), which was inspired by the colonial government's rural campaigns. Supported by the two ideological pillars of economic developmentalism and anticommunism,[1] the military government enforced chemical farming practices as an essential element of South Korea's reconstruction as a wealthy military power. Thus, rural villages were incorporated into a centralized social and economic system controlled by the government.

The example of high-yield rice demonstrates the political nature of South Korea's Green Revolution.[2] The high-yield rice varieties were expected to end food shortages and, in the process, mobilize political support in rural areas. The government gave the new "miracle rice" various political names, such as "unification" (統一, *t'ongil*) or "restoration" (維新, *yusin*), and enforced its cultivation across the country. New administrative and economic structures controlled the entire farming process, from the supply of the seeds to the purchase of the harvest.[3] The National Agricultural Cooperative Federation (NACF) controlled the supply of fertilizers and pesticides and the procurement of the harvests, while the Rural Development Administration (RDA) supervised the farming process.

The economic liberalization of the 1980s led to the intensification of chemical farming as the mainstream practice for commercial agriculture. As Anders Riel Muller shows in this volume (chapter 6), the government came to favor food importation over domestic food production and retreated from its earlier commitment to rural development, instead focusing on subsidizing the rural economy to alleviate the impacts of economic liberalization.[4] Policies that enforced low food prices created a vicious cycle of rural exodus, agricultural labor shortages, and overuse of costly chemicals. As more people left rural areas because of economic difficulties, more agrochemicals had to be used to maintain low food prices by reducing labor costs and maximizing harvests. With the increased use of fertilizers, crops became more vulnerable to attacks by insects and diseases, leading to the use of more pesticides.[5]

Whether state-led or market-driven, the intensive chemical farming in South Korea caused a wide range of environmental and health problems, and farmers, as a part of their local ecosystems, were directly affected by the resulting environmental crisis. Specifically, pesticide poisoning became a life-threatening issue for farmers. Pesticides were made easily available during the Green Revolution, and their overuse became widespread, as many farmers did not fully understand how to use them, sometimes assuming that more was better.[6] A survey in 1976 reported that 41 percent of farmers were suffering from chronic pesticide poisoning;[7] 81.9 percent suffered some level of poisoning in 1982.[8] By the 1980s, this was a common rural phenomenon, with more than one thousand farmers dying from pesticide poisoning every year.[9] These fatalities were a symptom of the exploitative relationships of mainstream agriculture, manifested in the farmers; but exploitation also existed in the relationship between consumers and farmers and between farmers and nature.

Communal versus National: The Beginning of the Organic Farming Movement

The beginning of South Korea's organic farming movement, with the creation of Chŏngnonghoe in 1976, included two important features: it was started by farmers and it was started when the government's Green Revolution was at its peak. The movement's members were Protestant farmers and intellectuals who believed that chemical farming was against God's will because it threatened people's health. As "awakened ones" who realized the risk of chemical farming to both human bodies and human minds, the members were urged to sacrifice themselves gladly and overcome the temptation to make more money through chemical farming,[10] which was equated to worshipping Baal, meaning materialism in this context.[11] The P'ulmu Agricultural School, a Christian school in Hongdong village, Hongsŏng County, joined the movement the following year by becoming the first agricultural school in South Korea to teach organic farming.[12] As successors to the Christian rural development movement of the colonial period, Chŏngnonghoe and the P'ulmu School spread the gospel of organic farming in South Korea as a communal lifestyle based on Christian belief.

For Chŏngnonghoe and the P'ulmu School, a communal ethos of self-sufficiency was the key to religious, political, and economic autonomy. First, the commune was a space outside mainstream church organizations. Wŏn Kyŏng-sŏn (1914–2013), who led the creation of Chŏngnonghoe, was an independent evangelist, and the P'ulmu School belonged to the Non-Church Movement,[13] which favored informal assemblies (called ecclesia) and avoided organized structure.

Second, the commune was a politically autonomous space. In the 1970s, the state-oriented nationalism of the Yusin ideology conferred on the South Korean state the authority to enforce national campaigns like the NVM. Inspired by the Christian ideal village movement of the Osan School in the 1920s, Chŏngnonghoe and the P'ulmu School pursued a Christian model of modernization vis-à-vis the militaristic, state-oriented modernization being pursued by the government.[14] In doing so, the P'ulmu School advocated a "commoner" (平民, p'yŏngmin) identity as an alternative to the "national subject" (國民, kungmin) identity defined by the state.

The case of Wŏn Kyŏng-sŏn's P'ulmuwŏn Farm, at the center of the Chŏngnonghoe movement, shows the challenges of creating such communal spaces.[15] The first challenge arose from readjusting farming's relationship with nature. The farmers were determined not to use pesticides but had little knowledge of how to grow crops without them. They removed weeds and insects manually, but the soil was conditioned by the previous use of chemical fertilizers and pesticides and produced only sparse, small, and ugly crops. Wŏn's new farm in Yangju suffered losses of five million *won* in the first year and another three million *won* in the second year; only in the third year did the farm begin to break even, as the soil and the farmers' techniques improved.[16] After a difficult early period, the farm was able to attain food self-sufficiency.[17]

A more serious challenge of life in an autonomous commune was social and political isolation. In general, nonorganic farmers did not understand "weed growers" who would not accept the evidently superior techniques of modern scientific farming. Farmers in general believed that if some farms did not use pesticides, the neighboring farms would suffer greater insect infestations.[18] More dangerously, Chŏngnonghoe members' deviation from the national farming project offended local officials and village leaders. Local authorities and neighbors often accused organic farmers of being Reds or pro-North Korea,[19] and even of taking orders from North Korea to hinder South Korea's growth.[20] At the annual meeting of Chŏngnonghoe, police officers attended to record the participants' names and the content of their conversations. Some members had their backgrounds checked by local police or village officers, while others had their seedbeds or rice paddies marked with red flags or even sabotaged by RDA officers. In the face of such reactions from their families, neighbors, consumers, and officials, not all of Chŏngnonghoe's members continued organic farming.

To overcome the members' isolation and strengthen their commitment to organic farming, Chŏngnonghoe focused on education emphasizing the movement's moral basis. For ten years, Wŏn Kyŏng-sŏn's P'ulmuwŏn Farm held training sessions, gatherings, and educational classes. In 1978 Wŏn and a younger commune member, Kim Chong-buk,[21] started the Short-Term Bible School, which met in January to take advantage of the farming off-season. The school had twenty to thirty students, some of whom were trainees at P'ulmuwŏn Farm. The program took about three weeks, and Chŏngnonghoe's annual meeting was held in the middle of this period so that the students could meet the Chŏngnonghoe members. The curriculum covered a wide range of topics, including religion, the environment, agriculture, history, education, and psychology.[22] The communal ethos was an important theme. For instance, Ham Sŏk-hŏn's lecture in 1979 specified the communal life as a way of overcoming the repressive nation-state system. He explained that communal life had emerged at that time because the state could not solve people's problems even if people could confront the government.[23] The school continued until 1986 or 1987, the period that marked the farming commune's heyday.

This communal space developed a certain autonomy for practicing righteous farming and redressing the exploitative relationships of state-led chemical farming, but its excessive reliance on the role of leaders like Wŏn Kyŏng-sŏn limited the movement's growth. In the case of the P'ulmuwŏn Farm, Wŏn's personal network and financial support were crucial in running the farm and the classes. Therefore, despite its egalitarian ideals of working together and sharing the harvest, the relationships within the commune were based on Wŏn's paternal and patriarchal roles.[24] This conflict between the commune's egalitarian ethos and its internal hierarchy stood out as the main reason for the commune's dissolution in the 1990s, after an internal dispute over the farm's for-profit business.[25]

The P'ulmu School was critical in overcoming the precariousness of the farming communes and providing stability to the movement. The school's involvement started with its organic farming education and experiments at the school farm. In September 1977, the school reported the outcomes of the first experiments: their organic rice farm yielded 60 per cent of what would be expected with chemical farming, and the fruit failed completely. It was suggested that it would take four to five years for dry-field crops and seven to eight years for fruit from their organic farming to become viable, and therefore, a long-term perspective would be required.[26] Like other Chŏngnonghoe members, the P'ulmu School was not admired by its neighbors. Ch'oe Sŏng-bong, who was among the first teachers of organic farming at the school, recollected that he would not have dared recommend organic farming to someone outside the school, even to his family members, who knew what he was teaching. He recalled the 1970s as a time when every farmer was asked to expand production, and almost every farmer was interested in increasing harvests and farm income; the other village farmers did not understand why an agricultural school should teach such a "useless" technique as organic farming.[27] The school's deviation from the national education system and the national farming campaign brought ridicule and suspicion. They were called everything from "the manure tub school" to communists.

Despite the challenges, the school adhered to its communal ethos. Hong Sun-myŏng, a P'ulmu School teacher who became the principal in 1982, summarized their pursuit of rural autonomy as a "theory of intentional local society" (意圖的 地域社會論, *ŭidojŏk chiyŏk sahoeron*). According to Hong, "intentional local society" refers to a local, economically self-reliant group of a minimum of three to five households with a shared lifestyle. It is not an attempt to return to a traditional society, nor does it seek to be a small replica of urban culture. To create cooperative communities based on face-to-face relationships, each group should have no more than fifty to one hundred members, splitting into new groups rather than growing larger. In this view of rural autonomy, local schools are important for practical and cultural purposes.[28] As more P'ulmu graduates joined Chŏngnonghoe, Hongdong village came to be the movement's hub, renowned as a mecca of organic farming in South Korea. Today, Hongdong village is a model of an autonomous and sustainable rural lifestyle, inspiring many activists, farmers, and ordinary urban people who are interested in alternative ways of life.

Commercial versus Communal: Hansalim's Organic Cooperative Movement

The liberalization of South Korea's agricultural market in the 1980s not only dismantled rural communities[29]—the basis of the nascent organic farming movement—but also changed the main source of challenge from the state to the global market system. An accelerated rural exodus seriously weakened the nascent organic farming movement based on rural communes.[30] A breakthrough was made by Hansalim, which expanded the basis of the movement from rural communes to an organic cooperative, an alternative market system that organized urban consumers and farmers into small communities. Creating a market for organic products was beyond the capacity of any single organization, but Hansalim was able to make it happen by using the nationwide networks of the Catholic Church, more specifically, the Corea Catholic Farmers' Movement (CCFM) and the churches in big cities.[31] Begun as a small organic shop in 1986, Hansalim rapidly grew to have the largest membership of any organic cooperative in Korea.[32] Unlike other organic consumer co-ops that mainly reflect consumers' interests, Hansalim promoted the concept of food as a source of life rather than a commodity, and aimed to overcome the commercial relationship between consumers and farmers by organizing them in communal spaces, which they called "urban-rural communities" (都-農 共同體, *to-nong kongdongch'e*).[33] The consumer support organized by Hansalim was crucial in spreading the organic farming movement by enabling more farmers to convert to organic agriculture.

The urban-rural community is a communal space alternative to the capitalist market, and the relationship among members is based on mutual help rather than competition. As an organized movement, Hansalim is directed by an ideology called "life philosophy" (生命思想, *saengmyŏng sasang*). This ideology originates from Tonghak, an indigenous religion and egalitarian social movement that arose during the late Chosŏn dynasty.[34] Tonghak proposed a holistic (physical and metaphysical) concept of life, encapsulated in the native Korean word *hanul* (the substance of the cosmos), and taught that people should serve, nurture, and practice this holistic concept of life. The movement's egalitarianism was not limited to humans but extended to nature, as the second leader of Tonghak, Ch'oe Si-hyŏng, taught that all living creatures were equal. Tonghak was critical of the repressive caste system, of Japanese imperialism, and of the Chosŏn dynasty, which led it to start a peasant revolution in 1894 against corrupt local and central governments and the Japanese Army. Tonghak's organizational form, based on secret communal groups called *chŏp* (接), provided an autonomous base on which a social and religious movement could create an egalitarian utopia.

Hansalim activists were inspired by Tonghak's egalitarian utopia as a vision of an agrarian society wherein farmers would be free from exploitation by corrupt officials and foreign powers. They saw the government's pursuit of industrial development in the 1980s as betraying farmers by collaborating with foreign countries and large companies that profited from importing foreign food. Capitalism and chemical farming were intertwined threats to the lives of farmers and consumers, as well as to nature. Hansalim's life philosophy took up Tonghak's antiestablishment ethos, declaring that the existing political structure was an "order of death" supported by various social elites.[35] The new military regime of Chun Doo-hwan, which came to power through a coup and was responsible for a massacre in Kwangju in 1980, was seen as similar to the Chosŏn dynasty, which suppressed the Tonghak revolution.

Hansalim's concept of the urban-rural community as a politically autonomous space originated in a rural reconstruction movement in the Wŏnju area in the 1970s.[36] With the financial support and the political protection of the Catholic Church, local intellectuals and democratization activists surrounding social educator Chang Il-sun[37] organized cooperatives and credit unions in Wŏnju diocese in a bottom-up approach to enlightening and empowering rural people. While the Yusin regime was promulgating the New Village Movement, Chang and other activists were trying to democratize rural villages by helping rural people run self-regulating economic organizations. Chŏng Ho-gyŏng, a Catholic priest and a member of CCFM, who participated in the development of life philosophy, described this communal space as a "living community"—a group of ten people or ten households in which people shared uncontaminated food as well as having an equal say in the affairs of the group. Chŏng criticized the monopoly and manipulation of public opinion by urban elites and condemned chemical farming that benefited the manufacturers and consumers in cities.[38] Still, life philosophy and its communal approach were also critical of the militant struggles of pro-democracy student activists in the 1980s who pursued a socialist revolution to create radical social changes. In life philosophy, both communism and capitalism were considered products of European rationalism and materialism that sustained the structures that threatened the environment and the life of the *minjung* (民衆, the people, or the masses). In contrast, life philosophy advocated gradual social change based on communal living in which life has priority over all political ideologies.[39]

In practice, pursuing the living community meant that Hansalim needed to organize farmers and consumers to create urban-rural communal ties. The organic farmers were already organized in the network of the CCFM, while the consumers had to be organized by Hansalim activists. They created consumer communities—each consisting of a minimum of five households—as the unit for the delivery of produce and a space for education.[40] Hansalim used organic produce as a familiar subject to begin to educate housewives and to build a cooperative ethos among members. The members of each potential consumer community had to attend an introductory class given by the Hansalim staff. The initial class was important to ensure that Hansalim activists visited the consumer communities to give lectures about food safety and environmental problems, while also explaining social issues like the government policies that favored big companies' profiting from importing food. This educational program was also designed to develop the groups' participatory processes for their everyday life practices, such as taking turns in representing the group, organizing study circles, inviting each other to their homes on delivery days, and sharing the produce fairly and unselfishly.

Once the consumer communities were organized, the communal relationship was extended to include farmers in face-to-face relationships. Hansalim staff organized various programs designed to build such relationships. For example, a spring festival was held every year at a farming village, where the consumer community members were invited to play games and experience farming life.[41] Every November, a Hansalim family night was organized to invite farmers to Seoul, where more than seven hundred participants shared food and took part in role-playing exercises to share their experiences in the Hansalim movement. Farmers' markets and farmstays for children were also organized from time to time. At the individual level, individual farmers were sometimes invited to a consumer member's home to stay overnight. The farmers and consumers were encouraged to write stories of their experiences for the newsletter, providing images of the desired model of urban-rural community. The consumers obtained a better understanding of the farmers' hardships and supported them by voluntarily buying surplus or unmarketable goods or exchanging letters with farmers to share their stories.

Still, the communal space created by Hansalim faced constant challenges from the capitalist economy. Conflicts often emerged between the communal relationships and the commercial relationships among members. Reciprocity between farmers and consumers could be sustained only when the consumers received quality organic food and the farmers could sell all their produce. In doing so, the dominant status of consumers over farmers was sustained within Hansalim's planned economy. Farmers were at a disadvantage, as selling their produce was central to their living, whereas consuming organic produce was a matter of choice for urban consumers. In addition, the consumer communities were greater in number than the farmers' communities. The disparity of power within the urban-rural communities did not matter as long as the planned economy functioned well. However, conflicts emerged when there was a shortage of supply or deterioration in quality.

An incident in 1991 exemplifies the weakness of Hansalim's community movement. From October 1990, consumers began to complain about the deteriorating quality of the eggs they were receiving—freshness, smell, the shape of the yolk, and so on—particularly those produced in the Ichǒn area. Hansalim staff visited the egg farms to find the cause and, at the same time, found alternative suppliers.[42] Although the egg farmers and Hansalim's Producers Council submitted written statements to the board of directors to explain the structural issues behind the quality problem, the board of directors decided to cancel the contract with the egg farmers. This decision provoked a sense of betrayal not only from those excluded, but also from other farmers' communities, and led to the dissolution of the Hansalim Producers Council in 1992.[43] Although it was one of the worst conflicts in the history of Hansalim, it shows that, unlike in a spontaneous community, a significant part of the communal relationship was also contractual.

The communities remained the main mode of Hansalim's organization until 1994, when growing membership led Hansalim to become an incorporated association, which used shops rather than consumer communities to distribute the farmers' organic produce. The shops, however, could not reproduce the face-to-face relationships of the communities. Nevertheless, the urban-rural community remained a defining feature of this movement, which aimed to overcome the exploitative relationships between consumers and farmers as well as between humans and nature in a capitalist market. Currently, as South Korea's first and largest organic cooperative, as well as an organized movement, Hansalim continues to spread its communal ideals to support a sustainable way of life.

This chapter has presented the role of community as a space autonomous from the centralized food system controlled by the state and the capitalist market system in South Korea's organic farming movement. By looking at how the relationship between humans and nature changed with the development of a capitalist nation-state system in South Korea, we see that communal environmentalism was the defining feature of the movement. Chemical farming focuses on maximizing human control over nature; it also entails state or market control over farmers, who live in and are members of a natural environment. Mainstream agricultural practices, reliant on chemical inputs and enforced first by the state and then by commercial interests, required the exploitation of both nature and farmers. Organic farming was an alternative for farmers who sought autonomy from exploitive social structures. Creating autonomous spaces entailed creating local economic systems such as self-sufficient farms and cooperatives, as well as new value systems based on reciprocity and face-to-face relationships among members.

The tradition of communal autonomy in the organic farming movement has spread to community-based rural revitalization movements (歸農運動, *kwinong undong*). The image of organic farming as a social movement became weakened with the government's intervention, such as the introduction of the organic food certification system in 1993, to make it a profit-making business.[44] Despite the growth of conventionalized organic farming, conducted in much the same way as chemical farming but using organic certified fertilizers and pesticides, the traditional way of organic farming continues to be practiced in the rural revitalization movement. Emerging from the mid-1990s, the rural revitalization movement has supported urban people's resettlement in farming villages that teach organic farming as a viable method for small family farms and, more importantly, as a way of preserving rural villages as a place of living rather than only a place of production. Organic farming's pursuit of communal relationship between consumers and farmers, as well as humans and nature, is still in progress.

9

GOTJAWAL

The Promise of Becoming Wild

Jeongsu Shin

Stones hold on to trees, and trees hold on to stones
(돌은 낭 으지허곡 낭은 돌 으지헌다)

—A proverb of Jeju Island

In early September 2018, in Eastern Bliss, a village on the eastern coast of Jeju Island (Cheju-do), a large banner hung on the side of the road. In bold white and yellow colors against a black background, the banner read as follows: "[Our] Ancestors know. [Our] village communal pastureland is not *gotjawal* [곶자왈] [조상들이 알고 있다. 공동목장은 곶자왈이 아니다]."[1] In the context of the recent political dispute between Eastern Bliss village and environmental activists, this banner represented support for a newly proposed development project called Eastern Bliss Safari World and opposition to the ongoing environmental activism fighting to protect the village's communal pasturelands from the project. The development plan for the project was proposed in 2014 by a business consortium that wanted to convert Eastern Bliss' communal pastureland into a safari resort by means of a fifty-year land lease. This proposal had caused an intense conflict between the environmental activists and the villagers over whether Eastern Bliss' communal pastureland is indeed *gotjawal*.

Gotjawal is a native Jeju term, newly coined in the mid-1990s, based on the local words *got* (곶, forest) and *jawal* (자왈, weedy volcanic rubble). It now refers to the "primeval" (원시적) forest areas indigenous to Jeju Island featured in recent media representations to lure domestic and international tourists to the island (see figure 9.1).[2] Eventually, *gotjawal* came to be one of the must-visit tourist attractions for those who wanted to feel the "real" Jeju. These previously anthropogenic pasturelands could not be made arable by the old plowing tools, so the lands were used mainly for grazing horses and cattle. However, these lands were abandoned (버려진) in the 1970s when people began farming

FIGURE 9.1.   Han'gyŏng Gotjawal. *Source:* Photo taken on May 20, 2017, by the author.

tangerine, onion, white radish, and carrot, which have become the island's most important commodity crops. Since then, these abandoned pasturelands have turned into places of rich biodiversity where plants and other nonhumans have thrived. Since the term was introduced to the public, these secondary forest spaces have been considered the quintessence of Jeju Island's unique ecology system, as *gotjawal* is the result of the *longue durée* of entanglement of the natural history of the volcanic island with the human history on South Korea's periphery (변방). The geology, fauna, and flora, the semitropical climate, and the activities of the inhabitants of Jeju Island, together constitute *gotjawal.*

Eastern Bliss' communal pastureland is a case in point. Environmental activists have assessed that the area's ecology is transforming into woodland on the solid volcanic surface made by a pāhoehoe lava flow.[3] As the abandoned pastureland is auto-rewilding into forests, this area has become a large habitat for the heavenly sweet-scented Jeju *paeksŏhyang* (제주 백서향, *Daphne jejudoensis*), a species in the genus of the flowering shrub daphne that is listed as a rare species by the Korea Forest Service (see figure 9.2). Jeju *paeksŏhyang* on Jeju Island prefers half-shaded areas, so it is often found at the edge of the forests. It thrives in areas that are in the process of ecological succession from grassland to forest, which perfectly suits the working definition of *gotjawal.*

FIGURE 9.2. Jeju *paeksŏhyang*, a species of daphne. *Source*: Photo taken on April 4, 2017, in Ch'ŏngsu Gotjawal by the author.

Environmental activists contend that its geological features and the rare species clearly indicate this area is *gotjawal* and should be protected. Furthermore, environmental activists maintain that this pastureland has been restored to the so-called wild as *gotjawal*, whereas the villagers insist it has never been *gotjawal* and desperately want the development that will bring new jobs and monetary compensation from the fifty-year land lease. Thus, the banner described earlier is sending a message of "opposition" (반대), geared directly to the recent environmental activism aiming to protect the *gotjawal* areas from development. But what did the ancestors of Eastern Bliss village know? Put differently, who could have known what *gotjawal*, a concept that never existed in their time, would be?

This chapter is a landscape ethnography that considers the scope of the temporal trajectory that has shaped the spatial concept of *gotjawal* by pursuing the etymology and "intimate knowledge" of the terms that the local people in Jeju Island use to envision the social and natural meanings of this space.[4] Among the many cultural geographers and anthropologists who have theorized human-landscape relations, Laura Ogden investigates the scope of meanings that people use to understand and interpret changing relations with animals, plants, and material objects found in the landscape.[5] The recent burgeoning discussions in multispecies ethnography are particularly helpful in understanding how non-humans are actively participating in this meaning-making process.[6]

In this light, this chapter traces the ways that *gotjawal* gained its substantial meanings through the keen eyes of the Jeju natives, who observe the constant weed-growing dynamics that change the landscape into what they consider messiness. This state of messiness is a result or part of an ongoing and unyielding process through which plants and other organisms are participating in rewilding in human-disturbed landscapes—what Anna Tsing calls "auto-rewilding."[7] There have always been auto-rewilders and messy spaces where humans want or need to control the landscape or tame nature for their purposes. Given the ways the Jeju natives perceive it, as well as the scientific assessments of what constitutes wildness, *gotjawal* appears as a Jeju-esque (제주다운) space at the intersection of global concerns on biodiversity and the increasing awareness of the need for environmental justice for Jeju natives in the face of an unprecedented development boom and rapid globalization. *Gotjawal* is conceptualized and materializes out of etymology, the activities of auto-rewilders, local journalism, and scientific research— as a space of resilience for Jeju Island and against global capitalistic invasion.

Influenced by the push for global conservation of nature and indigenous culture, environmental activists and supporters enthusiastically celebrate the force of rewilding found in *gotjawal* nature as a sign of resilience. As I briefly stated above, *gotjawal* areas are mostly the previously communal pasturelands—namely, formerly controlled lands—that have gone wild. The process of ecological succession and so-called messy conditions caused by the growth of ferns and brambles have been interpreted as signs of potentiality and hope in a time of ecological decline and capitalistic destruction on Jeju Island. Most importantly, environmental activists strategically focus on the communal pasturelands and forests as commons and common-pool resources that Jeju ancestors had historically formed as a kind of reciprocal social system and that represented their shared formal and communal responsibilities.[8] Although the utility of many of the existing communal pasturelands is perhaps waning with shifts in socioeconomic structure, activists on the island have tried to expand the meanings and purpose of these forms of the commons, not only for the villages but for Jeju Island and beyond. They view them, first, as a space evoking indigenous Jeju history and memories and, second, as the sanctuary for the rights of future generations and the lives of nonhumans (a topic taken up more fully by Nan Kim in chapter 10).

By engaging with recent anthropological studies, this chapter traces the critical historiography of *gotjawal*, the emergent space of wilderness of Jeju Island. Here I explore how the material qualities and temporalities of rewilding weeds and trees on abandoned lands are leading to new ways of perceiving and relating to natural cultural spaces in contemporary Jeju Island. By tracing and parsing out local terms, signs, and meanings associated with this emergent concept of *gotjawal* and the environmental activism to protect *gotjawal*, I call into question the integrity of "the wilderness" as a coherent, universal, and transcendent concept. With my ethnographic study of *gotjawal*, I examine the ways in which the space of wilderness has been historically transformed, articulated, and, most importantly, situated in particular political, social, and historical moments.

Gotjawal, a Word That No One Ever Used or Heard Before

As of 2019, *gotjawal* has become a popular spatial concept considered endemic to Jeju Island. Like the Jeju term orŭm (오름), for a volcanic cone, there is no equivalent term in standard Korean for things and places existing only in Jeju Island. *Gotjawal* seems to be one of those words that sound foreign to people from the mainland (육지). However, *gotjawal* also sounds unfamiliar to native Jeju islanders. Interestingly, during my ethnographic field research (September 2016 to August 2018), I never encountered anyone or any documents that could tell me about the history of the word prior to 1995. Its origin has long been a mystery to me. Many interlocutors told me they had heard similar terms or concepts but never knew the word *gotjawal* per se. Many just said, "It's a new term." Yet *gotjawal* was listed in *A Dictionary of the Jeju Language*, published in 1995 by a group of Jeju native linguists under the supervision of Hyŏn Pyŏng-hyo (1920–2004), who dedicated his life to salvaging the Jeju language.[9] To date, *A Dictionary of the Jeju Language* is the first document in which the word *gotjawal* appears.

This dictionary defines *gotjawal* as follows: "[noun] a messy place like the forest where trees and vines are wildly entangled [나무와 덩굴 따위가 마구 엉클어져서 수풀같이 어수선하게 된 곳]."[10] It is noteworthy that the adjective *ŏsusŏnhada* (어수선하다), or messy, untidy, disordered is a salient characteristic of this spatial concept. The definition indicates that *gotjawal* is a natural wilderness condition limiting human access to the area. But *gotjawal*'s spatial history can be best understood when we look at the entangled stories of humans and nature, which many scholars have researched.[11] This "messy place" is the result of the auto-rewilding that ferns, thorny bushes, vines, and trees create. It is in total opposition to the state of "the regularity and neatness" that state-led fiscal and scientific forestry wants to achieve.[12] Local flora has always thrived and disturbed human control over the landscape. In this vein, an example of the use of the word, as established in the dictionary, shows how Jeju islanders have engaged with this space: "gotjawal was a total dense forest [밀림] but we cultivated it into a park [동산]."[13] This phrase implies that *gotjawal* has never remained total wilderness. Rather it is a place that Jeju islanders have constantly tried to tame and cultivate into useful and beneficial land.

Gotjawal's ecology has been created and uncreated through its interactions with humans and the animals that Jeju islanders introduced when this space was used for lumbering or communal pasturelands. Although now it might be seen as primeval, an untouched wilderness, it is actually an anthropogenic, human-made forest. Many tourists and visitors seek this primeval world, totally isolated from human civilization, while hiking in the *gotjawal* forests. However, these areas are mostly secondary forests, regrown from pasturelands or that which survived the scorched-earth strategy during the Jeju April 3 massacres (1947–1954).

In *Friction: An Ethnography of Global Connection* (2005), Anna Tsing introduces the concept "social-natural landscape" to fill the gap between the cultivated and the wild in the ways we approach anthropogenic landscapes such as *gotjawal*.[14] She explains that "we can explore how interactions among humans and nonhumans on this landscape create its patches and trajectories. We can follow how the forest becomes readable as a social space."[15] Reading the social space of *gotjawal* might begin with its etymology. The word made its debut in the dictionary in 1995, but there are many other vocabularies in the Jeju language to describe the dynamics of weed-filled space to guide investigations into how the islanders perceive the dynamics of the plants that create the particular *ŏsusŏnhan* weedy landscapes (see figure 9.3). These vocabularies explain the resilient, or auto-rewilding, activities of plants that demarcate "the wild" on a volcanic topology.

FIGURE 9.3. Sangdo Gotjawal. *Source:* Photo taken on April 27, 2018, by the author.

The two main terms *got* and *jawal* that together constitute the term *gotjawal* refer to two profoundly different yet interconnected types of ecologies.[16] Forest areas or woodlands are called *got* (곶, forest), *koji* (고지, forest), or *kotpat* (곶팟, the field of the forest), depending on the regional differences in the Jeju language. *Jawal* refers to bushy areas on the volcanic rubble and captures the characteristics of volcanic ground. *Got* and *jawal* refer to two totally different socioeconomic value systems. Whereas *got* is considered a valuable natural resource because it provides useful timber and charcoal, *jawal* is considered wasteland, namely, a messy space. Moreover, the synonyms of these two words align with these two op-posing value systems. *Mŏse* (머세), a synonym of *got*, is where scrub or miscella-neous trees grow thick on piles of stones.[17] *Jawal* has more variations and synonyms than the term for forest. For example, *kasi jawal* (가시 자왈) highlights the thorny, entangled scrubs and vines on *jawal*.[18] *Suwŏl* (수월) is defined as "a forest made of thorny vines," but people use this term to describe larger formations of thorny woodlands that are connected in ways similar to how flowing water makes certain spatial connections.[19] And *sŏmbŏl* (섬벌) describes the place where trees and vines are thickly entangled.[20] To Jeju natives, especially for people over seventy, each term connotes distinctive qualities and ecological conditions, which is not reduc-ible to the single term, *gotjawal*. Each implies various social landscapes that people perceive and connect to a particular type of natural landscape. Each highlights different modes of auto-rewilding. And each term implies the main driving actors in the weedy and messy landscape such as wild berries, thorns, ferns, or volcanic rubble.

To explore the sylvan world of Jeju Island, which the local glossaries invite us to do, I briefly introduce a forest area belonging to Giving Forest village. A neighboring village of Eastern Bliss, Giving Forest village is locally called an up-land (웃뜨르) village. The village's communal forest, Giving Forest, is the larg-est evergreen forest in South Korea and designated as part of the UNESCO Geopark (2007), placing it under the protection of the Ministry of Environment. This forest area was formerly shared and owned by the Giving Forest villagers, but now most of the lands have been purchased by the Korea Forest Service.[21]

This large forest, dominated by various evergreen oak trees and camellia trees, once provided timber, charcoal, and camellia seed oil for the villagers. During the Japanese colonial period, villagers organized a forestry fraternity (삼림계 or 삼림접), to claim their rights over their neighboring forest, and en-couraged village members to participate in the protection of the forest from fre-quent slash-and-burn fires and from fires people intentionally set to renew the grass every spring. More importantly, the initial goal in organizing the Giving Forest fraternity was to build and run a school for the village's children, supported by the profits from communal charcoal production using a variety of evergreen oaks, *kasinang* (가시낭). Giving Forest has been a source of great pride for everyone in the village. Such a large forest is rare, because most of the island has been cultivated as pastureland since the Mongol invasion and the establishment of horse ranches, a process outlined by John S. Lee in chapter 1.[22] When I met Ko Chʼŏng-myŏng in 2017, he was seventy-one years old. He had been born and raised in Giving Forest village and was proud of his beloved village and the forest, which represented the extensive efforts to improve the village's education and community solidarity by preserving the forest. He remarked that now "the whole world" recognizes the village's ancestors and current members' efforts. For him, the current conservation activities are a continuation of the caring work of their "ancestors" (옛날 어르신).[23]

On May 22, 2017, Ko Chʼŏng-myŏng brought me to his eighty-seven-year-old uncle's home to tell me more about the history of Giving Forest, with particular attention paid to Japanese colonial rule and the April 3 massacres (1947–1954). Ko Paek-ro experienced the Japanese occupation and the massacres. He was born in 1930 in Giving Forest village and has remained there ever since. He has made his living by horse ranching and later by tangerine farming. From time to time, our conversation went off the track, which led to misunderstandings, as I often could not follow the specific place names and local terms he was using. The root of this confusion was that I kept asking about *gotjawal*, but the term *gotjawal* has never been his way of seeing Giving Forest. I kept asking where *got* was and where *jawal* was in Giving Forest, provoking this calm and gentle old man to finally raise his voice as he emphatically stated, "I have always said it is totally wrong that people say Giving 'gotjawal.' It should be just Giving *got*. The word *jawal* indicates places that have thorny vines and that has not yet become a forest. When we say *got*, it is a very deep forest."

As I briefly stated above, *got* (forest) and *jawal* (socially recognized as wasteland) relate to different ecological imaginaries and social values. Mr. Ko seemed unhappy about people's intentional combining these two terms. *Got*, their community's beloved forest, is "a deep forest" and economically valuable to the community, whereas *jawal* is hard and difficult to conform to human needs. Mr. Ko added, "*Jawal* is *motssŭnŭn ttang* [못쓰는 땅]," which means derelict land or lands that cannot be used.

In our conversation, Mr. Ko used *sŏmbŏl* (섬벌) with the suffix *-jida* (지다), which adds the meaning of becoming. For instance, one could ask the question, "Can you go in there because it has become *sŏmbŏl* (섬벌져서)?" Here *sŏmbŏljida* (섬벌지다) describes the auto-rewilding activities of, particularly, plants with thorns such as fatsia, mysore thorn, and brambles, intermingled with various ferns in the understory and vines with a kudzu covering. These overgrown plants create the messy (어수선한) landscape that is considered uncultivated and unwelcoming to humans and their domesticated animals. According to Mr. Ko, *jawal* or *sŏmbŏl* were the places gone wild that even cattle avoided.

The term *gotjawal*, as a compound word meaning these two different ecological conditions or the various conditions of the in-between status of *got* and *jawal*, holds the extensive possibility of being applied to any messy area to be transformed into a forest. However, at the same time, the inherent complexity and uncertainty of the concept makes it hard to draw the geographical boundaries of *gotjawal*, which is currently causing many legal and social disputes over the development of the area. Mr. Ko, an old farmer and retired horse herder, considered Giving Forest to now be a full-grown forest, but Eastern Bliss village's former communal pastureland, to his mind, has only recently become wild, or *jawal*.

In other words, native Jeju islanders do not necessarily read these patches of land as one total spatial concept of *gotjawal*; *got* and *jawal* have different qualities. In the past, there was no equivalent concept for modern wilderness. A Korean term, *yasaeng* (야생), has been used to describe "wild" fauna and flora, those nondomesticated species and their territories; however, native Jeju islanders did not have a romanticized view of wilderness. These two different spaces, *got* and *jawal*, which together have become a representative of the spaces of wilderness in contemporary Jeju Island, have never been purely matters of nature. Its "rewilding" forces kept creating "messiness." Yet messy *jawal* has the potential to be useful, helpful, and valuable forest, though as Mr. Ko pointed out, it "has not yet become."

Interestingly, although this observation of *jawal* "becoming" *got* is based on firsthand experiences of witnessing ecological succession, the spatial transformation between *jawal* and *got* does not always operate on a linear timeline. As a commentary on the new term, *gotjawal*, there is the saying, "*Jawal* can become *got*, but not vice versa. Except in the case when it is burnt by fire." However, this exception was not a rare case. Given the history of pastoralism on Jeju Island, fire, locally called *pang'e* (방에), is a life-generative force in spring, as it clears the pasturelands and helps to create the clean grasslands. Along the spectrum between grasslands and forests, *jawal* and its messiness has mediated the multidirectional intra-actions among species, space, and human practices.[24]

How, then, has the compound *gotjawal* become the overarching term embracing the various ways of perceiving spatially enacted ecological differences? In the section that follows, I explore how, over the past three decades, this newly coined term has attained its meanings through scientific investigation and local environmental activism.

Scientific Investigation of Jeju Island's Interior

In 1997, *gotjawal* appeared as a substantial geographical concept in *A Comprehensive Study on Mid-Mountain Areas of Jeju Island.*[25] The term mid-mountain area (중산간) is now largely used in local and academic contexts to describe a highland area located at an altitude of 200–600 meters. This term implies that the entirety of Jeju Island is actually Mount Halla. Every village, pastureland, forest, and volcanic cone (오름) is seen as being on the gentle slope of Mount Halla. Thus, when someone asks, "Where does Mount Halla end?" Jeju islanders will always answer, "At the sea!" In the local geographical sense, the lands of Jeju Island fall into three categories: lowlands (알뜨르), highlands (웃뜨르or 중산간), and top areas (상산) of Mount Halla. In 1997, the mid-mountain area was measured at 589 square kilometers, which was 32.2 percent of Jeju Island's total area. However, its population was only 1.5 percent of the total population.[26] The vast mid-mountain area consists of only a few highland villages, forests, old swidden agricultural fields, and, most importantly, large pasturelands.

A Comprehensive Study on the Mid-Mountain Areas of Jeju Island was the first attempt to characterize and define the highlands' geographical boundaries using geographic information system (GIS) technology in a massive investigation of the area's vegetation, geology, and landscape ecology. The word *gotjawal* appears in the section relating to the tectonic structure and the permeability study marking the crucial areas for protecting underground water.[27] Japanese geologists had carried out the first research on underground water in 1921, and although the island's underground water has been of great interest, aboveground water management has been an ongoing issue because of the basalt composition of the ground, which quickly absorbs the rain.[28] After about a decade of trying to solve this problem, the Agriculture Promotion Public Corporation drilled and gained access to the underground aquifer in the 1970s, solving the water supply problems in the highlands.

In the 1980s, however, Hanjin, a parent company of Korean Air, started producing bottled mineral water from Jeju Island. This private corporation's underground mineral water extraction sparked social awareness about the island's preservation and the management of its public property. By the 1990s, Jeju islanders and the provincial government had become deeply invested in the management of the quality of the island's underground water, and the geological research for *A Comprehensive Study on the Mid-Mountain Areas of Jeju Island* was carried out in this context. In 1995, based on a special law regarding the management of the island's drinking water, the Jeju Island provincial government established a public cooperative with exclusive rights to extract the underground water. The Jeju

Island Public Cooperative built a water production facility and in 1998 started producing water called Samdasu, now South Korea's most famous and best-selling bottled mineral water.

The scientific expedition to the mid-mountain areas to understand the geological system that creates the island's quality mineral water led to unexpected results in demarcating the concept of *gotjawal*. Among the geologists who participated in the research, Song Si-t'ae was a doctoral student who did not know he would later become the famous "Dr. Gotjawal" who would spark an environmental movement to preserve the *gotjawal*. Back then, the research team was looking at the particular volcanic topographies with high water permeability, places where rainwater went directly underground. On Jeju Island there are places called breathing holes (숨골), not seen on any map and known only to locals. When many Koreans hear the term breathing holes, they might think of the soft part of a newborn baby's head, believed to be still open, through which babies "breathe" (숨). As a local term and spatial concept, however, calling them breathing holes is an anthropomorphic projection on the part of Jeju islanders for identifying these particular spots—holes, hollows, or cracks of rocks—where they feel cool air in the summer and warm air in the winter. They are considered the "lungs" of the island. Insofar as they filter rainwater into best-selling mineral water, they might alternatively be seen as the island's kidneys.

The research team hiked into the highlands to examine these areas that were directly affecting the underground water's quality. Yet there was no specific concept to encompass and define these breathing and water filtering places. However, part of their research included interviews with neighboring villagers to learn about the locations of these spots and find out what their names were. According to Dr. Song, "One person from village A said, 'We have called it *jawal*,' while another person from village B said, 'We call it *got*.' But when we [geologists] went out to see the geology and the tectonic structures, there was no difference [between *got* and *jawal*]." Both types of spaces, whether called *got* or *jawal*, were created on the top of the volcanic topology from relatively recent (circa 10,000 years ago) volcanic activities from a nearby volcanic cone (오름). These tough and uneven topologies are not arable, so they remained as the villages' communal pastureland. Dr. Song continued, "Our ancestors did not see the geology. They only paid attention to the vegetation on the rocks to get firewood. They named the spaces based on what they needed and what they got from those spaces. But from the geological perspective, those spaces were not really different. The geological traits of those places spoke about when and how they were formed by certain types of volcanic activities. And later they were covered in different types of vegetation and received different names."

To conceptualize this uneven and rough volcanic topology, the research team decided to take the word *gotjawal* from *The Dictionary of the Jeju Language*.[29]

According to the 1997 report, the *gotjawal* of Jeju Island is mostly "abandoned land," as its vegetation conditions are not worth protecting. Its highly water-permeable geological characteristics, however, called for it to be preserved, primarily to protect the area from development to secure the quality of the underground water.[30]

As a continuation of his research interest in Jeju Island's tectonic structure, in 2000 Song Si-t'ae finished his doctoral dissertation, "The Distributions and Lithology of the 'A'ā Rubble Flows on Cheju Island, Korea."[31] He defined *gotjawal* as "areas of the lava flows with high water permeability in the highlands."[32] Song's dissertation was the first work to attempt to draw the *gotjawal*'s boundaries. Soon after, *Jemin ilbo*, a local daily newspaper, approached Song and requested a series of articles. An investigative team of botanists and biologists was quickly organized, including the journalist Kim Hyo-ch'ŏl, who later established an NGO called the Descendants of Gotjawal. "The Exploration of the Gotjawal" (곶자왈 대탐사), a series of articles published from November 2002 to February 2004, is considered one of the greatest achievements of Jeju Island journalism in its introduction of the *gotjawal* as a unique natural ecosystem and repository of biodiversity found only on the island. The aniseed tree (붓순나무), red-bark oak (개가시나무), Jeju *kosarisam* (제주고사리삼), and other rare species prevalent in the *gotjawal* were introduced to readers.

One of the species introduced by the Exploration of the Gotjawal series was Jeju *kosarisam* (*Mankyua chejuense*), a dime-sized fern that grows only on Jeju Island. It prefers the swampy but well-drained *gotjawal* areas (see figure 9.4). Kim Mun-hong, a botanist and a professor at Jeju National University, discovered it in Giving Forest in 1995. After a long assessment of this newly found fern, it was registered as a new genus in 2001.[33] Known to grow only in or around Giving Forest, the fern was promptly registered as a critically endangered species on the International Union for Conservation of Nature (IUCN) Red List.[34]

Learning about species like Jeju *kosarisam* has shifted the ways the local newspaper readers are seeing, understanding, and connecting with the uncharted, uncultivated, and "messy" pasturelands. When the seemingly common wild weeds and shrubs were given names and botanical recognition, *gotjawal* become a sanctuary for rare or endangered species and a space of biodiversity. Should the Giving Forest be destroyed, the genus of the tiny fern would disappear from the earth. This logic in many ways marks a departure from the way the ancestors of Eastern Bliss village had seen the world around them. In Jeju, as elsewhere, environmentalism has introduced an entirely different way of determining the value of abandoned land.

FIGURE 9.4. Jeju *kosarisam* (*Mankyua chejuense*) in Giving Forest. *Source:* Photo taken on February 1, 2018, by the author.

Resilient Landscape

On June 18, 2017, about twenty people gathered on the side of a country lane connecting tangerine, potato, and garlic fields in the highland village of Sunny Mount. Some were native Jeju islanders; some, including myself, were not. This monthly field trip to the *gotjawal* was organized by the Descendants of Gotjawal; this trip, the fourth in 2017, aimed to publicize the value of the *gotjawal* to those unfamiliar with this newly emergent spatial concept so that participants could "feel" its distinctive ecology.

Kim Hun, one of three co-presidents of the organization, guided us along a narrow footpath. After a few steps, he pointed to an iron fence and asked, "What do you think that is (see figure 9.5)?" Smiling, he answered, "This Sunny Mount Gotjawal means that it has lived with (더불어 살아온) the villagers of Sunny Mount." In recent years, while many *gotjawal* areas have been sold and turned into sites for hotels, resorts, English education complexes, and the like, some are protected zones owned by the provincial government or the Korea Forest Service. Furthermore, some areas remained as communal pastureland but were recently developed as hiking trails to attract more tourists. Despite the promotion of eco-tourism as an alternative for Jeju Island's future, many villages

FIGURE 9.5.   At the entrance of Sunny Mount Gotjawal. *Source*: Photo taken on June 18, 2017, by the author.

still grapple with how to deal with this trend and its benefits. Yet after consulting the People of Gotjawal, Sunny Mount village opened its old pathways for tourists and hikers. The idea that "it has lived with" the villagers implies not only the ways in which Sunny Mount villagers have relied on the natural resources and environment, but also how nonhumans have collectively survived in troubled times. This iron fence was nothing special or surprising, merely a space where Sunny Mount villagers in the past regularly drove their cattle. On our way to the deep forest, Kim reenacted the pastoral imaginaries by pointing out "relics" and showed us that the hiking trail we were on was a passageway used for cattle (목장길). As he led us into the woods, he cheerfully added, "This natural area was able to be protected and to become a deep forest because it has been abandoned; let's keep nature abandoned and see what happens!" Kim Hun suggested that to "keep nature abandoned"—meaning, removing humanity from nature—is the best act of care in contemporary environmental politics. Such care includes "making time" for care by opening up space for repair and other modes of "living as well as possible" in the time of the Anthropocene.[35]

The concept of *gotjawal* inherently includes the shifting nature of the area's ecology as grassland thrives to become *jawal*, and *jawal* thrives to become a forest. *Gotjawal*, once considered messy, abandoned, and less valuable land, has the potential for becoming a wild space. The once-unwelcoming signs of becoming messy have gained new meanings as signals for potential biodiversity. The material quality of messiness that the rewilding nonhumans have aroused, according to Jane Bennett's language, is the mesmerizing "thing-power" that resides in the process of ecological succession.[36]

In a broad sense, *gotjawal* has come to represent new perspectives regarding environmentalism and biodiversity, as well as new ways of seeing, feeling, and thinking about this messy landscape and the wild. Especially in this context of massive displacement of landownership and the fear of losing the ethos of Jeju Island (제주다움), *gotjawal* is at the political forefront as it stands for the natural indigeneity of Jeju Island.

10

SOUTH KOREA'S NUCLEAR-ENERGY ENTANGLEMENTS AND THE TIMESCALES OF ECOLOGICAL DEMOCRACY

Nan Kim

On the evening of September 12, 2016, two earthquakes shook the surface and crust of the Earth at the Korean peninsula. They shared roughly the same epicenter at the city of Kyŏngju in South Korea and could be felt throughout most parts of the country, occurring less than an hour apart. One of them would prove to be the largest earthquake recorded on the peninsula since the collection of data from instrumental measurements began there in 1908. Yet, that description could easily overstate the earthquake's severity. At magnitude 5.8, the second and larger of the two earthquakes at Kyŏngju was by no means a massive earthquake. It caused extensive damage but yielded little in the way of irreparable destruction. It resulted in no deaths. The quakes nonetheless came as a shock because Korea had long been regarded as "earthquake-free."[1] Compounding the sense of public alarm was the proximity of these earthquakes to an area with a high density of nuclear reactors along Korea's southeastern coast.

Thus, a new and unpredictable factor arose in the calculus of risk that had, for several decades, shadowed the development and expansion of South Korea's nuclear-energy program. With twenty-four operable nuclear reactors as of 2021, South Korea derives a little less than a third of its electrical supply nationwide from nuclear power. The size of South Korea's civilian nuclear-energy program currently ranks fifth in the world, but given the country's compact geographical footprint, the density of reactors is twice that of Japan and more than 150 times that of Russia or China. Indeed, compared to all other countries with large nuclear-energy programs, South Korea maintains by far the most densely concentrated cluster of nuclear reactors in the world. Until recent years, however, antinuclear activists could only estimate as much by using World Nuclear Association data; and not until 2014 could South Korean civic groups finally confirm this, using data produced by their own government's Nuclear Safety and Security Commission (NSSC).[2]

Following the 2016 earthquakes, seismologists concluded that these temblors had *not* in fact been triggered by North Korean underground nuclear tests, countering a dubious speculation that had circulated on social media and in the news. Yet, the idea of naturally occurring seismic activity was hardly more reassuring. In South Korea, retrofitting of nuclear power plants had already been under way by that juncture. In an attempt to allay anxieties triggered by the Kyŏngju earthquakes, the NSSC responded by releasing a statement that the country's nuclear reactors were designed to withstand a quake of up to magnitude 6.5 or 7.0, a standard adopted following Japan's triple disaster at Fukushima. Though intended to calm a nervous public, such pronouncements also recalled how the shock following Fukushima had reverberated anew in South Korea during a 2013 scandal when four reactors were ordered shut down in the wake of an investigation exposing the use of counterfeit parts and falsified certifications.[3] However insistently the technocrats and other spokespeople at official agencies tried to project confidence about more recent safety upgrades, it has remained a sobering reality that—to a degree arguably unparalleled anywhere—those in South Korea reside in the midst of nuclear energy's generation, its fuel cycles, and its biopolitics. Given that the country's significant reliance on nuclear energy is itself rooted in the period of authoritarian developmentalism that characterized South Korea in the mid-to-late twentieth century, what does the inheritance of an authoritarian-era energy infrastructure mean for contemporary democratic politics in thinking and practice?

This chapter analyzes a series of key controversies over nuclear-energy infrastructure in South Korea. I explore how the 2016 earthquakes in Kyŏngju brought to light an improbable convergence of circumstances, connecting nodes of protest, deferral, and the unknown. This co-occurrence—as it arose within the context of South Korean modern and contemporary history—highlights more broadly the ethical dilemmas embedded in ongoing public decision-making processes about the contingent futures of nuclear energy. Given that the radioactivity of the most dangerous forms of nuclear waste can extend over eons, the contestation of nuclear energy in South Korea plays out myriad implications relevant to an ethical framework of ecological democracy, challenging how the uncanny timescales of nuclear-fuel cycles are inevitably at odds with the expedient timelines of politically driven negotiation over calculated interests that inform decisions surrounding nuclear infrastructure.

Ecological Democracy across Generations

In South Korea's post-authoritarian era, questions regarding energy transition, or the shift away from unsustainable energy sources, have raised greater public awareness of the risks associated with the country's overbuilt nuclear power plant clusters. In the context of South Korea, Dowan Ku has investigated the concept of ecological democracy as it informs both the strategic and ethical thinking of the discourses and practices of antinuclear activists.[4] Ku highlights how advocates of ecological democracy seek to extend notions of democracy beyond state-centric and anthropocentric assumptions, respecting the inherent value of creatures other than human beings as well as the rights of future human generations.

Regarding the implications of ecological democracy, a sense of ethical obligation projects far into the future, but real-time deliberation is key. Recognizing that all those affected by a given policy should ideally be entitled to participate in decision making, Robyn Eckersley has framed ecological democracy within the principle of "democracy of the affected."[5] In other words, those unable to defend their own interests would be afforded representation through discursive proxy or forms of advocacy on their behalf. Moreover, recognizing how the interests of future generations must be taken into account is not to discount the importance of nonhuman biotic communities in political imaginaries, as indeed the concept of future generations may encompass all forms of life.

An intergenerational understanding of ecological democracy has also informed recent climate action calling for a rapid wide-scale response in light of the vanishing window for reducing carbon emissions. The intergenerational aspects of ecological democracy underscore how those affected by present-day decisions include all who must cope with potentially irreversible ecological disruption.[6] Seizing the long view—engaging in "deep time reckoning," as Vincent Ialenti has advocated[7]—also challenges more moderate approaches and "shallow-time thinking" preoccupied with using conventional procedures that can induce apathy or would yield, at best, incremental change.

With regard to relationships across generations, one response to the climate-action debate has been the promotion of nuclear power as a so-called green technology based on the assumption that it is carbon-neutral and therefore inherently sustainable.[8] However, antinuclear activists have rejected and critiqued this claim in South Korea as elsewhere. Lauren Richardson has traced how Korean members of the antinuclear movement articulated their refutation in a post-Fukushima campaign with the following points: (1) calling nuclear power carbon-neutral is misleading because that ignores the emissions required for the mining and processing of uranium; (2) reactor fuel extracted from uranium deposits will eventually be exhausted and is therefore not sustainable; and (3) the claim of nuclear energy's cost-effectiveness is undermined by social costs and risks, such as those exposed by the Fukushima disaster.[9] For deliberations relevant to decisions regarding nuclear-energy infrastructure, radical ecological democrats take a stand on principle that current and future generations of the affected, regardless of their geographical location, are entitled to the life-supporting conditions for surviving, if not flourishing.

Whatever potential hazards may result from the construction of facilities for nuclear energy, the public perception of danger often focuses on *possibility*—namely, the possibility of a nuclear accident. Yet, another hazard to humans and to the biosphere is not a matter of contingency. Such hazard is neither accidental nor hypothetical; rather, it is integral to the production of nuclear energy as the back-end of the nuclear-fuel cycle: that is, the production of nuclear waste, particularly spent fuel. The vast majority of the waste stream from nuclear-power production comprises low-level waste, which has only short-lived radioactivity and can be handled safely with simple precautions. However, small amounts of high-level waste in the form of spent nuclear fuel are what must be contained for many millennia and can remain dangerously radioactive for hundreds of thousands or millions of years.

To handle the waste stream from nuclear-energy generation, a facility designed to store spent fuel or even low-level radioactive debris should not be mistaken for a "nuclear dump."[10] Unlike a dumping ground or conventional landfill site, nuclear-waste disposal facilities are technologically sophisticated operations requiring careful maintenance to keep the radioactive materials isolated from the biosphere. Leakage of high-level nuclear wastes must be avoided because they can remain hazardous on an order of time that is mind-bending and multimillennial, another example of what Joseph Masco has called the "nuclear uncanny."[11] Ialenti considers how such "intransigent wastes" not only change our orientation toward an abstract sense of the future but also create new relationships with those who inhabit a far-off but grounded future world. Drawing on his ethnographic research among Finnish scientists and technicians involved in construction of the world's first geological facility for the disposal of high-level nuclear waste, Ialenti writes that high-level waste "disposal regimes emerge as idiosyncratic scenes of engagement with distant future societies, bodies, and environments—as sites in which relations between living societies of the present and unborn societies [of] distant future worlds are imagined and reimagined."[12]

Navigating Long-Term Stewardship in Two Senses

"Long-term stewardship" is a term shared by two spheres that would otherwise seem remote from each other: (1) UNESCO has used the concept to describe the curation and care of World Heritage Sites, and (2) the technocratic field of nuclear-waste management uses the term to denote the process of maintaining high-level waste sealed from the environment to avoid radioactive contamination.[13] These differing senses of stewardship are directly and indirectly relevant to a site in South Korea that, since 2015, has housed a state-of-the-art underground nuclear-waste facility for storing low- and intermediate-level nuclear waste. The first of its kind to operate in Asia, the facility is located on the outskirts of Kyŏngju, a city that is far more widely known as the location of Korea's most prominent UNESCO World Heritage Sites. Notably, Kyŏngju also became the beneficiary of a sizable package of economic-development funds, won in a 2005 referendum process that furthered the interests of the national nuclear industry while ensuring high-level nuclear waste be ultimately directed elsewhere.

As a site synonymous with national cultural heritage and closely identified with the nuclear sector, Kyŏngju is best understood through the city's association with Park Chung-hee. South Korea's former president from 1963 to 1979, who led an anti-Communist military-authoritarian regime, Park was responsible for both launching a national nuclear program and making Kyŏngju the country's preeminent city of cultural heritage. Park commissioned a series of excavations as well as conservation efforts in the 1970s that went hand in hand with the construction of museums and facilities for national historic sites. In this way, Kyŏngju became elevated in the historical imaginary of South Korean nationalist ideology.[14] Promoting the cultural heritage of Kyŏngju furthermore established a claim to Korea's roots in the Silla dynasty (57 BCE–935 CE), whose geographic territory overlaps with modern-day Kyŏngsang Province, the seat of Park's political power.

While Kyŏngju would be intentionally set apart as a space of exception in the cultural and political landscape of South Korea, to understand how a state-of-the-art nuclear-waste facility eventually came to be sited in the city's vicinity, it is helpful to review some significant moments in the development of the South Korean nuclear industry and the antinuclear movement. After a modest start to nuclear activities in Korea during the 1950s, ambitions for South Korea to become a nuclear state coalesced into a more serious nuclear program during the Park Chung-hee military regime. The program was centered on dual-use technology, combining the development of a civilian nuclear-energy program with a clandestine nuclear-weapons program. In the South Korean "sociotechnical imaginary," as Sheila Jasanoff and Sang-Hyun Kim have written, harnessing "atoms for national development" had the aim of enhancing nuclear capability whether for peace or war.[15] They note that nuclear power was regarded as the ideal example of Park's style of state-led techno-economic development, whereby science would provide "the foundation for increasing productive forces and the source of power for accelerating economic development," while national sovereignty would be secured through the indigenization of nuclear power and technology.[16] By the late 1970s, the country's first pressurized water reactor, Kori 1, began operation. With it, South Korea gained the latent capacity to build nuclear weapons, as the use of spent fuels from nuclear reactors meant its civilian program had the potential to be converted into a military one.[17] The secret weapons program would eventually end in 1979, after Park was assassinated, but civilian nuclear energy would remain integral to state-led economic development.

By the turning point of Korea's democratization in 1987, nuclear reactors had been completed in three locations: Kori (1978), Wǒlsǒng (1983), and Yǒnggwang (1986), with construction at Uljin already under way since 1983 (see figure 10.1). After that point, the South Korean nuclear agency built new reactors only next to existing ones. The decision to build reactors strictly in sites adjacent to already existing nuclear power plants was understandable, given the limited number of suitable sites in South Korea. Moreover, this approach had the effect of minimizing the risk of triggering protests, which had become increasingly effective in mobilizing public opposition to the new construction. To place this decision into wider context, the early history of the antinuclear movement in South Korea could be roughly periodized as follows: First, in the 1960s, initial isolated protest demonstrations were suppressed as members of the fledgling antinuclear movement were subjected to physical beatings and red-baiting. Then, during the 1970s and 1980s, activists organized to block the construction of new nuclear power plants but were repeatedly pushed back. Finally, since the 1990s, a series of successful activist campaigns during the post-authoritarian period have helped defeat the proposals for building nuclear-waste disposal sites through the political momentum generated by collective protests.[18] Although local resistance to constructing nuclear reactors had largely been defused by dependence of the local economy on jobs related to the nuclear-energy industry, even areas in relatively close proximity to nuclear power plants saw strenuous protest movements to counter this new kind of construction for the disposal of nuclear waste.[19]

For example, in 1988, the South Korean government announced three possible sites for nuclear-waste storage, Uljin, Yǒnggil, and Yǒngdǒk, all on the southeastern coast. After that announcement, local residents and antinuclear activists converged on the area to organize protests. With the key involvement of the Korean Federation for Environmental Movements and South Korean Catholic dioceses, the success of that opposition movement was repeated in Anmyǒndo (1990)

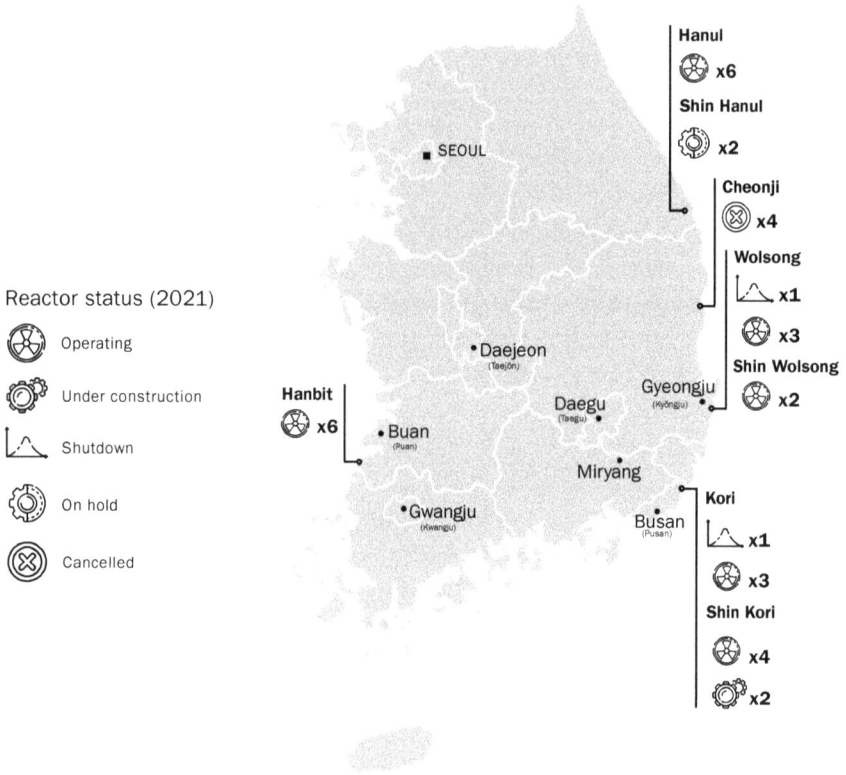

FIGURE 10.1. Nuclear power plants in South Korea, by status and number of reactors. The city names follow the South Korean revised romanization system. Image by Matthew Carlson. *Data source*: World Nuclear Association; Korea Hydro & Nuclear Power.

and Kurŏpto (1994), and in the particularly fierce protests in Puan County (부안군) in North Chŏlla Province (2003–2004).[20] Between 1986 and 2005, seven successive attempts to select a site for storing nuclear waste were all defeated by local resistance.

Since the mid-1990s, a push toward decentralization of policy decision making led to passage of the Local Referendum Act, first proposed in 1994 and eventually ratified in December 2003, during the first year of Roh Moo-hyun's presidency. It granted more autonomy to local governments in a range of policy areas including environmental issues, and that change has been attributed in part to the antinuclear protests of the early 1990s.[21] By the early 2000s, the Korea Radioactive Waste Agency (KORAD) had also been seeking a new strategy for securing approval to designate the site of its first radioactive-waste facility, after nearly two decades of facing stiff local resistance to site proposals.

Once the Local Referendum Act became government policy, KORAD applied the referendum format to the question of where to site a nuclear-waste storage facility. The referendum was framed in terms of economic incentives, creating a competition among various regions, which had been selected by virtue of having the necessary space and appropriate geological characteristics. At stake was a sizable package of incentives, including a state subsidy of 300 billion *won* (US$288 million), plus annual disposal fees estimated at approximately 8.5 billion *won* (US$8 million) per year. This approach thus took advantage of the strong interest among economically depressed regions to secure state subsidies for local revitalization and development.

In Kyŏngju, numerous cultural properties and archaeological sites—such as Sŏkkuram Grotto and Pulguksa Temple, Korea's first UNESCO World Heritage List designations—have shaped the city government's branding of Kyŏngju as a "museum without walls." Yet, such heritage designations have stipulated restrictions on development and construction, which local residents came to view as burdensome. As a result, factions emerged among the city's residents, who differ in opinion on how to cope with such limits on industrial and population growth. Growing anxiety over economic vulnerability among residents was not lost on the advocates for approving the waste site. Given that the city had been passed over in earlier competitions for state-sponsored development projects, the opportunity to win the contract for hosting the nuclear-waste facility was framed as a last chance for the region. Of the four participating regions, Kyŏngju ultimately secured the contract to host the facility by mobilizing the largest portion of favorable votes. Among the 70.8 percent voter turnout in the Kyŏngju area, the votes in favor of the plan exceeded expectations, amounting to 89.5 percent. The incongruity of a landslide referendum welcoming a radioactive-waste site is jarring, given that Kyŏngju is celebrated as Korea's preeminent "city of culture." What did it mean for a significant majority of Kyŏngju voters to approve the siting of a nuclear-waste storage facility in their own city?

In *Kyŏngju Things: Assembling Place*, Robert Oppenheim explores the latter-day creation of Kyŏngju in the twentieth century as not only the invention of tradition as a heritage site but also, more broadly, as the coalescence of having things, events, and social networks of expertise, all situated in proximate relationship with one another and their respective histories. Oppenheim characterizes Kyŏngju as "a national epicenter of historic objects," but it is one where the ancient and the futuristic exist in juxtaposition, as state cultural properties have been promoted alongside projects and things such as Korea's first high-speed rail line, which stand for advanced technological advancement.[22] Imported from France, the TGV—or Train à Grande Vitesse, the French high-speed train—came to Korea first not by way of the global megalopolis that is Seoul, but rather

via Kyŏngju, lending the provincial city an air of cosmopolitan glamor and technological advancement.

Members of the campaign to bring the nuclear-waste depository to Kyŏngju
similarly appealed to the identity of the city as one bridging the ancient past with
the imminent future. That orientation is evident in how the facility was eventually planned, constructed, and curated. For example, the location of KORAD's
public education center incorporates an adjacent winding hillside path dotted
with signs bearing panels of text that amount to an outdoor exhibition spotlight-
ing the nearby royal tomb of King Munmu (628–681), the first king of Unified
Silla. Clearly visible from the hillside, the tomb itself is located at sea, marked by
an outcropping of rocks just off the coast below where the facility is now located.
Though there had been speculation as to the historical authenticity of the site's
discovery, legend has come down that King Munmu is said to have instructed
that he be buried at sea so that he could become a dragon and protect the Silla
coastline.[23] Thus, a well-worn mythology of protecting the nation is reinforced at
the site of the nuclear-waste facility, anchoring a socio-technical imaginary while
imbuing it with nationalist projections onto the ancient historical past.

Returning to the question of why Kyŏngju residents would vote in favor of the
nuclear-waste facility in 2005, the referendum appeared to reflect a near-consensus
in favor, at least when perceived from a distance. On closer examination, however,
the voting outcome was in fact determined largely by those in Kyŏngju who would
be least affected by its consequences. Of the two hundred thousand Kyŏngju residents who participated in the referendum, more than 90 percent live on the opposite side of a mountain that separates their residential areas from the site. Less
than a tenth of those who voted in the Kyŏngju referendum lived within ten kilometers of the then-proposed site of the nuclear-waste facility.[24] Also, given that the
Kyŏngju site is specifically a low- and intermediate-level nuclear waste repository,
it matters that the waste generated by the nuclear-fuel cycle can be divided into
separate categories that represent vastly different degrees of radioactive exposure.
Low-level waste includes items such as protective clothing and gloves, and although this category represents over 90 percent of the waste that nuclear power
plants generate, it produces only 1 percent of the radioactivity. In contrast, *high-
level waste* comprises extremely radioactive materials such as spent fuel rods, and
while these make up only 3 percent of a nuclear reactor's waste-stream, they produce 95 percent of its radioactivity.[25]

In light of the highly divergent degrees of radioactive toxicity posed by the
wastes from nuclear-energy generation, Kyŏngju's referendum vote to accept the
nuclear-waste storage site takes on an entirely different meaning. In the context
of the South Korean government's strategy to secure approval through the referendum, the proposal not only included enormous economic incentives, it also

sweetened the deal by stipulating that the proposed underground repository would house *only* low- and intermediate-level nuclear waste and exclude high-level nuclear waste.[26] As part of the proposal, high-level wastes would be *legally mandated* to be transported elsewhere. Accepting the low-level waste nuclear facility in the short term therefore served as a strategy for Kyŏngju residents for taking their city out of the running to house high-level waste in the long run, exempting them from the next siting battle, which will eventually become the fate of another community in the future.

Contentious Nuclear Democracy

While South Korea's buildup of nuclear power plants dates primarily to its period of military authoritarian rule, another more recent wave of construction occurred during the conservative government of Lee Myung-bak. His administration had declared a Low Carbon Green Growth strategy as a national development policy in 2008, with nuclear plant enlargement and export at the center.[27] Although the Lee government won a contract with United Arab Emirates in 2009 to build and operate four nuclear power plants there, Korea did not manage to finalize further nuclear-reactor deals, despite Lee's target goal for the export of eighty Korean reactors by 2030.[28] The debate over nuclear energy then joined the issues at the heart of South Korea's ongoing transition toward a more open and participatory democratic system, the outcome of the 2016–2017 Candlelight Revolution that ousted Lee's conservative successor in the presidency, Park Geun-hye. That popular protest movement against government corruption and cronyism focused criticism on the failings of South Korea's system of "imperial presidency," characterized by a lack of accountability and transparency. By 2017 the question of Korea's nuclear-energy future no longer split along the conventional left-right divide of partisan politics.[29] Following Park's impeachment, every major candidate in the presidential election pledged to stop building nuclear reactors and to close down older ones.

After taking office as president in May of 2017, Moon Jae-in ordered the provisional halting of construction on two unfinished reactors, Sin'gori 5 and Sin'gori 6. However, the final decision was put to a three-month-long deliberative process of public review. Moon's new government assembled a "citizens' jury," which included experts representing both sides and a total of 471 randomly chosen citizens. Compared to the broader and more conventional means of holding a vote by public referendum, South Korea's recent citizens' jury provided a more focused and participatory deliberative process. The two questions on the ballot were (1) whether the Sin'gori 5 and 6 nuclear reactors should be constructed, and

(2), how much nuclear energy the country should rely on in the future. The vote of the citizens' jury yielded a mixed result. While 59.5 percent voted in favor of proceeding with the construction of the two reactors, a slightly smaller majority, 53.2 percent of the jurors, also supported a reduction of the country's reliance on nuclear energy. Critics of the process took issue with the short period of deliberation, only three months long, and South Korea's inexperience with the deliberative process, particularly given the issue's sensitivity and high stakes.[30] Environmentalists called out the unfairness of the significant imbalance in resources available to pro-nuclear groups, who could rely on an established network of government officials and research institutes. Nevertheless, the Moon administration ultimately decided to respect the vote rendered by the citizens' jury in this process. The concession to allow construction to resume on the Sin'gori reactors was a defeat for the antinuclear movement, though at the time it may have plausibly been calculated by the Moon administration as an attempt to secure greater support and legitimacy in the long run for the eventual phase-out of nuclear energy.[31]

Another aspect of South Korea's relationship with nuclear power that, surprisingly, became a lightning rod of national controversy was the power-transmission network, an aspect of energy infrastructure that is otherwise generally obscure. The grassroots activism by Miryang villagers and rural communities brought this into focus through their fight against the remote mountainside construction of high-voltage transmission towers, part of the network that sends electricity to Seoul from the Sin'gori nuclear reactor cluster. This struggle, waged by elderly residents who physically put their visibly frail bodies on the line to stop the advance of construction, drew public attention to how the high-consumption urban lifestyles in the metropole were sustained at the expense of those whose lives were upended by the expansion of energy infrastructure in the periphery.

In her study of the Miryang Halmaedŭl (밀양 할매들, Grannies of Miryang), Su-Young Choi analyzes how these rural grandmothers-turned-activists provide the visual embodiment of South Korea's culture of resistance against the neo-developmental state. She explores why the protests of these elderly rural residents gained striking momentum nationally among activists and other environmentally minded people who supported their fight against KEPCO, after the utility had determined the high-voltage transmission lines would run through their village. She discusses the Miryang controversy as an example of the sacrificial displacement and dispossession that is the modus operandi of neo-developmentalism, driven by vested interests and the state in South Korea. Choi writes,

> On the one hand, the government supports the nuclear-construction-industry complex's expansion of its domestic construction of nuclear power plants and accompanying substations and transmission lines. On

the other hand, the government also awards loans to these construction industries to promote the companies' commercial nuclear exports based on the domestic energy facilities as their references. In the case of the 765,000-voltage transmission line that cuts across Miryang, the line was a part of the newly developed Sin'gori III Nuclear Power Plant, while the plant's reactor was the reference model for the $18.6-billion export contract to build a nuclear power plant with the United Arab Emirates in 2009. Under "the infrastructural power" formed by "Korea's developmental alliance" between state and capital, . . . local residents have been forced to be displaced, "dispossessed," and sacrificed in order for the coalition of infrastructure businesses to generate its continuous profits.[32]

As reflected in Choi's analysis, residents of Miryang and surrounding villages were subject to unilateral decisions by KEPCO to install the high-power transmission towers. What has been insidious within these villages is the fractured ties that resulted from the fact that some residents, particularly male community leaders, eventually got co-opted and accepted compensation from KEPCO, alienating them from their neighbors and the residents who continued on in the long-term protest. Meanwhile, Miryang residents lived in fear and dread of an elevated risk of cancer, and among their grievances was the steep decline in their property values and the unlikelihood that younger generations would return to live near their ancestral homes. Anticipating the inevitable population loss came with melancholy over the untenability of preserving their long-standing communities and the inability to pass down "untainted" land to their children and descendants.[33]

The Soberingly Ironic Timing of Unforeseen Earthquakes

Whether manifested as fear of exposure to high-voltage electricity emanating from nuclear power plants or as fierce controversies over the long-term disposal of nuclear waste, the dilemmas presented by nuclear energy should not simply be taken as indications of how the "natural world" has become contaminated by toxic anthropogenic effects. Rather, they can be taken as aspects of what Drew Milne and John Kinsella have called "a dark ecology prefigured by the nuclear, and suffused with it."[34] Spanning epochs, the persistence of long-lived nuclear waste's radioactivity provides an index of how "nature" has become intertwined with the fate of resilient biohazards. One of the challenges presented by storing high-level nuclear waste is precisely the impossibility of foretelling what changes could occur over the extremely long periods when such material remains hazardous, the insurmountable gaps in what Hugh Gusterson calls "anticipatory knowledge" about nuclear futures.[35] That uncertainty extends to the occurrence of seismic activity, a possibility amply illustrated by the earthquakes-as-coincidence at Kyŏngju. Even though the newly opened underground facility in Korea contained only relatively benign low- and intermediate-level nuclear waste, the way the temblors caught everyone unawares was what proved most telling of all.

Although it is extremely unlikely that the recent earthquakes in Korea were triggered by climate change, their surrounding circumstances may nevertheless bring to light how human attempts at risk management in the evolving nuclear age must take into account global ecologies as the planet heats up. Indeed, given that ongoing glacial melt from the great ice sheets of Antarctica and Greenland will continue to hasten sea-level rise, it would be surprising if some of the innumerable faults beneath the Earth's surface did not respond to the ensuing redistribution of global water. As geoscientist Bill McGuire has argued, if the current trend of anthropogenic climate change continues, it may well lead to the reawakening of long dormant volcanoes and earthquakes in coming decades.[36] Were an increase in seismic activity to occur in areas where earthquakes might have once seemed unimaginable, that in turn changes the balance of risk when evaluating possible solutions for determining the "final" disposal of nuclear waste. Having to recalibrate such risk, moreover, raises questions regarding how deep geological disposal facilities operate on the assumption that the Earth's crust will remain stable over coming millennia, to ensure the necessary isolation of highly radioactive material into the distant future.[37]

In 2016 the state-of-the-art underground nuclear-waste repository in Kyŏngju had only recently started operations when Korea's strongest earthquake of modern times occurred in the same city. That soberingly ironic near-coincidence underscores the task burdening those charged with decisions regarding nuclear energy and the long-term storage and disposal of spent fuel. In South Korea, although it had previously been estimated that temporary sites storing used fuel rods would be filled by 2016, that year the Park Geun-hye government announced KORAD would nonetheless postpone until 2028 the selection of new sites for high-level nuclear wastes. As in virtually all other countries with nuclear-energy programs, spent fuel continues to accumulate in temporary storage near the nuclear reactors, waiting to be transported elsewhere for "permanent" disposal.[38]

Given the temporality of high-level waste from nuclear energy, proponents of ecological democracy may weigh the ethics of the current nuclear-energy debate in light of the responsibility to advocate for future generations, whether in 2028 for the next siting battle or far into the remotely distant future. Though the 2016 Kyŏngju earthquakes did not set any records of seismic magnitude outside of Korea, they did signify something momentous in their improbable timing and the layered irony of their location. Odds were vanishingly small, close to nil, that the epicenter of those quakes would be the same city where a historically signifi-cant nuclear-waste repository had just opened only months prior. As the site of Asia's first geological-disposal facility for nuclear waste, Kyŏngju's status as host city is important, in part, because KEPCO historically faced formidable chal-lenges by civil-society groups who had successfully protested and blocked the approval of several sites for storing nuclear waste in other parts of Korea. In Kyŏngju, the referendum vote enabling the siting of strictly low- and intermediate-level nuclear wastes there could in turn be understood as a gambit of opportun-ism and strategic deferral, sacrificing the interests of a minority of residents to gain economic benefits for the region while deflecting a far more consequential reckoning of the nuclear age regarding the disposal of high-level nuclear waste. That latter higher-stakes siting battle would be effectively pushed off to another region and community, where someone else's future descendants will have little choice but to inherit a proximity to sites of buried radioactive toxicity.

In light of such stacked events brought to light by a pair of earthquakes in a city with no expectation of seismic activity, their convergence at Kyŏngju can serve more broadly to expose technocratic blind spots while amplifying the ethi-cal compromises inherent in the compressed and highly consequential way that decisions over nuclear-energy infrastructure are made and executed. This is true not only in Korea but also elsewhere in the world, wherever nuclear reactors are constructed and wherever high-level waste is stored. Whether or not an attempt is undertaken to make such decision-making processes more deliberative, their relative haste and expedience can hardly answer for the duration of their impact over the exceedingly long-extended timescales of nuclear energy's dark ecology.

ON EVERYDAY ECOLOGIES AND SYSTEMS OF MEDIATION

Albert L. Park and Eleana J. Kim

Next Steps

This epilogue is being written at a momentous period in time. The global pandemic of COVID-19 has become a biological threat to human life inside and outside the Korean peninsula. Starting with the outbreak of cases among the followers of the religious group Sinch'ŏnji in February 2020, the global pandemic upended everyday life and any sense of normality in society and the economy in Korea. As the government scrambled to identify, trace, and contain the virus, it quickly became apparent that this deadly microbe had the power to ravage people's respiratory systems. Infected with the virus, countless numbers of people have experienced respiratory tract infections that have left them with severely compromised lungs and windpipes, a major factor behind COVID-19-related deaths. At the very beginning of the pandemic, Koreans were already being exposed to environmental dangers that were causing stress to their upper and lower respiratory tracts. Respiratory health was under assault by the massive air pollution in the country—known as "fine dust" (*misaemŏnji*). From the urban to the rural, no one in the country could escape the ubiquitous air pollution that had been releasing the dangerous fine particulate matter known as PM 2.5, which has the power to seep deeply into the respiratory tract of humans, causing shortness of breath, coughing, sneezing, runny nose, and irritation to the lungs, eyes, throat, and nose. The most serious consequence of the lung's absorption of PM 2.5 has been the onset of asthma and bronchitis and cardiovascular effects, such as heart disease and cardiac arrhythmias, particularly when absorbed into a person's bloodstream. Air pollution in Korea has caused an estimated forty thousand premature deaths annually, and nearly five thousand deaths related to chronic obstructive pulmonary disorder (COPD)—also related to PM 2.5.[1] The residual effects of air pollution left Korean bodies even more vulnerable to the damaging effects of COVID-19. Indeed, this situation has become even more apparent in Korea and elsewhere, with scientific studies showing a connection between high pollution exposure and increased rates of COVID-19 and in COVID-19 deaths.[2]

Severe air pollution in Korea has stemmed from a number of internal and external causes, including the shared air space between China and the Korean peninsula that has moved pollutants from China to Korea.[3] Across the Yellow Sea, Korea's neighbor, China, has had its own share of dangerously high levels of air pollution, with PM 2.5 that has ravaged the respiratory systems of its own citizens and left them more vulnerable to the dangers of COVID-19. The relationship between COVID-19 and air pollution took a fascinating turn during the period of the pandemic. Studies revealed that air pollution had decreased in both Korea and China since January 2020, and the air become cleaner during the pandemic. Even though the government had not rolled out a plan calling for the total lockdown of movement, more people stayed home and refrained from driving, manufacturing and heavy industry plants put a pause on production, a vast number of airplanes remained on the ground, and construction projects of all sorts were temporarily on hold. The reduction in the movement of people combined with lower than normal fossil fuel combustion produced conditions for improved air quality. Early scientific findings have reported that the levels of tropospheric nitrogen dioxide, a pollutant released by fossil fuel combustion, were reduced during the pandemic.[4] In South Korea, between January 1 and May 31, 2019, there were 191 fine dust advisories, 523 ultrafine dust advisories, and 52 ultrafine dust warnings. During the same period in 2020, by contrast, there were 82 fine dust advisories and 122 ultrafine dust advisories. The government did not issue a single ultrafine dust advisory in 2020.[5] Yet the irony of less pollution and cleaner air during the pandemic has been people's respiratory systems, especially lungs, have still been exposed to a dangerous biological force that could weaken and destroy people's health in a more rapid fashion—that is, COVID-19. The pandemic has replaced a dangerous nonhuman pollutant with a treacherous nonhuman microbe.

Even after the dangers of the pandemic subside, from measures put in place to control the spread of virus and the introduction of a vaccine, air pollution and its produced threats will still remain. Steady fossil fuel combustions without strict restrictions and regulations will only give way to more hazardous fine dust and a gradual assault against human bodies and nonhuman species. This type of assault against humans and nonhumans is in line with the overall trend of how environmental issues have unfolded on the peninsula. Far from being punctuated by rupturing events that have been sudden and forceful, the environmental history of modern Korea has been filled with a string of environmental events that have gradually unfolded and have affected human bodies and ecologies. Unlike China and Japan, modern Korea has never encountered a singular environmental catastrophe that had led to an abrupt, dramatic disruption of landscapes and patterns and rhythms of nonhuman life that led to large-scale human death and injuries—perhaps with the exception of the destruction during the three years of the Korean War and long-lasting famine in North Korea that spanned the 1990s and was partially caused by devastating floods in the summer of 1995. As the chapters in this book have laid out, significant environmental issues, such as deforestation, chemical-led industrial farming, the Little Ice Age, and the reengineering of fish ecologies through large-scale infrastructure projects, have given way to a gradual degradation of areas from the air to the soil to the water that have, in turn, steadily battered humans. Far from being immediately apparent and striking, the severe consequences of the damages and the poundings have appeared and been felt over time. Though not instantaneously visible, these alterations and transformations over time have been just as unsettling, disruptive, and corrosive as the changes produced from an immediate, catastrophic environmental event.

The way that environmental issues have unfolded on the Korean peninsula has required more nuanced approaches and observations to environmental issues. It has called for a closer examination of people's daily practices—their mundane moments in daily life—in relation with nonhuman entities, and how these interactions shape and reshape ecologies. This type of observation and study—which we refer to as everyday ecologies—seeks to scrutinize the routine rhythms, patterns, and depths of interactions among organisms in everyday life. Ecology refers to the relations of organisms to one another, and everyday ecologies particularly place emphasis on the daily contact and exchanges between humans and nonhumans. It connects those interactions to larger social, economic, political, and cultural systems and structures to explain ecological-social changes and the transformations of human and nonhuman landscapes on the Korean peninsula; the degree and intensity of these changes and transformations have often depended on the types of systems of power and mediation in place. With environment referring to the larger context or setting of ecological relations, the examination of everyday ecologies seeks, in short, to detect a diverse range of environmental issues and the changes, damage, and destruction that they may have caused on the scale of daily life. In this capacity, this paradigm serves as a way to make more environmental issues more visible. Chapters in this book have drawn out many nuanced and particular observations and points of view from this paradigm. In line with the chapters, this epilogue highlights potential areas of the environment that could be approached and explained through the paradigm of everyday ecologies in future studies. In particular, it offers subjects and themes in ethnography and history for drawing out new perspectives of everyday ecologies that would bring about creative approaches and viewpoints to the study of the environment from the past to the present.

Contemporary Ethnography and Everyday Ecologies

The framework of everyday ecologies expands the range of possible research areas and topical foci that could be included in a book such as this one, both temporally and spatially. It also extends how we think about what constitutes "environments" and their material and symbolic relationships to human societies. Climate change is aptly described by Timothy Morton as a "hyperobject"—something that exceeds our conceptual ability to grasp as a totality. As such, it defamiliarizes and dislodges what have been hegemonic master narratives, grounded in modernist and anthropocentric cartographies and epistemologies.[6] Categories such as "politics," "economy," "society," which had already been deconstructed as theoretical constructs, have been further problematized for their dependence on seemingly universal distinctions between human and nonhuman and nature and culture. These distinctions are now being questioned, not only because they are historically contingent but also because they are conceptually and politically limiting in the face of the enormity of the current planetary predicament.

In the discussion that follows, we outline three areas for ethnographic studies of Korean ecologies that can center the living and nonliving relationships that constitute everyday ecologies: critical ecologies, landscapes of militarized modernity, and vernacular climate changes.

First, critical ecologies examines the scientific and cultural dimensions of ecological discourses and knowledge projects. It extends the growing scholarship in environmental humanities and social sciences on South Korean environmental activism to ask how the categories of "environment" or "ecology" emerge out of a nexus of political, economic, cultural, and cosmological histories, discourses, and practices. Ecology has become a key word in environmental discourses and scholarship in South Korea, particularly since the early 1990s, when activists shifted their attention from "environment" (환경, *hwangyŏng*) to "ecology" (생태, *saengt'ae*), which also entailed a political shift from workers' struggles against industrial pollution to middle-class demands for sustainable environments. State projects have also embraced *saengt'ae* through science education and ecotourism, and a commitment to building and maintaining green spaces, even as it prioritizes economic growth based on capitalist values.

These trends reflect the desires of middle-class and elite consumers for eco-friendly lifestyles, which took the form of the well-being fad in South Korea at the turn of the millennium. Although these consumption-based choices are widely critiqued as complicit with capitalist greenwashing, the explosion in "well-being" arguably increased the critical environmentality of South Korean citizens, who embrace not only the values of eco-friendly products but also healthy environments. Related to these developments is a subculture of "return," inspired by a critique of neoliberal cultures of overwork, overproduction, and overconsumption. Urbanites in the late 1990s began seeking a slower pace of life, leading to an exodus. The trend of *gwinong* or *gwich'on*—literally, "returning to farming" or "returning to the country"—connoted a romantic nostalgia for Korea's premodern, agrarian past and a rejection of the rise of the consumer citizen, particularly in the aftermath of the Asian financial crisis (1997–1998).

In light of these cultural and social transformations, scholars in South Korea have increasingly turned their attention to ecology through the analysis of citizen science, ecological citizenship, ecotourism, human-nonhuman interactions, and eco-philosophy. The critical eco-logics proposed here would bring greater focus to how *saengt'ae* and *saengt'aegye* (생태계, ecosystems) are framed in relation to actually existing environments, scientific knowledge, political economic structures, and cultural narratives of the organic world. How are scientific epistemologies of "eco-," which are embedded in Western epistemologies and modernist natural sciences, translated and transformed in Korean contexts? Rather than risking an Orientalizing approach to Korean notions of "nature," this critical approach to ecologies asks how contemporary Koreans produce situated knowledge in ways that are informed, but not overdetermined, by modernist epistemologies and transnational environmentalist discourses.[7] What other logics, cosmologies, or human-nonhuman relations are encompassed in *saengt'ae*? A related discourse is that of *saengmyŏng*, which informs the Tonghak-inspired ecological thinking of Hansalim (see Paik, chapter 8).[8] Along these lines, what cultural histories, social memories, and everyday associations inform these ecological modes of understanding life, or *saeng*, as vital, relational, and multispecies? How do modern scientific discourses and paradigms inform, intersect, or contradict contemporary, everyday understandings of *saengmyŏng* and *saengt'ae*? What other transnational histories and disciplinary knowledge regimes—premodern, colonial, and postcolonial—are embedded in these discourses?

Second, a focus on landscapes of militarized modernity weds the militarized modernity and everyday militarisms of both North and South Korea to studies of its environments.[9] As this book has emphasized, forces of nature have often been entangled with state power and sovereignty, whether during the Chosŏn dynasty, the Japanese colonial period, or the Cold War authoritarian dictatorships. Given the centrality of premodern and modern technological war, warfare, and militarization on the peninsula, particularly since World War II, the Korean peninsula offers many sites for investigating questions about the effects of human violence and technological mastery on landscapes and human-nonhuman ecologies.

The Land of the Morning Calm is also the Land of Unending War—with a total of more than 1.6 million soldiers on the peninsula, an unverified number of military bases and installations on both sides of the border, and a million or more land mines and other deadly weapons. South Korea is also the site of highly contested US-ROK joint military exercises that have brought hundreds of thousands of US soldiers to South Korea over the past five decades for live-action drills, as well as an anti-base movement galvanized by activism in Gangjeong Village, Jeju Island, since the early 2010s.[10] Meanwhile, in the North, nuclear weapons and missile tests, both underground and aerial, have been ongoing sources of regional tension. How do these facts, materially and epistemologically, affect Korean landscapes while also shaping cultural and social discourses and experiences of nature, environment, and ecology?

In the context of the Anthropocene, and the significance of post–World War II intensifications of industrialization, referred to by geologists as the "great acceleration," Korea offers a particularly useful case study. After the devastation of the Korean War, Cold War antagonisms on the peninsula fueled the race to modernization between socialist North Korea and capitalist South Korea, as both states engaged in economic and military competition to buttress their claims to sovereign legitimacy. Today, it is clear that both socialist centrally planned development and state-driven capitalist development had terrible environmental costs. The north has suffered from the collapse of its industrialized agricultural systems, along with deforestation, soil erosion, and mass famine. In the south, unfettered development is exemplified by the expansion of "new towns" that extend the sprawl of the megalopolis of the Seoul Metropolitan area and by the smart city of Songdo, built on reclaimed wetlands and tidal flats, features that have now been recognized as ecologically crucial, natural flood control barriers for a future of rising sea levels. Given the stark realities of the two Koreas, it is no wonder that the DMZ has been celebrated as a "natural sanctuary," existing as an ecological parenthesis between the two world historical projects, both of which have brought us to the brink of human survival on the planet.[11]

Third, a vernacular approach to climate change would wed an ethnographic focus on emergent knowledges with a microhistorical approach that asks how climate change is constituted through everyday talk, social memory practices, and ties to land and landscapes. Climate change, as a hyperobject, is impossible to grasp as a totality, yet it is happening everywhere. On the Korean peninsula, climate-change-related events include longer and earlier monsoon seasons and related flooding disasters, longer periods of drought, warmer summers, rising sea levels, and shifting agricultural practices. An ethnographic attention to the phenomenological, affective, and embodied experiences of change, along with how it is perceived, measured, understood, and contested, can offer a more nuanced and humanistic interpretation of climate change than that offered by climatological models and discourses of crisis and disaster.

Historical Systems of Mediation and Everyday Ecologies

Critical ecologies, landscapes of militarized modernity, and vernacular climate changes furnish the ethnographic lens necessary to expose and interrogate the forces behind the contemporary unfolding of complex ecologies, militarized landscapes, climate change, and a variety of other environmental issues at the everyday level. This lens brings attention to discursive and material processes as well as ontological relations among humans and nonhumans that constitute what we refer to as the environment. This ethnographic approach to the paradigm of everyday ecologies is complemented by a historical approach, which traces the evolution of the relationship between humans and nonhumans and overall environments. It serves as the means to connect the present to the past and therefore constructs a more comprehensive narrative of everyday ecologies that explains how residual forces have intersected with emergent processes to create and alter environments across time and in the present.

Which angles of analysis best furnish a way to trace the transformations and alterations of the human and nonhuman relationship from the past to the present? In particular, reflecting on the establishment and effects of different types of systems of mediation over time can serve as useful framework to exploring relationships and changes in the environment. A system denotes "a set of units or elements" that are interconnected to the point that "changes in some elements or their relations produce changes in other parts of the system."[12] A system of mediation, then, specifically refers to a system with its forces, units, and entities, such as modes of production and exchange, that facilitates the interconnected relationship between humans and nonhumans and thus helps determine the historical outcome from that relationship. As Karatani Kojin points out, it is problematic to interpret alterations and exploitations of landscapes as simply the result of "a relation of man and nature."[13] For him, there are material and ideological mediums between humans and nonhumans that negotiate and determine the relationship between the two. Systems of mediation, therefore, alerts us to human-constructed systems that have powered, influenced and mediated the intersection between humans and nonhumans and created changes in the environment and society.

Capitalism is a clear example of a system of mediation. The most influential studies on the environment, such as works by Donald Worster, have painstakingly showed how capitalism and its distinctive features of production, exchange, and consumption have dramatically altered and reconfigured the relationship between humanity and nature.[14] Industrial capitalism's appearance in societies and its firm hold in organizing modern economies have particularly led to the revaluation of nature as a chief commodity for production and exchange. As a system, capitalism has created a culture that has celebrated and pushed for the exploitation of nature for human advancement and the accumulation of wealth. With the human autonomous self at the center, it has organized society in a way that would free individuals "(and corporations as collective individuals) from encumbrances on their aggressive use of nature, teach young people the proper behavior, and protect the successful from losing what they have gained."[15] Finally, capitalism has led to the creation of labor systems that has tied the exploitation of the environment to the control and abuse of workers—features of an era that some call "the Plantationocene"—as well as severed people's relationship to nature.

There is no shortage of examples of capitalism being a vehicle that has fundamentally reshaped the environment and the human relationship to nature in modern Korea. Take, for example, the drive to commodify and commercialize agriculture in the late nineteenth century by the Chosŏn state, which viewed agriculture as a key source for generating national wealth. The Japanese colonial period featured an intense push to commercialize agriculture further and Japanese capital fueling mining adventures to extract key minerals, such as tungsten and coal. At the same time, Korean peasants encountered a brutal regime of labor, as landlords intensified the production of rice, and a metabolic rift arose as rural inhabitants migrated to urban centers for work. South Korean corporations in the 1950s began to invest in the production of chemical pesticides that would lead to the poisoning of landscapes and bodies. North Korea industrialized its agricultural sector by pushing fossil-fuel-based technology and chemical farming, which, in turn, totally reconfigured land usage and the biodiversity of the rural. Industrialization quickly took off in urban centers in South Korea, and people violently extracted natural resources to fuel industrial growth. Supported by authoritarian governments, business conglomerates (재벌, *chaebol*) built industrial factories that spewed pollutants into the air and water, starting in the 1960s. Fast-paced urbanization has given way to the rapid escalation of real estate prices and new valuations and usages of land. Finally, the false and corrupt promises of green growth by Lee Myung-bak, the former South Korean president who has been arrested on corruption charges, led to the devastation of ecosystems and the reduction of biodiversity in areas affected by the Four Rivers Project in the early 2000s.

Capitalism in Korea cannot be ignored. It has been a powerful and pivotal system that has been the main cause of environmental change on the Korean peninsula. When employing capitalism as a lens through which to study the relationship between humans and nonhumans, it is crucial for any study to detail specifically what mechanisms, practices, beliefs, and values of capitalism have conditioned this relationship on different levels. Frequently, studies on the environment and capitalism have a tendency to state simply that "capitalism" has been behind all changes, exploitation, and destruction, instead of laying out the specific aspect of capitalism that has caused changes at the macro and everyday level. This general explanation omits the minute details of daily life that help produce nuanced explanations of *how* capitalism has touched the environment; it leaves out the causes of change and reduces capitalism to a simple, innocuous system that is like any other system, when, in fact, its power has made it into one of the most transformative systems of mediation under the Anthropocene. Furnishing details alerts readers to trace and understand precisely the anthropocentric effects of capitalism on ecosystems and complex ecologies

Alongside capitalism, religion has been a powerful system of mediation between humans and nature on the Korean peninsula. Through beliefs, practices, and institutions, religion has expressed itself as a collective paradigm through which people have interpreted and valuated the environment. As such, religion has functioned as an instrument for filtering and shaping people's approach to and interaction with the environment and its nonhuman entities. From Buddhism to Islam to Judaism, all religions have carried a sacred/profane paradigm that helps distinguish religion from other systems of mediation. This paradigm has served as the foundation for informing and structuring a spiritual reading and treatment of nature, including animals. Religion has therefore codified and regulated a spiritual experience between humans and nonhumans.

Take, for example, the role of animism in negotiating relationships between people and the environment. In animism, all entities, places, and objects possess a spiritual essence; thus, animism has configured nature as a sacred entity that should be respected and valued. Animistic religions in East Asia, such as Daoism, Shintoism, and Shamanism, have traditionally framed nature and animals as sacred entities based on their views that a single spiritual force is the underlying, foundational energy behind all creations. Theoretically speaking, then, animism has called for people to value and respect the nonhuman world. Yet, despite religious language that frames the environment as sacred, religious institutions and groups and their followers have nevertheless exploited and have sought to dominate and domesticate the environment for human purposes. The mistreatment and manipulation of nature through everyday practices by religious figures and institutions, such as those groups who have been influenced by the evangelical theology of Prosperity Gospel, which places the human as the center of all, testifies to how religion can operate as a force that fuels environmental destruction.

Religion has been one of the most influential systems to structure and guide the day-to-day lives of Koreans from the premodern to modern periods. Religions ranging from Buddhism to Christianity to Shamanism have nurtured a complex relationship with the environment. Religious doctrine and practices in Korea ostensibly promote the reverence and protection of nature, but these religions have also espoused ideas that have authorized and legitimized abuse. Protestant Christianity in Korea, which is one of the largest religions in the country, has legitimized human control over the nonhuman world, which laid the foundation for Christians to abuse the nonhuman world. From the very first day Protestant missionaries entered the country in the late nineteenth century, Western missionaries and Korean Christians, including leaders like Yun Ch'i-ho, spoke about God giving humans dominion over nature based on biblical principles. Grounded by theology, many conservative Korean Christians have freely treated nature as a commodity to be managed through political, business, and cultural practices. These efforts by Protestant Christians to control nature have been countered by movements to restore a healthy relationship between humans and nature in an industrial capitalist world. In particular, Buddhists, progressive Christian groups (Catholic and Protestant), and groups influenced by Tonghak have rolled out organic farming movements to counter chemical-based farming and pursued drives for social renewal through the construction of autonomous living associations between humans and nonhumans. Guided by the principle of oneness, these groups have connected environmental protection to social renewal. That is, they have maintained that the arrival of harmonious ecological relations could only occur through fundamental social transformations.

Religion absolutely cannot be ignored when studying the environment in the Korean peninsula. Not only have religious doctrines held powerful sway over the moral and ethical lives of Koreans, but they have also been the basis for the rise of environmental movements in South Korea. In approaching the intersection between religion and the environment, a "lived-religion" form of study should be at the center. This approach views "things as a result of social processes," in that religious ideas and practices originate and gain meaning in the context of social relationships, interactions, and events.[16] In particular, the lived-religion approach emphasizes practice as a process and calls attention to "its embeddedness and relations within a range of settings and concepts" rather than studying practice as an isolated object of study.[17] Broadly put, lived religion looks at the intersection between religion, social context, and nature. This triangular approach ultimately enables a deep understanding of the intersection between social context, religious practices, and the human connection to the nonhuman world over time.

Next to religion, science and technology have served as systems of mediation that have configured and transformed the environment on the Korean peninsula. They have functioned as a system of mediation that has directly connected humanity and nature. From the premodern to modern era in Korea, scientific surveys have recorded with increasing precision the biological, chemical, and physical rhythms and patterns of nature. From these studies and experiments, a cataloguing of the nonhuman world appeared in which species, organisms, landscapes, geological formations, microbes, and bodies of water, among other things, were identified, named, and listed in records with their characteristics. The sciences have helped make the natural world and its entities more visible to humans and have established them as "facts" or objects of investigation; technology has often become the direct site through which to manipulate and concretely transform the environment. It has served as the scientific apparatus for creating material changes in the world. In these capacities, science and technology have long operated as mediums that have guided and structured people's everyday approaches to and contacts with the environment. Scientific and technological networks have combined human and nonhuman entities to create a collective power that has reshaped human society and the nonhuman world simultaneously.

The production and employment of scientific knowledge and practices in premodern and modern Korea have, of course, never taken place in a vacuum. The modern era has featured plenty of instances of science and technology being relied on to increase national wealth, security, and prosperity, especially during the "civilization and enlightenment" campaigns of the late nineteenth century. Both the North Korean and South Korean governments have long viewed science and technology as tools for national empowerment and therefore have generously supported scientific and technological research. Science and technology, as such, have been regularly employed as instruments of power, development, and growth to achieve economic and political objectives. How have the relationships among science, technology, and state power changed over time? How has their use and promotion changed or remained the same across the full sweep of Korea's history? What networks in society have shaped and structured the world of science in Korea? In particular, how have political and economic influences, from the small scale to the large scale, guided scientific processes in relation to the environment?

How have science and technology directly shaped and reshaped ecological systems and biodiversity on the Korean peninsula? Tackling these questions opens up a new avenue for viewing and interpreting the role of science and technology in influencing and shaping everyday ecologies.

Capitalism, religion, and science and technology are just a few of the systems of mediation that could be further covered in the study of the environment in the Korean context. Of course, each of these systems of mediation have overlapped and intersected with one another. So, the environment and people's everyday lives have often been conditioned by multiple systems concurrently. Layered on one another, these interlocking systems have collectively shaped each entity or factor in the environment. Indeed, as campaigns to protect the environment have made clear, changing the circumstances of a single species or community cannot be achieved unless the system in which it is embedded has been modified. Consequently, all parts of the environment cannot be understood without accounting for all types of systems and their full web of influences. As such, this historical approach to the study of the environment opens up new pathways for working with ethnographic lenses in order to link the past to the present. Together, then, the ethnographic and historical serve as the cornerstones of everyday ecologies, allowing us to deepen our understanding of the forces of nature on the Korean peninsula.

Notes

GENERAL INTRODUCTION

1. "Peace Dam Still Waits for the Flood That Never Came," *New York Times*, August 28, 2007.

2. "金剛山水電 댐건설 中止하라 [Suspend the construction of Mt. Kŭmgang hydropower dam]," 동아일보 [*Tonga ilbo*], October 30, 1986.

3. "平和의 댐 着工 [Construction on the Peace Dam begins]," 동아일보 [*Tonga ilbo*], February 28, 1987.

4. "平和의 댐 의혹 [Doubts about the Peace Dam]," 연합뉴스 [*Yonhap News*], June 15, 1993.

5. On the downstream implications of North Korea's Imnam Dam, see Kyudok Hong, "Inter-Korean Environmental Cooperation: Options for Improving Environmental Quality in North Korea," in *The Environmental Dimensions of Asian Security: Conflict and Cooperation over Energy, Resources, and Pollution*, ed. In-Taek Hyun and Miranda Schreurs (Washington, DC: United States Institute of Peace Press, 2007), 185–207.

6. On the politics of inter-Korean environmental management, see Kyudok Hong, "A New Threat Currently Ignored: Need for Inter-Korean Environmental Cooperation," *Journal of East Asian Affairs* 20, no. 2 (2006): 79–108.

7. David Fedman, "Can Green Diplomacy Take Root in the DMZ?" *Edge-Effects*, June 5, 2018.

8. For a thoughtful examination of the history of tigers in Korea, and their place in the Korean environmental imagination, see Joseph Seeley and Aaron Skabelund, "Tigers—Real and Imagined—in Korea's Physical and Cultural Landscape," *Environmental History* 20, no. 3 (2015): 475–503.

9. On the cultural diplomacy of these games, see Jung Woo Lee, "A Game for the Global North: The 2018 Winter Olympic Games in Pyeongchang and South Korean Cultural Politics," *International Journal of the History of Sport* 33 (2016): 1411–1426.

10. The online petition, drawn up by Korea Green United under the title "Stop Ancient Forest Destruction," received more than 1,200,000 signatures. It can be read in full online at https://secure.avaaz.org/campaign/en/save_ancient_korean_forest_loc/ (accessed November 2, 2021).

11. "1회성 행사에 너무 큰 희생 [Too great a sacrifice for a one-time event]," 중앙일보 [*Chungang ilbo*], August 10, 2014.

12. "500년 원시 가리왕산' 주장에 강원도는 '최대 70년' [500-year-old Mt Gariwang is up to 70-years-old, Kangwŏn province officials claim]," 오마이뉴스 [*OhmyNews*], September 23, 2014.

13. This book may be read as a companion to the numerous English-language edited books dedicated to the environmental histories of Japan and China. See, for example, Ian Miller, Brett Walker, and Julia Adeney Thomas, eds., *Japan at Nature's Edge: The Environmental Context of a Global Power* (Honolulu: University of Hawaiʻi Press, 2011); Bruce Batten and Philip Brown, eds., *Environment and Society in the Japanese Islands: From Prehistory to the Present* (Corvallis: Oregon State University Press, 2015); and Mark Elvin, Cuirong Liu, and Ts'ui-Jung Liu, eds., *Sediments of Time: Environment and Society in Chinese History* (Cambridge, UK: Cambridge University Press, 1998). A broader, region-wide

analysis can be found in Ts'ui-Jung Liu and Micah Muscolino, *Perspectives on Environmental History in East Asia: Changes in the Land, Water, and Air* (London: Routledge, 2021).

14. The establishment in 2015 of the Society for Ecological and Environmental History [한국생태환경사학회], the first scholarly body of its kind in Korea, marks a major milestone in the fruition of the field in South Korea. Now publishing its own journal, this academic society has become a major driver of research as well as an important institutional touch point with similar scholarly bodies abroad. On the origins and objectives of this society, see Donald Hughes, "Welcoming a New Star in the Environmental History World," 생태환경과역사 [*Saengt'ae hwan'gyŏng kwa yŏksa*] 1 (2015): 8–10.

15. This is not to suggest that nationalist thinkers did not draw inspiration from the environment or touch on environmental topics in their writings. As Sunyoung Park points out, Korean dissident writers in the colonial period routinely invoked both a "harmonious, utopian" nature and a "violent, revolutionary" nature to articulate their socialist politics. See Sunyoung Park, "Anarchism and Culture in Colonial Korea: *Minjung* Revolution, Mutual Aid, and the Appeal of Nature," *Cross-Currents: East Asian History and Culture Review* 28 (2018): 93–115. On the broader intellectual currents behind this movement, see, for example, Namhee Lee, *The Making of Minjung: Democracy and the Politics of Representation* (Ithaca, NY: Cornell University Press, 2009).

16. On the ideological underpinnings of environmental thought in North Korea, see Robert Winstanley-Chesters, *Environment, Politics, and Ideology in North Korea: Landscape as Political Project* (London: Rowman and Littlefield, 2014).

17. Two recent special journal issues have laid the groundwork for English-language scholarship on Korean environmental history. In 2018, the *Journal of Asian Studies* published a special issue on war and the environment in Korea. This was followed in 2020 by a collection of essays published in the *International Journal of Korean Studies* covering a wide range of environmental topics. Looking at work currently in the publication pipeline, it is clear that the dearth in Anglophone scholarship on Korea's environmental history will not last long.

18. One important exception that foregrounds the environmental implications of Korean cuisine is Jaenyeong Jeong and Joong Hwan-Oh, eds., *Communicating Food in Korea* (Lanham, MD: Lexington Books, 2021).

19. One canonical account makes this very point in its title. See David Halberstam, *The Coldest Winter: America and the Korean War* (New York: Hachette Books, 2008).

20. This point is elaborated in John S. Lee, "Editor's Introduction: New Perspectives from Korean Environmental History," *International Journal of Korean History* 25, no. 1 (2020): 1–13. For a broader discussion of the intellectual currents shaping approaches to Korean environmental history, see Lee Jongmin, "Engineers for Seoul: Sewage Treatment and the Professionalization of Sanitary Engineering in Korea," *Korean Journal for the History of Science* 43, no. 2 (2021): 484–488. On the growth of environmental history as a field in South Korea, see 김도균 [Kim Do-Kyun], "한국 환경사 연구의 동향과 과제: 한국사 관련 학술지를 중심으로 [Trends in research of Korean environmental history and its future directions: A literature review based assessment]," *ECO* 12, no. 1 (2008): 217–249; 고태우 [Ko Tae-woo], "한국 근대 생태환경사 연구의 동향과 과제 [The research trends and challenges of Korean modern ecological and environmental history]," 생태환경과역사 [*Saengt'ae hwan'gyŏng kwa yŏksa*] 2 (2016): 31–70; and 洪錦洙 [Hong Kŭm-soo], "環境史 [Environmental History] 어떻게 해야 할 것인가 [A methodological discourse on environmental history]," 진단학보 [*Chindan hakpo*] 116 (2012): 149–181.

21. Eun-su Cho, "From Ascetic to Activist: Jiyul Sunim's Korean Buddhist Eco-Movement," in *Nature, Environment and Culture in East Asia: The Challenge of Climate Change*, ed. Carmen Meinert (Leiden: Brill, 2013), 259–283.

22. Normal Eder, *Poisoned Prosperity: Development, Modernization, and the Environment in South Korea* (London: Routledge, 2016).

23. An extended analysis of the environmental activism surrounding Onsan disease can be found in Hwa-Jen Liu, *Leverage of the Weak: Labor and Environmental Movements in Taiwan and South Korea* (Minneapolis: University of Minnesota Press, 2015).

24. For an extended analysis of this nascent activism, see Su-Hoon Lee, "Environmental Movements in South Korea," in *Asia's Environmental Movements: Comparative Perspectives*, ed. Yok Shiu Lee and Alvin So (Armonk, NY: M.E. Sharpe, 1999), 90–120.

25. For a brief discussion of the poetry of Kim Kwang-sŏp and a pathbreaking analysis of how Korea's literary world responded to this environmental degradation, see Karen Thornber, *Eco-Ambiguity: Environmental Crises and East Asian Literatures* (Ann Arbor: University of Michigan Press, 2012), 74–84.

26. Nancy Abelmann, *Echoes of the Past, Epics of Dissent: A South Korean Social Movement* (Berkeley: University of California Press, 1996), 228–231.

27. On these literary trends, see Simon Estok, "Discourse of Nation, National Ecopoetics, and Ecocriticism in the Face of the US: Canada and Korea as Case Studies," *Comparative American Studies* 7, no. 2 (2009): 85–97.

28. On this literature, see Kim Won-Chung, "Environmental Literature and the Change of Its Canon in Korea," *Comparative Literature and Culture* 16, no. 6 (2016): 1–9.

29. As cited in Thomas Kern, "Translating Global Values into National Contexts: The Rise of Environmentalism in South Korea," *International Sociology* 25, no. 6 (2010): 874.

30. For a fascinating case study of one such grand scheme of environmental reclamation in the heart of Seoul, see Chihyung Jeon and Yeonsil Jang, "Restoring and Re-restoring the Cheonggyecheon: Nature, Technology, and History in Seoul, South Korea," *Environmental History* 24 (2019): 736–765. On the South Korean government's efforts to promote "green growth" at home, see, for example, Jackson Ewing and Min-young Shin, "South Korea Paves the Way for an Eco-Friendly Asia," *East Asia Forum*, October 5, 2020.

31. For a critical examination of the planning and implementation of this project, see T. J. Lah, Yeoul Park, and Yoon Jik Cho, "The Four Major Rivers Restoration Project of South Korea," *Journal of Environment and Development* 24, no. 4 (2015): 375–394.

32. 김동진 [Kim Tong-jin], 조선의 생태 환경사 [An ecological-environmental history of Choson Korea] (Seoul: 푸른역사 [P'urŭnyŏksa], 2017), 15.

33. See, for example, 노성룡 [No Sŏng-ryong] and 배재수 [Pae Chae-su], 조선후기 송정(松政)의 전개과 특성: 국방 (国防) 문제를 중심으로 [The development and character of pine management policies in the Late Chosŏn dynasty: Focusing on issues of defense]," 아세아연구 [*Asea yŏn'gu*] 63, no. 3 (2020): 39–78.

34. For a critical examination of the Koreanization of environmental thought, see Wonsik Hong, "Confucianism, Korean Confucianism and Ecological Discourse," *Acta Koreana* 14, no. 2 (2011): 15–40.

35. See, for example, Seong Ho Jun, *Agriculture and Korean Economic History: Concise Farming Talk* (Singapore: Springer Nature, 2019).

36. If a consensus has emerged from this scholarship it is that deforestation was but one of several forces in the eighteenth and nineteenth centuries (including a population boom, economic instability, and social unrest) that contributed to the collapse of the ruling regime. For this perspective see, for example, 이우연 [Yi U-yŏn], 한국 의 산림 소유 제도 와 정책 의 역사, 1600–1987 [A history of Korea's forest tenure system and policies, 1600–1987] (Seoul: 일조각 [Ilchogak], 2010); 김흥순 [Kim Hŭng-sun], "조선후기 산림정책 및 산림황폐화: 시장주의적 고찰과 그에 대한 비판 [Forestry policy and the devastation of forests in the late Chosŏn dynasty: Review from and critique of the market principle]," 한국지역개발학회지 [*Han'guk Chiyŏk Kaebal Hakhoe chi*] 20, no. 2 (2008): 169–192.

37. See, for example, 고태우 [Ko Tae-woo], "일제 식민권력의 재해대책 추이와 성격 [The development and characteristics of disaster relief under Japanese colonial rule]," 역사문제연구 [*Yŏksa munje yŏn'gu*] 31 (2014): 352–398; Jung Lee, "Mutual Transformation of Colonial and Imperial Botanizing? The Intimate yet Remote Collaboration in Colonial Korea," *Science in Context* 29, no. 2 (2016): 179–211; Aaron S. Moore, *Constructing East Asia: Technology, Ideology, and Empire in Japan's Wartime Era, 1931–1945* (Stanford, CA: Stanford University Press, 2013); Joseph Seeley, "Liquid Geography: The Yalu River and the Boundaries of Empire in East Asia, 1894–1945" (PhD diss., Stanford University, 2019); and David Fedman, *Seeds of Control: Japan's Empire of Forestry in Colonial Korea* (Seattle: University of Washington Press, 2020).

38. On environmental reclamation projects during and in the immediate wake of the Korean War, see Lisa Brady, "Sowing War, Reaping Peace: The United Nations Resource Development Programs in Korea, 1950–1953," *Journal of Asian Studies* 77, no. 2 (2018): 351–363.

39. Julia Adeney Thomas, "The Exquisite Corpses of Nature and History: The Case of the Korean DMZ," *Asia-Pacific Journal* 43, no. 7 (2009), https://apjjf.org/-Julia-Adeney -Thomas/3242/article.html.

40. Rhetoric of this sort is examined in Lisa Brady, "Korea's Green Ribbon of Hope: History, Ecology, and Activism in the DMZ," *Solutions* 3, no. 1 (2012): 94–98.

41. This is discussed in depth in Eleana J. Kim, *Making Peace with Nature: Ecological Encounters Along the Korean DMZ* (Durham, NC: Duke University Press, 2022).

42. For rhetoric of this sort, see, for example, 환경부 [Hwan'gyŏngbu], ed., 환경 30 년사 [The environment: A thirty year history] (Seoul: 환경부 [Hwan'gyŏngbu], 2010).

43. These policies are examined in depth in Byung-Kook Kim and Ezra Vogel, eds., *The Park Chung Hee Era: The Transformation of South Korea* (Cambridge, MA: Harvard University Press, 2011).

44. On the relationship between landscape and political legitimacy in North Korea, see P. J. Atkins, "The Dialectics of Environment and Culture: Kimilsungism and the North Korean Landscape," in *Environment and Development: Views from the East and the West*, ed. A. Mukherjee and V. K. Agnihotri (New Delhi: Concept, 1993), 309–332.

45. See, for example, Lisa Brady, "Mountain, Militarized: North Korea, Nuclear Tests, and Nature," *Arcadia* 8 (Spring 2019), http://www.environmentandsociety.org/node/8496.

46. A comprehensive study of the economic forces underlying North Korea's "arduous march" famine is Stephan Haggard and Marcus Noland, *Famine in North Korea: Markets, Aid, and Reform* (New York: Columbia University Press, 2009).

47. Jung-Ho Hyun et al., "Climate Change and Anthropogenic Impact around Korean Coastal Ecosystems: Korean Long-Term Marine Ecological Research," *Estuaries and Coasts* 43 (2020): 441–448.

48. Jung Il-Won, Bae Deg-Hyo, and Kim Gwangseob, "Recent Trends of Mean and Extreme Precipitation in Korea," *International Journal of Climatology* 31, no 3 (2011): 359–370.

49. For a recent assessment of the threat of climate change in North Korea and policies to ameliorate these risks, see Catherine Dill, Alexandra Naegele, Natalie Baillargeon, et al., "Converging Crises in North Korea: Security, Stability, and Climate Change," Woodwell Climate Research Center, accessed November 8, 2021, https://climateandsecurity.org/2021 /07/brief-report-north-korea-climate-change-and-security/.

50. On the Korean peninsula's place in global environmental history see 이종찬 [Jong-Chan Lee], "한국에서 생태환경사를 세계사적 지평에서 탐구하기 [Investigating ecological and environmental history from the world history perspective—How to write Korea in it]," 서양사론 [*Sŏyangsaron*] 100 (2009): 127–153.

51. On the ecological implications of this geomorphology, see Conrad Totman, *Preindustrial Korea and Japan in Environmental Perspective* (Leiden: Brill, 2004).

52. For more on these regional and climatic zones, see, for example, 옥한석 [Han-sŏk Uk] and 서태열 [Sŏ T'ae-yŏl], 세계화 시대의 한국 지리읽기 [Reading Korean regional variation in global context] (P'aju: 한울 아카데미 [Hanul Academi], 2009); and 김종욱 [Kim Chong-uk], ed., 한국의 자연 지리 [Physical geography of Korea] (Seoul: 서울대학교 출판문화원 transliteration, 2012). See also Ministry of Land Infrastructure and Transport, ed., *National Atlas of Korea: Comprehensive Edition* (Seoul: Ministry of Land Infrastructure and Transport, 2020), http://nationalatlas.ngii.go.kr/us /index.php.

GEOGRAPHICAL INTRODUCTION

1. "Child of Magohalm and the Echoes of Creation," *Crossing Cultures*, accessed September 30, 2021, https://blogs.brighton.ac.uk/crossingcultures/leejoo-chang-on-xadie-za/.

2. "Grandmother Mago," *Encyclopedia of Korean Folk Culture*, accessed November 25, 2021, https://folkency.nfm.go.kr/en/topic/detail/5344.

3. See, for example, Robert Ji-Song Ku and Sonja M. Kim, eds., *Future Yet to Come: Sociotechnical Imaginaries in Modern Korea* (Honolulu: University of Hawai'i Press, 2021).

4. Amitav Ghosh, *The Great Derangement* (Chicago: University of Chicago Press, 2016), 19.

5. Ghosh, *Great Derangement*, 20.

6. Woo-seok Kong and David Watts, *The Plant Geography of Korea* (Dordrecht: Kluwer Academic Publishers, 1993), 5–6.

7. Bryan Harris and Kang Buseong, "South Korea Joins Ranks of World's Most Polluted Countries," *Financial Times*, accessed December 21, 2021, https://www.ft.com /content/b49a9878-141b-11e7-80f4-13e067d5072c.

8. Youngsin Chun and Sang-woon Jeon, "Chugugi, Supyo, and Punggi: Meteorological Instruments of the 15th Century in Korea," *History of Meteorology* 2 (2005), http:// www.meteohistory.org/2005historyofmeteorology2/02chun_jeon.pdf.

9. United States Department of Agriculture, Foreign Agricultural Service, "Torrential Rainfall Causes Flooding in North Korea," July 29, 2013, https://ipad.fas.usda.gov /highlights/2013/07/NorthKoreaFlood/.

10. Food and Agricultural Association (FAO), "Fishery Country Profile: The Republic of Korea," accessed October 1, 2021, https://www.fao.org/fishery/docs/DOCUMENT/fcp /en/FI_CP_KR.pdf.

11. World Wildlife Foundation, "Eastern Asia: Korea, China and Russia," accessed July 1, 2021, https://www.worldwildlife.org/ecoregions/pa0426; https://www.worldwildlife .org/ecoregions/pa0413; https://www.worldwildlife.org/ecoregions/pa0439.

12. "Plants," *National Atlas of Korea II,* accessed July 1, 2021, http://nationalatlas.ngii .go.kr/pages/page_689.php.

13. "Mudflats," *Agricultural and Environmental Data Archive*, accessed January 9, 2021, http://www.environmentdata.org/archive/vocabpref:21642.

14. "Getbol, Korean Tidal Flats," World Heritage Convention, UNESCO, accessed January 7, 2022, https://whc.unesco.org/en/list/1591/.

15. "Soil Genesis and Development, Lesson 1-Rocks, Minerals and Soils," *Plant and Soil Sciences eLibrary*, accessed July 1, 2021, http://passel-test.unl.edu/beta/pages /informationmodule.php?idinformationmodule=1130447023&topicorder=6&maxto =6&minto=0.

1. A STATE OF RANCHES AND FORESTS

Acknowledgments: This research was supported by the Korean Studies Grant Program of the Academy of Korean Studies (AKS-2019-R54). Earlier versions of this chapter received key feedback at the Korea with Empire conference organized by Sixiang Wang at the University of Pennsylvania in 2016; the annual meeting of the New England Association for Asian Studies at Boston College in 2017; the Environmental History Colloquium at Yale University in 2018; and the Korea at Nature's Edge conference at the University of California, Irvine, in 2018. I thank David Fedman, Eleana J. Kim, and Albert L. Park for their exemplary guidance, organization, and comments; and Aaron Moore and Robert Oppenheim for their kind feedback. Portions of this chapter are drawn from a previous article, John S. Lee, "Postwar Pines: The Military and the Expansion of State Forests in Post-Imjin Korea, 1598–1684," *Journal of Asian Studies* 77, no. 2 (May 2018), and have been reused with permission from Cambridge University Press.

1. In this chapter, I use "Yuan" and "Mongols" interchangeably, though I recognize that the Yuan dynasty was the relevant political entity in northeast Asia. The context of Mongol-Koryŏ relations is elucidated when necessary, though any detailed description of the political context are beyond the scope of this paper. For more information about Koryŏ under Yuan vassalage, see David Robinson, *In the Shadow of the Mongol Empire: Ming China and Eurasia* (Cambridge, UK: Cambridge University Press, 2019); and David Robinson, *Empire's Twilight: Northeast Asia under the Mongols* (Cambridge, MA: Harvard University Asia Center, 2009).

2. Pekka Hämäläinen, *The Comanche Empire* (New Haven, CT: Yale University Press, 2008); Peter Mitchell, *Horse Nations: The Worldwide Impact of the Horse on Indigenous Societies Post-1942* (Oxford: Oxford University Press, 2015); Greg Bankoff and Sandra Swart, eds., *Breeds of Empire: The "Invention" of the Horse in Southeast Asia and Southern Africa 1500–1950* (Copenhagen: NIAS Press, 2007); Pamela Kyle Crossley, *Hammer and Anvil: Nomad Rulers and the Forge of the Modern World* (London: Rowman and Littlefield, 2019).

3. Jos Gommans, "Warhorse and Post-Nomadic Empire in Asia, c. 1000–1800," *Journal of Global History* 2 (2007): 1–21.

4. For studies of Mongol and Inner Asian equine legacies in late imperial China, see Noa Grass, "A Million Horses: Raising Government Horses in Early Ming China," in *Animals and Human Society in Asia: Historical, Cultural and Ethical Perspectives*, ed. Rotem Kowner, Guy Bar-Oz, Michal Biran, Meir Shahar, and Gideon Shelach-Lavi (New York: Palgrave Macmillan, 2019), 299–324; Sare Aricanli, "Reconsidering the Boundaries: Multicultural and Multilingual Perspectives on the Care and Management of the Emperor's Horses in the Qing," in *Animals through Chinese History: Earliest Times to 1911*, ed. Roel Sterckx, Martina Siebert, and Dagmar Schäfer (Cambridge, UK: Cambridge University Press, 2019), 199–216; Yan Gao, "The Retreat of the Horses: The Manchus, Land Reclamation, and Local Ecology in the Jianghan Plain (ca. 1700s–1850s)," in *Environmental History in East Asia: Interdisciplinary Perspectives*, ed. Tsui-jung Liu (London: Routledge, 2013), 100–125.

5. Much of the existing literature on empire and environment has been preoccupied with the "biological expansion of Europe," to quote Albert Crosby's influential work. Crosby, *Ecological Imperialism: The Biological Expansion of Europe, 900–1900* (Cambridge, UK: Cambridge University Press, 2004). Even studies that critique Crosby and find roots of environmentalist ethics in European imperialism, notably Richard Grove's *Green Imperialism*, still find its source in European empires and their subjects. See Grove, *Green Imperialism: Colonial Expansion, Tropical Island Edens and the Origins of Environmentalism, 1600–1860* (Cambridge, UK: Cambridge University Press, 1994).

6. For more information on pre-Koryŏ horses and related archaeological and textual sources, see 남도영 [Nam Toyŏng], 한국마정사 [A history of horse governance in Korea]

(Kwach'ŏn: 한국마사회 마사박물관 [Han'guk Masahoe Masa Pangmulgwan], 1996), 61–117.

7. Particularly prominent is Jeju's rich mixed forest. Known locally as "Gotjawal [곶자왈]" the forest covers about 12 percent of contemporary Jeju and is central to the island's unique ecology. For more information and context, see Jeongsu Shin's chapter 9 in this volume.

8. 고려사 高麗史 [Standard Koryŏ history], 82.24a–24b.

9. 고려사 高麗史 [Standard Koryŏ history], 82.26b–27a.

10. Robinson, *Empire's Twilight*, 58; and Robinson, *In the Shadow of the Mongol Empire*, 281–282.

11. *Yuan shi* [History of Yuan], vol. 208, accessed August 1, 2022, https://zh.wikisource .org/wiki/元史.

12. *Yuan shi* [History of Yuan], vol. 100.

13. 고려사 高麗史 [Standard Koryŏ history], 28.17b.

14. *Yuan shi* [History of Yuan], vol. 100.

15. 고려사 高麗史 [Standard Koryŏ history], 44.25b–26a.

16. 고려사 高麗史 [Standard Koryŏ history], 82.26b.

17. 고려사 高麗史 [Standard Koryŏ history], 31.3a.

18. For more examples, see 남도영 [Nam Toyŏng], 제주도 목장사 [A history of ranches on Jeju Island] (Kwach'ŏn: 한국마사회 마사박물관 [Han'guk Masahoe Masa Pangmulgwan], 2001), 149.

19. 고려사절요 高麗史節要 [Essentials of Koryŏ history], vol. 21, 충열 忠烈 22.11.

20. Larry Moses, "Triplicated Triplets: The Number Nine in the *Secret History* of the Mongols," *Asian Folklore Studies* 45, no. 2 (1986): 287–294.

21. 허균 [許筠, Hŏ Kyun], 성소부부고 惺所覆瓿藁 [Minor writings of Sŏngso] (Seoul: 한국고전번역원 [Han'guk Kojŏn Pŏnyŏgwŏn], 1991), 22:48. "Heavenly horses" are a reference to the Akhal-Teke horses that originated in the Ferghana Valley of central Asia, famed for their speed and beauty.

22. Hŏ, 성소부부고 惺所覆瓿藁 [Minor writings of Sŏngso], 22:48.

23. W. E. Henthorn, *Korea: The Mongols Invasions* (Leiden: E.J. Brill, 1963), 207–208, 223.

24. For examples of late Chosŏn forestry statutes concerning the southwest, see 비변사등록 備邊司謄錄 [Records of the Border Defense Command], 숙종 肅宗 10.2.30; 10.5.3; 17.8.24. *Note*: Entries are in "reign year.month.day" format.

25. Randall Sasaki, *The Origins of the Lost Fleet of the Mongol Empire* (College Station: Texas A&M University Press, 2015), 37–40, 118–119, 142–146.

26. 박원규 [Pak Wŏn'gyu], 이광희 [Yi Kwanghŭi], "우리나라 건축물에 사용된 목재수종의 변천 [Changes in tree species used in Korean architecture]," 건축역사연구 [*Kŏnch'uk yŏksa yŏn'gu*] 16, no. 1 (2007): 9–27.

27. Pak and Yi, "Changes in Tree Species Used in Korean Architecture," 23; 전영우 [Chŏn Yŏng'u], ed., 소나무와 우리문화 [Pines and Korean culture] (Seoul: 수문출판사 [Sumun Ch'ulp'ansa], 1999).

28. Remco Breuker, "Mountains and Streams: Architecturalizing Landscapes in Medieval Korea," in *Architecturalized Asia: Mapping a Continent through History*, ed. Vimalin Rujivacharakul (Honolulu: University of Hawai'i Press, 2014), 55–57.

29. 고려사 高麗史 [Standard Koryŏ history], 54.1a–1b.

30. The moniker can be traced back to a founding legend of the Koryŏ dynasty. Planting pines, geomantic prophecy, and political legitimacy were intricately linked during the Koryŏ era. Michael Rodgers, "Pyŏnnyŏn T'ongnok: The Foundation Legend of the Koryŏ State," *Journal of Korean Studies* 4 (1982/3): 6–7.

31. 이색 [李穡, Yi Saek], "초동 樵童 [Woodcutting youth]," 목은고 牧隱藁 [Collected works of Mokŭn] 22.32a [1626] (Seoul: 한국고전번역원 [Han'guk Kojŏn Pŏnyŏgwŏn], 1990).

32. 고려사 高麗史 [Standard Koryŏ history], 78.53a.

33. Representative works on Mongol imperial legacies in these regions include Crossley, *Hammer and Anvil*; Morris Rossabi, ed., *Eurasian Influences on Yuan China* (Singapore: Institute of Southeast Asian Studies, 2013); Judith Pfeiffer and Sholeh A. Quinn, eds., Ernest Tucker, collab., *History and Historiography of Post-Mongol Central Asia and the Middle East: Studies in Honor of John E. Woods* (Wiesbaden: Harrassowitz Verlag, 2006); Morris Rossabi "The Legacy of the Mongols," in *Central Asia in Historical Perspective*, ed. Beatrice F. Manz (Boulder, CO: Westview Press, 1998), 27–44; Donald Ostrowski, "The Mongol Origins of Muscovite Political Institutions," *Slavic Review* 49, no. 4 (1990): 525–542; Charles J. Halperin, "Russia in the Mongol Empire in Comparative Perspective," *Harvard Journal of Asiatic Studies* 43, no. 1 (1983): 239–261.

34. 조선왕조실록 朝鮮王朝實錄 [The veritable records of the Chosŏn dynasty], 태종실록 太宗實錄 [The veritable records of T'aejong], 7.4.7.

35. Robert Hellyer, "Poor but Not Pirates: The Tsushima Domain and Foreign Relations in Early Modern Japan," in *Elusive Pirates, Pervasive Smugglers*, ed. Robert J. Antony (Hong Kong: Hong Kong University Press, 2012), 118.

36. 김일환 [Kim Ilhwan], "세종 대마도 정벌의 군사적 전개 [The process of King Sejong's military actions toward Tsushima]," 순천향인문과학논청 [*Sunch'ŏnghyang inmun kwahak nonch'ong*] 31, no. 2 (2012): 97–98.

37. 세종실록 世宗實錄 [Annals of King Sejong], 1.6.20.

38. 세종실록 世宗實錄 [Annals of King Sejong], 1.7.28.

39. Contrary to the Chosŏn state's assertions, the Waegu was not solely a Tsushima problem, as the raids were part of a broader fifteenth-century network of "sea bandits" and "sea lords" of diverse regional origins. Peter D. Shapinsky, "From Sea Bandits to Sea Lords: Nonstate Violence and Pirate Identities in Fifteenth- and Sixteenth-Century Japan," in *Elusive Pirates, Pervasive Smugglers*, ed. Robert J. Antony (Hong Kong: Hong Kong University Press, 2012), 27–42.

40. 세종실록 世宗實錄 [Annals of King Sejong], 8.27.30.

41. 태종실록 太宗實錄 [Annals of King T'aejong], 7.10.24.

42. For examples, see 남도영 [Nam Toyŏng], 한국마정사, 219; 강만익 [Kang Manik], "고려말 탐라목장의 운영과 영향 [A study of the management and influence of Tamna ranches in the late Koryŏ era]," 탐라 문화 [*T'amna munhwa*] 52 (June 2016): 83–93.

43. 노사신 [盧思愼, No Sasin] et al., 경국대전 經國大典 [The Great Code of Administration], 4.67a–68a (Seoul: Yŏgang ch'ulp'ansa, 2001).

44. No, et al., 경국대전 經國大典 [The Great Code of Administration], 4.67a–68a. See also 남도영 [Nam Toyŏng], 한국마정사, 313–331. According to Nam, the identities of herders were mixed. Some were public slaves (공노公奴); others could be of commoner status and herding as part of corvée duty.

45. 단종실록 端宗實錄 [Annals of King Tanjong], 2.6.4.

46. 세종실록 世宗實錄 [Annals of King Sejong], 8.27.30.

47. 역주 조선의 임수 [The forests of Korea, Korean-language edition], ed., trans. 생명의숲 국민운동 [Forest for Life] (Seoul: Geobook, 2007), 663.

48. F. W. M Vera, *Grazing Ecology and Forest History* (Wallingford, UK: CABI, 2000), 26–28.

49. Gordon G. Whitney, *From Coastal Wilderness to Fruited Plain: A History of Environmental Change in Temperate North America, 1500 to the Present* (Cambridge, UK: Cambridge University Press, 1994), 170.

50. John S. Lee, "Postwar Pines: The Military and the Expansion of State Forests in Post-Imjin Korea, 1598–1684," *Journal of Asian Studies* 77, no. 2 (2018): 326.

51. 김경옥 [Kim Kyŏngok], 조선후기 도서연구 [A study of islands in the late Chosŏn era] (Seoul: 혜안 [Hyean], 2004), 117.

52. Lee, "Postwar Pines," 326–237.

53. 숙종실록 肅宗實錄 [Annals of King Sukchong], 2.3.6.

54. 성종실록 成宗實錄 [Annals of King Sŏngjong], 1.1.4; 허목 [許穆, Hŏ Mok], 목장지도 牧場地圖 [Map of ranches] (Seoul: National Library of Korea, 1678).

55. 정약용 [丁若鏞, Chŏng Yagyong], "목민심서 牧民心書 [Admonitions for governing the people]," 8:32b; Choi Byonghyon, trans., *Admonitions for the Governing the People: Manual for All Administrators* (Berkeley: University of California Press, 2010), 595.

56. Lee, "Postwar Pines," 327.

57. Hermann Lautensach, *Korea: A Geography Based on the Author's Travel and Literature*, trans. Eckart Dege and Katherine Dege (Berlin: Springer Verlag, 1988), 363.

58. Lautensach, *Korea*, 369.

59. Martina Deuchler, *Under the Ancestor's Eyes: Kinship, Status, and Locality in Premodern Korea* (Cambridge, MA: Harvard University Asia Center, 2015), 1–3.

2. DAMMED FISH

1. "鴨綠江水電을비롯해 人工湖에서養殖魚 [Raising fish in reservoirs starting with the Sup'ung Dam]," 조선일보 [*Chosŏn ilbo*], May 13, 1939.

2. "Sekai ichi no yōgyojō," 매일신보 [*Maeil sinbo*], January 30, 1944.

3. See, for example, David Fedman, *Seeds of Control: Japan's Empire of Forestry in Colonial Korea* (Seattle: University of Washington Press, 2020); and Lim Chaisung, "The Development of a Control Policy over the Coal Industry and the Management of the Coal Mining Industry in Wartime Colonial Korea," *Review of Korean Studies* 14, no. 4 (2011): 85–133.

4. Hirose Teizō, "'Manshūkoku' ni okeru Suihō Damu kensetsu," *Niigata kokusai jōhō daigaku jōhō bunka gakubu kiyo* 6 (March 2003): 1–25; Aaron Stephen Moore, "'The Yalu River Era of Developing Asia': Japanese Expertise, Colonial Power, and the Construction of the Sup'ung Dam," *Journal of Asian Studies* 72, no. 1 (2013): 115–139.

5. Wang Shoukun, "Zhongguo zhuyao heliu yulei fenbu qi zhonglei duoyanxing yu liuyu tezheng de guanxi," *Shengwu duoyangxing* 3 (May 1997): 198.

6. For two essays from the same edited volume on the expansion of Japan's marine fisheries, see William Tsutsui, "The Pelagic Empire: Reconsidering Japanese Expansion"; and Micah Muscolino, "Fisheries Build Up on the Nation: Marine Environmental Encounters between Japan and China," in *Japan at Nature's Edge: The Environmental Context of a Global Power*, ed. Ian Jared Miller et al. (Honolulu: University of Hawai'i Press, 2013), 21–38 and 56–72.

7. 국사편찬위원회 [Kuksa Py'ŏnch'an Wiwŏnhoe], 통감부문서 [Documents of the Residency-General of Korea], vol. 10, pt. 19, no. 35: "Kantei haken ni kansuru ken," (June 9, 1909); 통감부문서 [Documents of the Residency-General of Korea], vol. 10, pt. 19, no. 55: "密漁 단속 출장 復命書 移牒 [Communication of expedition to crack down on poaching]," (November 5, 1909), National Institute of Korean History database, http://db.history.go.kr/.

8. "Ōryokkō gyogyō kankei zassan," JACAR (Japan Center for Asian Historical Records), B11091940400.

9. "Yalu Jiang Huaren yuye shili zhi shu wen," *Huashang lianhe bao*, June 1909; "Ya Jiang yuye quan jiang jue jing yi," *Shen bao*, May 7, 1910.

10. Minami Manshū Tetsudō Kabushiki Kaisha Chōsaka, *Manshū no suisangyō* (Dairen: Minami Manshū Tetsudō, 1931), 57.

11. Chōsen Sōtokufu Suisan Shikenjō, *Ōryokkō no sakana* (Fuzan: Chōsen Sōtokufu Suisan Shikenjō, 1940), 2.

12. Chōsen Sōtokufu Suisan Shikenjō, *Ōryokkō no sakana,* 3.

13. "朝鮮的名物인白魚漁撈開始 [Harvesting of Korean specialty product icefish begins]," 매일신보 [*Maeil sinbo*], April 13, 1933.

14. Heian Hokudō Gyogyō Kumiai Rengōkai, *Heian hokudō suisan tōkei: Shōwa 11 nen* (Shingishū: Heian HokudōoGyogyō Kumiai Rengōkai, 1936), 9.

15. Moore, "Yalu River Era," 119.

16. Chōsen Sōtokufu Teishinkyoku, *Chōsen suiryoku chōsasho dai 2 ken* (Keijō: Chōsen Sōtokufu Teishinkyoku, 1930), 19.

17. For the original discussion of the concept of "legibility" as referring to government's efforts to render a society or environment in terms that would allow for more effective governance, see James Scott, *Seeing Like a State* (New Haven, CT: Yale University Press, 1998), 2.

18. "'세멘트'의 流下로 鴨綠江白魚減少 [Icefish decrease due to downstream flow of cement]," 조선일보 [*Chosŏn ilbo*], June 1, 1938.

19. Carter Eckert, *Offspring of Empire: Koch'ang Kims and the Colonial Origins of Korean Capitalism, 1876–1945* (Seattle: University of Washington Press, 1991), 116.

20. "'세멘트'의流下로 鴨綠江白魚減少 [Icefish decrease]."

21. " 朝鮮水産의名産인 白魚生産이激減 [Harvest of icefish, specialty product of Korean fisheries, decreases rapidly]," 동아일보 [*Tonga ilbo*], December 13, 1938.

22. "工場地帶排水淨化對策講究 [Deliberations about measures for purifying factory area drainage]," 조선일보 [*Chosŏn ilbo*], February 24, 1939.

23. Katō Keiki, "Chōsen shokuminchi shihai to kōgai: senjika no Hwanhedo Hūsangun o chūshin ni," *Shikai* 61 (June 2014): 78.

24. In 1926, Seoul-based educator and natural historian Mori Tamezō conducted a limited series of fish collections on the river, the results of which were published in both Japanese and English articles. See Tamezo Mori, "On the Fresh Water Fishes from the Yalu River, Korea, with Descriptions of New Species," *Journal of Chosen Natural History Society* 6 (March 25, 1928): 54–70; and Mori Tamezō, "Ōryokkō, Ryōga oyobi Shōkakō no tansuigyo no bunpu tsuketari Shōkakō tansuigyo no keiziteki kachi ni tsuite," in *Chōsen nōgaku kankei sho gaku ronbunshū*, ed. Onodera Jirō (Keijō: Nōgaku Kankei Sho Gakkai Rengō Taikai, 1931), 230–238.

25. Minami Manshū Tetsudō Kabushiki Kaisha Chōsaka, *Manshū no suisangyō*, 57.

26. "蹂躪되는鴨江魚族棲息調査報告 [Research report on fish species in the ravaged Yalu]," 동아일보 [*Tonga ilbo*], December 9, 1938. Fisheries experiment stations (*suisan shikenjō*) were part of a bureaucratic infrastructure created by the Japanese government in the late nineteenth century to advance scientific fishery practice and later exported to Japan's overseas colonies. Tsutsui, "Pelagic Empire," 27–28.

27. Moore, "Yalu River Era."

28. "蹂躪되는鴨江魚族棲息調査報告 [Research report on fish species]."

29. "水電化에蹂躪된鴨江流域의 魚道設置를 計劃中 [Plans for construction of fish ladder in the Yalu River ravaged by dam construction]," 동아일보 [*Tonga ilbo*], November 20, 1938.

30. Mantetsu sangyōbu, "Ōryokkō suiryoku hatsuden ni okeru gyodō oyobi shūbatsuro ni kansuru ni, san no chosa kekka," in *Mantie diaocha baogao*, pt. 1, vol. 14, ed. Heilongjiang sheng danganguan (Guilin: Guangxi shifan daxue chubanshe, 2005), 167.

31. "Suihō suiden damu riyō ōgakari no tansuigyō shiyō," *Nishi sen nippō*, March 5, 1938.

32. "Suihō suiden damu riyō ōgakari no tansuigyō shiyō."

33. "鴨綠江上流-魚類를調査 [Study of fish species in the upper Yalu River]," 매일신보 [*Maeil sinbo*], December 12, 1939.

34. Minami Manshū Tetsudō Kabushiki Kaisha, *Manshū suisan jigyō hōsaku* (Dairen [Dalian]: Minami Manshū Tetsudō Keizai Chōsakai, 1935), 209.

35. "許多한漁民을犧牲 [The sacrifice of numerous fishermen]," 매일신보 [*Maeil sinbo*], September 9, 1940.

36. "鴨江貯水池利用問題 [Usage problems surrounding the Yalu River reservoir]," 매일신보 [*Maeil sinbo*], March 28, 1940.

37. "'세멘트'의流下로 鴨綠江白魚減少 [Icefish decrease]."

38. "累年激減되던白魚 今年은意外로好調 [Surprisingly good icefish harvest after previous years' rapid decline]," 동아일보 [*Tonga ilbo*], April 22, 1939; 鴨江의名物 白魚는豊漁 [Bounteous harvest of Yalu specialty icefish]," 매일신보 [*Maeil sinbo*], May 19, 1940.

39. "氷點下의鴨江水没地 [Below freezing temperatures in the lands flooded by the Yalu River]," 만선일보 [*Mansŏn ilbo*], February 1, 1940.

40. "水豊養魚計畫 明年度에實現 [Sup'ung aquaculture plan to be realized in following year]," 매일신보 [*Maeil sinbo*], July 19, 1941.

41. "世界一의人工湖水 [The largest manmade lake in the world]," 매일신보 [*Maeil sinbo*], July 4, 1941.

42. For two studies that discuss issues of labor migration in the Japanese colonial empire, see Hyun Ok Park, *Two Dreams in One Bed: Empire, Social Life, and the Origins of the North Korean Revolution in Manchuria* (Durham, NC: Duke University Press, 2005); and Paul H. Krotska, ed., *Asian Labor in the Wartime Japanese Empire: Unknown Histories* (Armonk, NY: M.E. Sharpe, 2005).

43. William M. Tsutsui, "Landscapes in the Dark Valley: Towards an Environmental History of Wartime Japan," *Environmental History* 8, no. 2 (2003), 294–311.

44. "淡水魚增殖 [Increase cultivation of freshwater fish]," 매일신보 [*Maeil sinbo*], October 21, 1943.

45. "Tansuigyo no sōsyoku," *Keijo nippō*, February 14, 1944; "水豊댐에淡水魚 [Freshwater fish in the Sup'ung Reservoir]," 매일신보 [*Maeil sinbo*], February 14, 1944.

46. "Tansuigyo no sōsyoku."

47. "大量의淡水魚 [Large amounts of freshwater fish]," 매일신보 [*Maeil sinbo*], August 13, 1944.

48. "'세멘트'의流下로 鴨綠江白魚減少 [Icefish decrease]."

49. 최정화 [Ch'oe Chŏng-hwa], 朔州郡誌 [*Sakchu County Gazetteer*] (Seoul: 삭주군민회 Sakchu kunminhoe, 1991), 132.

50. Ch'oe, *Sakchu County Gazetteer*, 81.

51. Ch'oe, *Sakchu County Gazetteer*, 141. Such oral testimony may contain an element of nostalgic embellishment. Both Pak and Kim had fled their homes along the Yalu during the 1940s–1950s as part of a mass exodus of Koreans to the newly formed country of South Korea, never to return to the river of their youth.

52. Walter Simmons, "Report Chinese Red Army Uses Jap Prisoners: So. Korean Officers Tell of Drive to Border," *Chicago Daily Tribune*, November 8, 1950.

53. Danshuiyu yanjiusuo, "Shuifeng shuiku yulei diaocha suode de ji dian ziliao," *Taipingyang xibu yuye yanjiu weiyuanhui di si ci quan ti huiyi lunwen ji*, ed. Taipingyang xi bu yuye yanjiu weiyuanhui zhongguo weiyuan zhuanjia bangongshi (Beijing: Kexue Chubanshe, 1963), 201–202.

54. Xie Han et al., "Shuifeng shuiku yuhuo bianhua he yulei ziyuan xianzhuang ji xiaoxing jingji yu xia zhong jian guanxi fenxi," *Shuichan xue zazhi* 15, no. 1 (2002): 38.

55. Special Report, "The Promise of a Blue Revolution," *The Economist*, August 7, 2003.

56. Xie Han et al., "Shuifeng shuiku yuhuo bianhua," 37.

57. De Lie, "Shuifeng hu xin mao," *Renmin ribao* [People's Daily], January 29, 1963.

58. 김행륜 [Kim Haeng-nyun], "담수에서 중층 자망을 도입 [Introduction of middle layer gill nets in freshwater aquaculture]," 조선수산 [*Chosŏn susan*], May 1963; Huh Hang Jong, "Along the Amrok River," *Korea Today*, July 1965.

59. Zhang Shidong, "Yalu Jiang yinyu ziyuan huisheng de xiangguan yinsu fenxi," *Zhongguo yuye jingji yanjiu*, March 1999, 32.

60. Xie Han et al., "Shuifeng shuiku yuhuo bianhua," 38.

61. *Youzhi jiangshui yi fang hao yu, Liaoning Shuifeng shuiku quan Yazhou zui da de wangxiang yang yu jidi*, YouTube video, 2:39, posted by Zhongguo Liaoning weishi guanfang pindao, May 25, 2018, https://www.youtube.com/watch?v=O5hUwCRQN4c.

62. Examples include 최경수 [Ch'oe Kyŏng-su], "<만리마속도창조대전에서 강원도 정신을 높이 발휘하자!> 이동식그물우리양어의 된바람을 [Let us raise high the banner of the Kangwon Province spirit: Mobile fish farming cages are the strong wind]," 민주조선 [*Minju Chosŏn*], June 13, 2017; 최경수 [Ch'oe Kyŏng-su], "<어버이수령님의 숭고한 뜻을 가슴깊이 간직하고 인민을 위해 더 많은 일을 하자> 이동식그물우리양어에 큰 힘을 [Let us preserve the lofty goals of the fatherly great leader and work more for the people: Contributing our all for mobile fish farming cages]," 로동신문 [*Rodong sinmun*], July 9, 2017. For more on the significance of fishing and "fishy matters" in the contemporary DPRK, see Robert Winstanley-Chesters, *Fish, Fishing and Community in North Korea and Neighbours* (Singapore: Springer, 2020).

63. "사회주의조선의 강용한 기상떨치며 계속혁신, 계속전진 [The strong spirit of socialist Korea spreads forth, continually innovating and marching forward]," 로동신문 [*Rodong sinmun*], November 17, 2017.

64. See, for example, Richard White, *The Organic Machine: The Remaking of the Columbia River* (New York: Hill and Wang, 1995); and Mark Cioc, *The Rhine: An Eco-Biography, 1815–2000* (Seattle: University of Washington Press, 2002), 159.

PART 2

1. Ho Gyong Pil, "Slaughter and Destruction without Gunshot," *Korean Nature* 45 (1977): 32.

2. Chong Rak Won, "Korea, the People's Paradise Turning Ever More Fertile and Scenic," *Korean Nature* 47 (1977): 26–29.

3. THE POLITICS OF FRUGALITY

1. On scholarly reappraisals that debunk the pro-colonial view about the late Chosŏn dynasty, see Christopher Lovins, *King Chŏngjo: An Enlightened Despot in Early Modern Korea* (Albany: State University of New York Press), x–xvii.

2. JaHyun Kim Haboush, "Rescoring the Universal in a Korean Mode," in *Korean Arts of the Eighteenth Century: Splendor and Simplicity* (New York: Asian Society Galleries, 1994), 23.

3. 김덕진 [Kim Tŏk-chin], 대기근 조선을 뒤덮다 [Great famines, which plagued Chosŏn] (Seoul: 푸른역사 [P'urŭn yŏksa], 2008).

4. This "innate" aesthetic framing was started by Yanagi Muneyoshi (1889–1961). Yanagi characterized Korean art, especially ceramics of the Chosŏn dynasty, as "sad" and "lonely," descriptions that reflect how Korean culture was interpreted by successive foreign invaders. Yanagi's aesthetics of colonialism directly influenced Korean scholars' unending search for "innate" Korean aesthetics. For Yanagi's folk art movement and its colonialist nature, see Kim Brandt, *Kingdom of Beauty: Mingei and the Politics of Folk Art in Imperial Japan* (Durham, NC: Duke University Press, 2007).

5. Lee E-Wha, *Korea's Pastimes and Customs: A Social History* (Paramus, NJ: Homa and Sekey Book, 2001), 193.

6. The term Little Ice Age was coined in the late 1930s by the US glaciologist Francois Matthes (1875–1949). Major studies on the Little Ice Age and its impact on European history are Geoffrey Parker and Lesley M. Smith, eds., *The General Crisis of the Seventeenth Century* (Routledge and Kegan Paul, 1978); T. M. L. Wigley, M. J. Ingram, and G. Farmer, eds., *Climate and History: Studies in Past Climates and Their Impact on Man* (Cambridge, UK: Cambridge University Press, 1981); Jean M. Grove, *The Little Ice Age* (New York: Routledge, 1988); and Brian Fagan, *The Little Ice Age: How Climate Made History, 1300–1850* (New York: Basic Books, 2000). For the works by Atwell, see William S. Atwell, "Some Observations on the 'Seventeenth-Century Crisis' in China and Japan," *Journal of Asian Studies* 45, no. 2 (1986); "Volcanism and Short-Term Climate Change in East Asia and World History, c.1200–1699," *Journal of World History* 12, no. 1 (2001): 29–98.

7. The discussion on the Little Ice Age in Korea, roughly from the sixteenth century to the first half of the nineteenth century, includes 박근필 [Pak Geun-pil], "17세기 소빙기 기후 연구의 현황과 과제 [Current research status and prospectus of 17th-century Little Ice Age]," 대구사학회 [*Daegu sahakhoe*] 18 (2005): 287–318; 김연옥 [Kim Yŏn-ok], "역사속의 소빙기 [The Little Ice Age in Korean history]," 역사학회 [*Yŏksa hakhoe*] 149 (1996): 253–265; 이태진 [Yi T'ae-jin], "小氷期 (1500–1750) 천변재이 연구와 조선 왕조 실록 [Disasters in the Little Ice Age recorded in the veritable records]," 역사학보 [*Yŏksa hakbo*] 149 (1996): 203–236.

8. 김문기 [Kim Moon-kee], "17세기 중국과 조선의 기근과 국제적 곡물유통 [Famines in 17th-century China and Korea and international grain tradings]," 역사와 경계 [*Yŏksa wa kyŏnggye*] 85 (2012): 323–367; 김성우 [Kim Sŏng-u], "17세기의 위기와 숙종 대 사회상 [Korea in peril during the reign of King Sukchong]," 역사와 현실 [*Yŏksa wa hyŏnsil*] 25 (1997): 12–47.

9. For late Chosŏn farming and environmental crisis, see 김재호 [Kim Chae-ho], "조선후기 한국 농업의 특징과 기후생태학적 배경 [Characteristics of agriculture in late Chosŏn-period Korea in relation to ecological circumstance]," 비교민속학 [*Pigyo minsokhak*] 41 (2010): 97–127. For epidemics, see 이규근 [Yi Kyu-keun], "조선후기 질병사 연구: 조선왕조실록의 전염병 발생기록을 중심으로 [Study on the history of disease during the late Chosŏn-period through the records about epidemic outbreaks in the *Veritable Records*]," 국사관 논총 [*Kuksagwan nonch'ong*] 96 (2001): 1–42.

10. See the *Veritable Records*, 25th day of the 8th month of 1686. Henceforth, references to entries in the *Veritable Records* will use the convention YYYY/MM/DD. Thus, the preceding example would be 1686/08/25.

11. The original entry can be found in a daily log dated to 1709/7/21 in the *Veritable Records*.

12. 김문기 [Kim Moon-kee], "소빙기의 성찬: 근세 동아시아 청어어업 [Feast amid the Little Ice Age: Early modern East Asian fishing for herring]," 역사와 경계 [*Yŏksa wa kyŏnggye*] 9 (2015): 461–520.

13. 박희진 [Pak Hŭi-chin], "역사인구학 관점으로 해석하는 조선후기 [Understanding the late Chosŏn-period Korea based on the sources of historical demographics]," 역사와 현실 [*Yŏksa wa hyŏnsil*] 93 (2014): 505–528; Sang-guk Yi and Byŏng-ju Son "Long-Term Patterns of Seasonality of Mortality in Korea from the Seventeenth to the Twentieth Century," *Journal of Family History* 37, no. 3 (2012): 270–283.

14. See the incidents of cannibalism dated to 1732/12/10 and 1735/10/20 documented in the *Veritable Records*.

15. JaHyun Kim Haboush argues that Yŏngjo's ritualization of royal lecture was an important way to fashion his image as a sage-king. JaHyun Kim Haboush, "Confucian

Rhetoric and Ritual as Techniques of Political Dominance: Yŏngjo's Use of the Royal Lecture," *Journal of Korean Studies* 5 (1984): 39–62.

16. For the discussion of genre paintings as the truthful portrayal of eighteenth-century Korea, see 이태호 [Yi Tae-ho], 조선후기 회화의 사실 정신 [Zeitgeist of Korean paintings from the late Chosŏn-period] (Seoul: 학고재 [Hakgojae], 1999); 강관식 [Kang Kwan-sik]," 진경시대 후기 회화의 실학적 사실성 [Realism of practical learning in the paintings of the late True-View period]," 간송문화 [*Kansong munhwa*] 49 (1995): 58–60; and 유봉학 [Yu Bong-hak], "조선후기 풍속화 변천의 사상적 검토 [Examining the ideological aspects in the development of late Chosŏn-period Korean genre paintings]," 간송문화 [*Kansong munhwa*] 36 (1989): 87–110. Recent scholarly investigations rebut the conventional reading of Korean genre paintings. McCormick, for example, asserts that "tilling and weaving imagery in *Sokhwa* works was made to lend legitimacy, as a potent inspirational omen, to eighteenth-century Korean ruling elites, who maintained an optimistic attitude toward the resilience of human spirit, which leads to overcoming environmental and economic challenges." For further readings, see Sooa Im McCormick, "Re-Reading Imagery of Tilling and Weaving in the Context of the Little Ice Age," in *Eco-Art History in East and Southeast Asia* (Newcastle upon Tyne, UK: Cambridge Scholars Publishing, 2019), 1–46; and J. P. Park, *A New Middle Kingdom: Painting and Cultural Politics in Late Chosŏn Korea (1700–1850)* (Seattle: University of Washington Press, 2018), 66–99.

17. *The Arts of Korea: A Resource for Educators* (New York: Metropolitan Museum of Art, 2001), 7.

18. 강경숙 [Kang Kyŏng-suk], 한국 도자사 [History of Korean ceramics] (Seoul: 예경 [Yekyŏng], 2012), 17.

19. 강태규 [Tae-kyu Kang], "Overviews of Joseon Blue-and-White Porcelain," in *In Blue and White: Porcelain of the Joseon Dynasty*, ed. National Museum of Korea (Seoul: National Museum of Korea, 2015), 11.

20. Excellent examples of extremely decorative blue-and-white porcelains dated to early Chosŏn period can be found in the collection of Leeum and Dongkuk University Museum. For early Chosŏn court imports of Chinese Ming-period blue-and-white porcelains, see 방병선 [Bang Byŏng-sun], 왕조실록을 통해 본 조선도자사 [Examining history of Chosŏn period ceramics through the *Veritable Records*] (Seoul: Korea University Press, 2005); and 전승창 [Chŏn Sŭng-ch'ang], "조선 초기 명나라 청화백자의 유입과 수용 고찰 [Examination on the introduction and adoption of Ming-period Chinese blue-and-white porcelains during the early Chosŏn-period Korea]," 미술사학연구 [*Misulsahak yŏn'gu*] 12 (2009): 35–62.

21. For Tudor-period sumptuary laws, see Wilfrid Hooper, "The Tudor Sumptuary Laws," *English Historical Review* 30, no. 119 (1915): 433–449. For early modern colonized India's cases, see Nandini Chaturvedula, "On the Precipice of Ruin: Consumption, Sumptuary Laws, and Decadence in Early Modern Portuguese India," *Journal of World History* 26, no. 2 (2015): 355–384.

22. Craig Clunas, *Superfluous Things: Material Culture and Social Status in Early Modern China* (Honolulu: University of Hawai'i Press), 149.

23. Tax relief programs were instituted numerous times throughout Sukjong's reign. Some of the notable cases, dating to 1680/08/26, 1684/07/17, 1684/08/20, 1692/08/03, and 1698/09/15, are documented in the *Veritable Records*.

24. 송인희 [Song In-hee], "조선 17세기 전반의 假畵龍樽 [Faux-dragon jars in the 17th-century Chosŏn]," 미술사 논단 [*Misulsa nondan*] 38 (2014): 67–91.

25. *Daily Records*, 1729/01/14.

26. Pak Mun-su served as the king special inspector who oversaw the impact of natural disasters on the livelihood of the public. For more readings, see 원재영 [Won Jaeyoung], "17–18세기 재해행정과 御史의 역할 [Roles of secret government inspector and

natural disaster administration in the 17th and 18th centuries]," 한국문화 [*Han'guk munhwa*] 75 (2016): 233–267.

27. *Veritable Records*, 1757/06/20.

28. About the staggering deficit of the Chosŏn central government, see 조영준 [Cho Yŏng-chun], 조선후기 왕실재정과 서울상업 [Royal house's finance during the late Chosŏn period and commerce in Seoul] (Seoul: 소명출판 [Somyong ch'ulp'an], 2016).

29. Christopher Lovins focuses on the effectiveness of Chŏngjo's sage-king politics. See Lovins, *King Chŏngjo*, 42–47.

30. 정양모 [Chŏng Yang-mo], *Arts of Korea* (New York: Metropolitan Museum of Art, 1998), 243.

31. 강경숙 [Kang Kyŏng-suk], 한국 도자사 [History of Korean ceramics], 522–523.

32. As early as the nineteenth century, a wide variety of color-coated porcelains with decorative patterns enjoyed much popularity.

33. 방병선 [Bang Byŏng-sun], 왕조실록을 통해 본 조선도자사 [Examining history of Chosŏn period ceramics], 238.

34. Banning the usage of saggar is mentioned in the *Veritable Records* for 1791, 1793, and 1795. 송영은 [Song Yŏng-ŭn], "正祖의 도자인식과 18세기 후반 조선의 도자 생산 [King Chŏngjo's perception of ceramics and its impacts on late 18th-century ceramic production]," 한국학연구 [*Han'gukhak yŏn'gu*] 49 (2014): 138.

35. *Veritable Records*, 1714/08/23.

36. *Veritable Records*, 1795/08/06.

37. 정정남 [Chung Jung-Nam], "18세기 이후 조선사회의 온돌에 대한 인식변화와 난방효율 증대를 위한 건축적 모색 [Changes in perceptions toward the floor heating system ondol since the 18th century]," 건축역사연구 [*Kŏnch'uk yŏksa yŏn'gu*] 23, no. 3 (2018): 15–26.

38. 정약전 [Chŏng Yak-chŏn], A Personal Treatise on Pine Administration 松政私議 (1804).

39. 김동진 [Kim Tong-jin], "한반도 산림의 민간 개방과 숲의 변화 [Opening the state-owned forests to the pubic during the period spanning from the 15th to 19th centuries and changes in Korean forests]," 역사와 현실 [*Yŏksa wa hyŏnsil*] 103 (2017): 77–118.

40. *Veritable Records*, 1794/07/17.

41. 장성욱 [Chang Sŏng-uk], "Official Kilns in Gwangju: The Production Sites of Royal Vessels," in *In Blue and White: Porcelain of the Joseon Dynasty* (Seoul: National Museum of Korea, 2015), 49.

42. 장성욱 [Chang Sŏng-uk], "Official Kilns in Gwangju," 49.

43. The original text regarding Pak's assessment is found in a chapter dedicated to ceramics in 박제가 [Pak Che-ga], 북학의 [Northern learning]. As quoted in 임종태 [Lim Jong-t'ae], "조선 후기 북학론(北學論)의 수사(修辭)전략과 중국 기술 도입론 [The northern learning policy for introducing China's technology and its rhetorical strategy in late Chosŏn period]," 한국문화 [*Han'guk munhwa*] 90 (2020): 186.

44. 송영은 [Song Yŏng-ŭn], "正祖의 도자인식과 18세기 후반 조선의 도자 생산 [King Chŏngjo's perception of ceramics and its impacts on late 18th-century ceramic production]," 134.

45. V. K. Rahmathulla, "Management of Climatic Factors for Successful Silkworm (*Bombyx mori* L.) Crop and Higher Silk Production: A Review," *Psyche: A Journal of Entomology* (August 2012): 1–12.

46. One incident is recorded in a daily log dated to 1767/02/26 in the *Veritable Records*.

47. For further information about the queen's personal sericulture ceremony, see 한형주 [Han Hyŏng-chu], 밭 가는 영조와 누에 치는 정순왕후 [King Yŏngcho plowing,

Queen Chŏngsun] (Sŏngnam: 한국학중앙연구원 [Han'gukhak chungang yŏn'guwŏn], 2013).

48. For further reading about eighteenth-century Chosŏn ruling house's ban on patterned silk, see 이수현 [Yi Su-hyŏn], "조선시대 문직문의 수입에 관한 연구 [Study on the importation of patterned silks during the Chosŏn period]," MA thesis, Ehwa University, 2016.

49. One such instance can be found in a daily log dated to 1733/03/17 in the *Veritable Records*.

50. It is recorded in a daily log of the *Veritable Records* dated to 1733/03/22.

51. *Veritable Records*, 1746/12/15.

52. *Veritable Records*, 1746/12/15.

53. *Veritable Records*, 1733/12/22.

54. 이수현 [Yi Su-hyŏn], "조선시대 문직문의 수입에 관한 연구 [Study on the importation of patterned silks]," 62.

55. 심연옥 [Sim Yŏn-ok], "대한제국 적의 직물 제직에 대한 고찰 [Examination of textiles used in women's ceremonial robe]," 고궁문화 [*Kokung munhwa*] 4 (2011): 88.

56. 심연옥 [Sim Yŏn-ok], "대한제국 적의 직물 제직에 대한 고찰 [Examination of textiles]," 92.

4. BETWEEN MEMORY AND AMNESIA

1. 월드컵 공원 관리 사업소 [Wŏldŭcŏp Kongwŏn Kwalli Saŏpso], 난지도 그 향기를 되찾다 [Nanjido regained its scents] (Seoul: 월드컵공원관리사업소 [Wŏldŭcŏp Kongwŏn Kwalli Saŏpso], 1995).

2. Jeong Hye Kim, *Waste and Urban Regeneration: An Urban Ecology of Seoul's Nanjido Post-landfill Park* (London: Routledge, 2020), 114; 임태훈 [Yim T'ae-hun], "난지도가 인류세에 묻는 것들 [What Nanjido asks Anthropocene]," 문화과학 [*Munhwa kwahak*] 97 (2019): 131.

3. 전경수 [Chŏn Kyŏng-su], "쓰레기를 먹고 사는 사람들 [People living off waste]," in 한국문화론: 현대편 [*Korean Culture: Contemporary Period*] (Seoul, 일지사 [Ilchisa], 1995), 99; Ik Ki Kim, "Differentiation among the Urban Poor and the Reproduction of Poverty: The Case of Nanjido," *Environment and Urbanization* 7, no. 2 (1995): 194.

4. Myra Hird suggests that landfills, with their institutional and technological support systems, ultimately work as "sites of forgetting." See Myra J. Hird, "Waste, Landfills, and an Environmental Ethic of Vulnerability," *Ethics and the Environment* 18, no. 1 (2013): 105.

5. Gay Hawkins, *The Ethics of Waste: How We Relate to Rubbish* (Lanham, MD: Rowman and Littlefield, 2006), 72.

6. Robin Nagel, "To Love a Landfill: The History and Future of Fresh Kills," in *Dirt: The Filthy Reality of Everyday Life*, ed. Nadine Monem (London: Profile Books, 2011), 187–205.

7. 서울특별시 [Sŏult'ŭkpyŏlsi], 쓰레기 종말처리장 확보 계획 [A plan for securing waste disposal site] (Seoul: 서울특별시[Sŏult'ŭkpyŏlsi], 1977).

8. 서울특별시 [Sŏult'ŭkpyŏlsi], 난지도 매립지 안정화공사 건설지 [White paper on Nanjido landfill stabilization] (Seoul: 서울특별시 [Sŏult'ŭkpyŏlsi], 2003).

9. 서울특별시 [Sŏult'ŭkpyŏlsi], 서울시 도시고형페기물 처리장 건설 기본계획에 관한 연구 [A study on the basic plan for construction of Seoul's urban solid waste treatment facility] (Seoul: 서울특별시 [Sŏult'ŭkpyŏlsi], 1983).

10. 서울특별시 [Sŏult'ŭkpyŏlsi], 서울시 난지도 폐기물 입체위생매립사업 기본계획 보고서 [A basic plan report for sanitary mounding landfilling in Seoul's Nanjido landfill] (Seoul: 서울특별시 [Sŏult'ŭkpyŏlsi], 1985).

11. The plant, built with Danish technology, adopted wind-blowing, spinning, and magnet-sorting to separate waste. However, without source separation, much of Seoul's household waste was too wet for the automated machines to function properly. "난지도 쓰레기 처리장 가동 못 해 [Unable to operate the Nanjido waste treatment facility]," 동아일보 (*Tonga ilbo*), April 11, 1987.

12. It was only in 1987 that the city secured a new landfill site in Kimp'o.

13. In the 1983 Han River Basin Environmental Master Plan, investigators suggested continuing the Nanjido landfill on the condition that the city adopt sanitary landfill practices. Office of Environment and Engineering Science Inc., *Han River Basin Environment Master Plan Project Final Report on Solid Waste Sector Studies* (Seoul: Office of Environment, 1983). See also Japan International Cooperation Agency (JICA), *Master Plan and Feasibility Study on Seoul Municipal Solid Waste Management System in the Republic of Korea* (Tokyo: JICA, 1985).

14. The city introduced brick production with ash, constructing a factory in Nanjido, but it ultimately failed. "연탄재 벽돌 첫선 [The first introduction of ash brick]," 동아일보 (*Tonga ilbo*), February 2, 1978.

15. The main cause for decreased ashes derived from household heating sources. 국토통일 연구원 [Kukt'o t'ongil yŏn'guwŏn], 도시고형폐기물의 효율적 수거방안 연구 [A study on effective collection methods of urban solid waste] (Seoul: 국토통일연구원 [Kukt'o t'ongil yŏn'guwŏn], 1983), 7.

16. The Nanjido Management Office (NMO) was originally established to manage the waste treatment plant in December 1985. 서울시 의회 [Sŏul-si ŭihoe], 1992년도 행정감사—난지도관리사업소 업무보고 [1992 administrative auditing—Nanjido Management Office Report] (Seoul: 서울특별시 [Sŏult'ŭkpyŏlsi], 1992).

17. The soil truck section ran their own "business" with their own bulldozers and other landfill equipment, charging drivers landfill entrance fees. Lacking managerial capacity, the city condoned it. The city and the prosecutors brought charges against the gangs on accusations of fraud and blackmail, but lawsuits did not eradicate their illicit practices. "난지도 통행세 8억 갈취 [Nanjido toll fee, extorting 8 billion wŏn]," 중앙일보 (*Chungang ilbo*), May 18, 1990.

18. "쓰레기터서 폐품 주워 남편 학비 벌던 주부가 불도저에 치여 숨져 [A housewife, who collected waste in the dump to support her husband's tuition, was hit by a bulldozer and died]," 중앙일보 (*Chungang ilbo*), August 26, 1981.

19. KERA/Nanjido staff, in interview with the author, June 26, 2016.

20. Waste picker in the private section, in interview with the author, April 9 and June 22, 2015.

21. While certain waste types can be used as daily cover or road base, it requires careful profiling and characterization of incoming waste. Nicholas P. Cheremisinoff, *Handbook of Solid Waste Management and Waste Minimization Technologies* (Oxford: Butterworth-Heinemann, 2003), 104.

22. Front-line waste picker/district drew leader, in interview with the author, May 15, 2015.

23. "난지도 쓰레기 무너져 소동 [Waste collapse in Nanjido]," 경향신문 (*Kyŏnghyang sinmun*), April 4, 1990.

24. In one instance, a garbage truck rolled over the dumpsite slope while unloading, fell onto a shack, killing a waste picker couple that was sleeping in it. "난지도 폐품수집 부부 움막 덮친 트럭에 압사 [Waste picker couple crushed to death by a truck]," 동아일보 (*Tonga ilbo*), January 17, 1990.

25. Waste collection truck drivers, in interview with the author, June 15, 2015.

26. Second-line picker, in interview with the author, April 13, 2015.

27. "하치장 분리 요구 난지도주민 농성 [Nanjido residents protest for separating dumpsites]," 중앙일보 (*Chungang ilbo*), June 25, 1988; "난지도 고물수집원 농성," 조선일보 (*Chosŏn ilbo*), June 26, 1988.

28. "난지도 '유해 산업쓰레기' 마구 버려 [Disposing 'hazardous industrial waste' in Nanjido]," 한겨레 (*Han'gyŏre*), July 19, 1988.

29. Administrator, an interview with the author, March 20, 2015; and field superintendent, an interview with the author, March 23, 2015.

30. "청소차 시위 [Garbage truck protest]," 경향신문 (*Kyŏnghyang sinmun*), November 10, 1989.

31. Mary Douglas, *Purity and Danger: An Analysis of Concepts of Pollution and Taboo* (London: Routledge, 2001 [1966]), 36.

32. "난지도 진입로 포장 [Paving Nanjido accessway]," 동아일보 (*Tonga ilbo*), November 11, 1989.

33. It is worth noting that these protests all occurred in the late 1980s—a time of tumult for South Korea. The June Democratic Uprising and the Great Worker Struggle in 1987 provided an impetus to widespread political action. Under these circumstances, both the informal waste pickers and the drivers—occupying the lowest rung of the civil service—could voice their demands and even exercise power in the city's landfill operation. See Hagen Koo, *Korean Workers: The Culture and Politics of Class Formation* (Ithaca, NY: Cornell University Press, 2001); Namhee Lee, *The Making of Minjung: Democracy and the Politics of Representation in South Korea* (Ithaca, NY: Cornell University Press, 2007).

34. "부당노동행위의 현장 (13) 남성전기산업 [The scene of unjust labor practice (13) Namsŏng electricity industry]," 한겨레 (*Han'gyŏre*), July 2, 1988; "닭장차에 실어 내동댕이 [Dragged in a caged riot police vehicle then being thrown out]," 한겨레 (*Han'gyŏre*), February 11, 1989.

35. The 1980s saw the flourishing of writings by laborers—ranging from memoirs to reportage to poetry—in the literary sphere. Many laborers formed a literary coterie and created literary works based on their experiences. For labor literature and detailed analysis of this poem, see 박지영 [Pak Chi-yŏng] "'현장'의 노래, '광장'의 시—1980-90년대 초반 노동자문예운동과 시쓰기 [Songs of the workplace, and poems of the agora: Labor literary movement and poem composition in the 1980s–the early 1990s]," 상허학보 (*Sanghŏ hakbo*) 50 (2017): 168–185.

36. This poem illustrates the protest experiences of Pico Korea, an American subsidiary factory based in Puch'ŏn, that fought against the company's disguised bankruptcy and factory closure. 부천노동자문학회 [Puch'ŏn nodongja munhakhoe], "아들아 이젠 말하리라—한국 피코 어머니들의 완전 승리를 위하여 [Our sons, we shall speak now—For the full victory of Pico Korea mothers]," in 작업화 굵은 자국을 찍으며 [Stepping the work shoes], ed. 전국 노동자 문학회 시 모음 [A poetry anthology of nationwide laborers' literature coteries] (Seoul, 개마고원 [Kaemagowŏn], 1989), 55–56. Also see Hyun Mee Kim, "The Politics of Korean Working Class Women," *Asia Journal* 3, no. 1 (1996): 72.

37. It is beyond the scope of this chapter to analyze the entire poem, but it is worth noting that this particular contrast, set in Nanjido, signals the social position and marginalization of waste pickers. In South Korea in the 1980s, the laboring class was typically central to social movements. Ironically, this centrality of laborers tended to silence other segments of the underclass, with waste pickers here being a case in point: even the proximity of waste pickers to laborers abandoned in Nanjido was insufficient to bring them notice, let alone any awareness or solidarity for them as part of the oppressed class.

38. 대한민국 국회 [Taehanmin'guk kukhoe], 국회 회의록 [National Assembly minutes], 제13대, 제145차, 제5차 본회의 [The 13th National Assembly, 145th session, 5th plenary session], February 24, 1989, p. 2.

39. 대한민국 국회 [Taehanmin'guk kukhoe], National Assembly minutes, 24.

40. Scholars conceptualize waste as capturing various instances where "humans take on the form of waste." For example, Zygmunt Bauman, *Wasted Lives: Modernity and Its Outcasts* (Cambridge, UK: Polity, 2004); Michelle Yates, "The Human-as-Waste, the Labor Theory of Value and Disposability in Contemporary Capitalism," *Antipode* 43, no. 5 (2011): 1680. For criticism of this language of waste, see Kathleen M. Millar, *Reclaiming the Discarded: Life and Labor on Rio's Garbage Dump* (Durham, NC: Duke University Press, 2018), 5–8.

41. Colin Marshall, "Learning from Seoul's Sampoong Department Store Disaster," *The Guardian*, May 27, 2015, https://www.theguardian.com/cities/2015/may/27/seoul-sampoong-department-store-disaster-history-cities-50-buildings.

42. "'제2의 삼풍 현장' 난지도 비애 ['The second Samp'ung site' grief in Nanjido]," 한겨레 (*Han'gyŏre*), July 23, 1995; 서울특별시 [Sŏult'ŭkpyŏlsi], 삼풍백화점 붕괴사고 백서 [White paper on the collapse of Samp'ung Department Store] (Seoul: 서울특별시 [Sŏult'ŭkpyŏlsi, 1996), 389.

43. 구도완, 홍덕화 [Ku To-wan, Hong Dŏk-hwa], "한국 환경운동의 성장과 분화: 제도화 논의를 중심으로 [The growth and diversification of the Korean environmental movement: Focusing on institutionalization]," 환경사회학연구 ECO (*Hwan'gyŏng sahoehak yŏn'gu*) 17, no. 1 (2013): 95–97.

44. Agenda 21 is one of the action plans of the 1992 United Nations Conference on Environment and Development (UNCED) to achieve sustainable development goals at the local level.

45. The government indeed strategically framed Nanjido's restoration as a success model for developing countries. The Seoul Institute, *Nanjido Eco Park Restoration from Waste Dumping Site* (Seoul: The Seoul Institute, 2014).

46. 정규호 [Chŏng Kyu-ho], "지속가능성을 위한 거버넌스에서 합의형성 실패 문제—녹색서울시민위원회의 경험 [The consensus building in sustainability governance—A case study of the Green Seoul Citizens Committee]," 환경사회학연구 ECO (*Hwan'gyŏng sahoehak yŏn'gu*) 2 (2002): 43–67.

47. The Seoul Institute, *Nanjido*, 111–112.

5. NORTH KOREA CAUGHT BETWEEN DEVELOPMENTALISM AND HUMANITARIANISM

Acknowledgements: An earlier, much condensed form of this chapter appeared online in the January 2020 issue of *episteme*, available at https://positionspolitics.org/episteme-1-1-4fortier-kim/. The authors would like to thank Patrick Fox and Aengus Ryan for their input and support at various stages in the development of this chapter.

1. Brain H. Hook, "Opinion: The Parasites Feeding on North Koreans," *New York Times*, November 24, 2017.

2. Josee Ng, "Professor Tôn Thất Tùng: Patriotic Liver Surgeon and Author of World-Class Medical Advancements," *TheSmartLocal Vietnam*, September 1, 2021, https://thesmartlocal.com/vietnam/ton-that-tung-surgeon/.

3. See, also, Peter Hayes, "Unbearable Legacies: The Politics of Environmental Degradation in North Korea," *Asia-Pacific Journal* 41, no. 2 (2009), http://apjjf.org/-Peter-Hayes/3233/article.html.

4. "North Korean Defector Had 27cm Parasitic Worm in His Stomach," *The Guardian*, November 17, 2017.

5. Multiple authorities from the IFRC to UN agencies have underscored the unintended negative impact of sanctions on humanitarian work. For example, see Robert R. King, "Humanitarian Engagement with North Korea—Great Need but Increasingly Difficult," Center for Strategic and International Studies, September 4, 2018, https://www

.csis.org/analysis/humanitarian-engagement-north-korea-great-need-increasingly
-difficult.

6. IFRC Beijing Press Release, December 21, 2018, https://oldmedia.ifrc.org/ifrc/press
-release/dprk-assistance-not-less-needed-humanitarian-challenges-rise/.

7. Chong-Ae Yu, "The Rise and Demise of Industrial Agriculture in North Korea,"
Journal of Korean Studies 12, no. 1 (2007): 75–110. Pointing to North Korea's record grain
production at eight million tons in 1984 under the socialist system and a dip to 5.44 million tons in 1993 before the onset of adverse weather conditions, Yu argues that systemic
arguments about socialist inefficiencies as well as climate change are inadequate to fully
explain North Korea's food shortages. Rather, she argues, North Korea's food crisis is part
and parcel of the unsustainable practices of modern industrial agriculture that require
increasing amounts of synthetic inputs with worsening environmental and ecological impacts. For arguments that emphasize the inherent inefficiencies of rural collectivization
under a command economy, see Ruediger Frank, "Classical Socialism in North Korea and
Its Transformation: The Role and the Future of Agriculture," *Harvard Asia Quarterly* 10,
no. 2 (2006): 15–33; and Nam Sung-wook, "Chronic Food Shortages and the Collective
Farm System in North Korea," *Journal of East Asian Studies* 7 (2007): 93–123.

8. Even before the additional sanctions imposed in 2017 and thereafter, UNICEF reported that "due to sanctions imposed on DPR Korea, bilateral and multilateral donor
support plummeted in 2015 to the lowest level in the region," which resulted in "a sharp
increase in malnutrition and hunger" for children. They further explain that the sanctions have closed off banking channels, which are integral in the transfer of funds for
continued humanitarian work. See Christopher Davids, Sylvie Morel-Seytoux, Laura
Wicks, and David Solomon Bassiouni, *Situation Analysis of Children and Women in the
Democratic People's Republic of Korea—2017* (Pyongyang: United Nations Children's
Fund, 2016), 26.

9. The International Federation of Red Cross and Red Crescent Societies (IFRC) is the
world's largest humanitarian organization, providing assistance without discrimination
as to nationality, race, religious beliefs, class or political opinions. The IFRC works with
member national societies, and should be differentiated from the International Committee of the Red Cross, which is an independent organization. For more information,
see the IFRC information on national societies, accessed December 18, 2021, https://www
.ifrc.org/national-societies-directory/374.

10. References to *Rodong sinmun* [Workers newspaper, 로동신문] were collated
through keyword searches of the digital database of North Korean publications in December 2017 at the Information Center on North Korea run by the Ministry of Unification in South Korea. All translations of *Rodong sinmun* are by Suzy Kim. For IFRC
evaluations, see IFRC Evaluations, accessed December 19, 2021, https://www.ifrc.org
/evaluations?organisational_structure%5B%5D=6422&date_from=&date_to=&title=.

11. Christopher Flavelle, "Climate Change Threatens the World's Food Supply, United
Nations Warns," *New York Times*, August 8, 2019.

12. The World Bank estimates 120,410 m^2, whereas the DPRK's own Ministry of Land
and Environment Protection (MoLEP) provides 123,138 km^2. See *Democratic People's
Republic of Korea: Environment and Climate Change Outlook* (Pyongyang: MoLEP and
UNEP, 2012), 3, https://europa.eu/capacity4dev/unep/document/democratic-peoples
-republic-korea-environment-and-climate-change-outlook.

13. *Democratic People's Republic of Korea: Environment and Climate Change Outlook*, 49.

14. FAO/WFP Joint Rapid Food Security Assessment, May 2019, p. 10, https://www
.fao.org/3/ca4447en/ca4447en.pdf.

15. UN DPR Korea Needs and Priorities Plan, April 22, 2020, https://dprkorea.un.org.

16. IFRC website, accessed December 18, 2021, https://www.ifrc.org/donor-response.

17. For more on the environmental destruction from the Korean War, see Su-kyoung Hwang, "The Korean War and the Environment," *Critical Asian Studies* 53, no. 4 (2021): 517–537.

18. For details, see https://www.icrc.org/en/document/dprk-weapon-contamination -2017. In June 2019, the ICRC worked with the DPRK Ministry of People's Security to distribute thousands of posters to raise awareness on the dangers of unexploded bombs; North Korea is one of the worst affected regions of weapons contamination in the world. See Koh Byung-joon, "ICRC distributes to N. Korean schools posters warning of dangers from unexploded bombs," *Yonhap News Agency*, June 10, 2019.

19. See *Democratic People's Republic of Korea: Environment and Climate Change Outlook*, 14.

20. "지구의 기후 변화는 앞으로 더욱 심하게 나타날 것이다 [Earth's climate change will become more severe]," 로동신문 [*Rodong sinmun*], March 30, 1979, p. 4.

21. 전영희 [Chŏn Yŏng-hǔi], "식량 위기와 기후 변화 [Food crisis and climate change]," 로동신문 [*Rodong sinmun*], October 27, 2009, p. 6.

22. According to the Information Center on North Korea database, there seems to be just a single reference in 1991 to world food problems in the 로동신문 [*Rodong sinmun*] between 1985 and 2008.

23. 김세진 [Kim Se-jin], "한랭전선의 파국적 영향으로 많은 나라들이 식량난에 허덕이고 있으며 무서운 기근이 세계를 휩쓸고 있다 [Due to the catastrophic effects of the cold front, many countries suffer from food shortages and a terrible famine sweeps the world]," 로동신문 [*Rodong sinmun*], June 9, 1977, p. 6.

24. 김재식 [Kim Chae-sik], "한랭전선의 영향으로 더욱 심해지는 농업위기, 식량난 [Increasing agricultural crisis and food shortage due to the effects of the cold front]," 로동신문 [*Rodong sinmun*], January 28, 1978, p. 6; "식량난으로 아우성치는 세계, 굶주림과 영양실조 [World clamoring with food shortage, hunger and malnutrition]," 로동신문 [*Rodong sinmun*], November 17, 1980, p. 4.

25. 류용식 Ryu Yong-sik, "식량문제 해결은 발전도상나라들의 새 사회건설의 중요한 요구 [Solution of the food problem is an important mandate in the construction of a new society by developing countries]," 로동신문 [*Rodong sinmun*], May 2, 1981, p. 6.

26. See the various reports of the UN Intergovernmental Panel on Climate Change, accessed December 19, 2021, http://www.ipcc.ch/.

27. Benjamin Habib, "North Korea: An Unlikely Champion in the Fight against Climate Change," *The Guardian*, May 20, 2014.

28. "DPRK Will Actively Engage in International Efforts for Environmental Protection," DPRK Ministry of Foreign Affairs, September 27, 2019, http://www.mfa.gov.kp/en /dprk-will-actively-engage-in-international-efforts-for-environmental-protection-head -of-its-delegation/.

29. 채일출 [Ch'ae Il-ch'ul], "기후 변화와 에네르기 [Climate change and energy]," 로동신문 [*Rodong sinmun*], June 5, 2008, p. 6.

30. *Democratic People's Republic of Korea: Environment and Climate Change Outlook*, 76–83.

31. The full text of the DPRK Environmental Protection Law is available at "조선민주주의인민공화국 환경보호법," 로동신문 [*Rodong sinmun*], April 10, 1986, p. 2. The law was subsequently amended in 1999, 2000, 2005, 2011, 2013, and 2014, with a significant revision in 2013, which we discuss in the final section. For an overview of the legislation and the subsequent amendment in 1999, to include environmental impact assessments, as well as discussion of other related environmental legislations in North Korea, see Sangmin Nam, "The Legal Development of the Environmental Policy in the Democratic People's Republic of Korea," *Fordham International Law Journal* 27, no. 4 (2003): 1322–1342.

32. "부주석 리종옥 대의원의 보고 [Report by Vice President Ri Chong-ok on the adoption of the Environmental Protection Law]," 로동신문 [*Rodong sinmun*], April 8, 1986, p. 2.

33. "환경보호사업에 이바지하게될 은혜로운 조치 [Gracious policy to contribute to the work of environmental protection]," 로동신문 [*Rodong sinmun*], March 8, 1987, p. 4.

34. 전영희 [Chŏn Yŏng-hŭi], "주목을 끄는 핵에네르기 개발 움직임 [Movement to develop nuclear energy attracts attention]," 로동신문 [*Rodong sinmun*], July 17, 2009, p. 6.

35. *DPR Korea Multiple Indicator Cluster Survey 2017, Survey Findings Report* (Pyongyang: Central Bureau of Statistics and UNICEF, 2017), June 2018, p. 13, https://www.unicef.org/dprk/reports/2017-dpr-korea-mics-survey.

36. Christopher Davids, Sylvie Morel-Seytoux, Laura Wicks, and David Solomon Bassiouni, *Situation Analysis of Children and Women in the Democratic People's Republic of Korea—2017* (Pyongyang: United Nations Children's Fund, 2016), 37–40. Overall, the report estimates that more than 5.6 million people in North Korea were affected by natural disasters between 2004 and 2015 (p. 21), and approximately 10.5 million people or 42 percent of the North Korean population are considered undernourished (p. 40).

37. 리승철 [Ri Sŭng-ch'ŏl], "과학 기술적 문제를 잘 알고: 국토환경보호성, 환경보호국, 환경보호연구소 일꾼들과 나눈 이야기 [Understanding science and technology issues: Interview with workers of Ministry of Land and Environmental Protection, Department of Environmental Protection, Institute of Environmental Protection]," 로동신문 [*Rodong sinmun*], September 6, 2005, p. 3. The article seems to have mistakenly added a zero to some of its statistics, off by a factor of ten, which I have corrected in the citation.

38. For the latest statistics, see the World Water Council website, accessed December 19, 2021, http://www.worldwatercouncil.org/en/water-supply-sanitation. According to the WHO/UNICEF Joint Monitoring Program, 1.1 billion people live without clean drinking water and 2.6 billion people lack adequate sanitation, resulting in 1.8 million deaths from waterborne diseases.

39. "환경보호를 위한 에네르기 개발과 그 리용 [New energy development and use to protect the environment]," 로동신문 [*Rodong sinmun*], June 1, 2003, p. 6.

40. "환경보호에 좋은 아카시아 나무: 환경보호에 적극 리용하자 [Acacia trees good for environmental protection: Let's actively use it to protect the environment]," 로동신문 [*Rodong sinmun*], June 28, 2002, p. 3. According to the 2012 *Environment and Climate Change Outlook* report, the quality and extent of forest cover has declined between 1990 and 2002: "The area of timber forest was reduced at a rate of approximately 480 km^2 per year due to harvest of fuel wood, building materials but also flooding, droughts, fires and pest. In 2000 and 2002, 365 forest fires were recorded affecting 128 km^2 of forests and approximately 300 km^2 of forest were damaged by pest" (p. 48). Reforestation efforts have been ongoing since the mid-1990s, which has partly reversed the trend. As 75 percent of the rural population use wood as their primary fuel for cooking and heating, however, pressures on forest resources will continue until alternative forms of energy are introduced and food security improves.

41. Paradoxically, recent efforts at reforestation in North Korea have reportedly led to declines in food production and availability of firewood. See Benjamin Katzeff Silberstein, "The North Korean Economy—June 2019: Kim Jong Un's Reforestation Plans: The Dilemma of Forests Versus Food and Fuel," *38 North*, July 1, 2019, https://www.38north.org/2019/07/bkatzeffsilberstein070119/.

42. Michael Russell, "Red Cross Tree Planting in the DPR of Korea: A Management Review," IFRC Report, June/July 2008, p. 5. The IFRC and DPRK RC conducted an external management review in 2008 to assess the effectiveness of the Red Cross contribution to the national reforestation effort. The report gave specific recommendations to national authorities such as MoLEP and the Red Cross at the national, provincial, county, and village

levels. Among the key recommendations was a focus on multipurpose seedlings such as acacia trees (the acacia tree is a legume and therefore a soil improver, useful as fuel wood and food for goats and oxen, and the flowers are excellent for bees and honey production), and modernizing seedling production and planting techniques through targeted training.

43. See, for example, 전국녀성사회주의건설자회의 문헌집 [Documents of the national meeting of women socialist builders] (Pyongyang: 조선녀성사 [Chosŏn nyŏsŏngsa], 1959). See, also, 녀성천리마기수들 [Women Chollima engineers] (Pyongyang: 조선녀성사 [Chosŏn nyŏsŏngsa], 1960).

44. Chong-Ae Yu, "Rise and Demise of Industrial Agriculture," 79.

45. Knud Falk, "A Review of Red Cross DM Management in DPR Korea," IFRC Evaluations, accessed December 19, 2021, https://www.ifrc.org/media/13944.

46. Aengus Ryan, "WatSan Impact Study Review DPRK, Stage 4," IFRC, December 31, 2007, p. 4, https://www.ifrc.org/media/13945.

47. "Humanitarian Sanctions Requests, Humanitarian Exemptions in Effect," UNSC 1718 Sanctions Committee DPRK, accessed December 18, 2021, https://www.un.org/securitycouncil/sanctions/1718/exemptions-measures/humanitarian-exemption-requests.

48. "Democratic People's Republic of Korea: Measles Epidemic," IFRC Operations Update, March 21, 2007, http://www.ifrc.org/docs/appeals/07/DPRKRFAou01.pdf.

49. Since 2000, the IFRC has launched twenty-two official Emergency Appeals, or DREF (Disaster Relief Emergency Fund), allocations for floods and droughts in the DPRK. See "IFRC Appeals DPRK," accessed December 18, 2021, https://www.ifrc.org/appeals?date_from=&date_to=&location%5B6422%5D=6422&type%5B2%5D=2&type%5B19%5D=19&appeal_code=&text=&page=1. These documents contain detailed data about affected areas, casualties and people missing, homes destroyed, and crops lost.

50. Solar panels have become widely popular throughout North Korea, seen on apartment balconies, street lamps, factories, and fields, often used to supplement power shortages and favored by the government as part of its push toward renewable energy. See Julie Makinen, "Off the (Failing) Grid in North Korea, Where Solar Energy Is a Hot Commodity," *Los Angeles Times*, May 23, 2016.

51. "Food and Nutrition Security and Sustainable Agriculture under the Global Public Goods and Challenges Thematic Programme," Internal Report of the Swedish Red Cross Budget line: BGUE-B2015–21.020704-C1-DEVCO. For the graphic of the loop production system published by the DPRK Academy of Science, see https://positionspolitics.org/episteme-1-1-4fortier-kim/.

52. "Why Soil Is Disappearing from Farms," *BBC News*, July 8, 2019, https://www.bbc.com/reel/video/p07gbzsz/why-soil-is-disappearing-from-farms.

53. Recognizing the need to replenish the soil, North Korea has evidenced growing interest and developments in biotechnology and organic fertilizers. See, for example, discussion of the Patriot Compound Microbial Fertilizer Factory by Soobok Kim, "N Korea Science and Technology Part 3: Enriching the Soil—Producing beyond Subsistence," *ZoominKorea*, April 20, 2018, http://p3nlhclust404.shr.prod.phx3.secureserver.net/SharedContent/redirect_0.html.

54. Alice Slater, "The United Nations Votes to Start Negotiations to Ban the Bomb," *The Nation,* November 1, 2016.

55. 조선민주주의인민공화국 법전 [Laws of the Democratic People's Republic of Korea] (Moranbong: 법률출판사 [Pŏbryul Ch'ulpansa], 2016), 214.

56. 조선민주주의인민공화국 법전 [Laws of the Democratic People's Republic of Korea], 338–346.

57. "Towards Sustainable and Resilient Human Development: The Strategic Framework for Cooperation between the United Nations and the Government of the

Democratic People's Republic of Korea, 2017–2021," UN-DPRK Office of the Resident Coordinator 2016, https://unsdg.un.org/sites/default/files/cf-documents/2223c130-ffdd -412a-a9f3-f77b9cf0337c_DPRK_UN_Strategic_Framework_2017-2021_Final.pdf.

58. Mirva Helenius, "IFRC President Commends Community Resilience Building Efforts in Democratic People's Republic of Korea," IFRC, December 22, 2016, https:// oldmedia.ifrc.org/ifrc/2016/12/22/ifrc-president-commends-community-resilience -building-efforts-democratic-peoples-republic-korea/.

59. The IPCC report also urged better soil management, crop diversification, fewer restrictions on trade, and changes in consumer behavior for less waste and shifts away from meat. See Christopher Flavelle, "Climate Change Threatens the World's Food Supply, United Nations Warns," *New York Times*, August 8, 2019.

6. RICE FIELDS, MOUNTAINS, AND THE INVISIBLE MEATIFICATION OF KOREAN AGRICULTURE

1. Kyoung-Hee Park, "State and Food in South Korea: Moulding the National Diet in Wartime and Beyond," PhD diss., Leiden University, 2013; Hanhee Hahm, "Rice and Koreans: Three Identities and Meanings," *Korea Journal* 45, no. 2 (2005): 89–106; and Katarzyna Cwiertka, *Cuisine, Colonialism and Cold War: Food in Twentieth-Century Korea* (London: Reaktion Books, 2012).

2. Laura C. Nelson, *Measured Excess: Status, Gender, and Consumer Nationalism in South Korea* (New York: Columbia University Press, 2000).

3. Mick Moore, "Mobilization and Disillusion in Rural Korea: The Saemaul Movement in Retrospect," *Pacific Affairs* 57, no. 4 (1984): 577–598; Larry L. Burmeister, "State, Industrialization and Agricultural Policy in Korea," *Development and Change* 21, no. 2 (1990): 197–223; Hsin-Huang Michael Hsiao, *Government Agricultural Strategies in Taiwan and South Korea: A Macrosociological Assessment* (Taipei: Institute of Ethnology Academia Sinica, 1981); and Chul-kyoo Kim, "The Rise and Decline of Statist Agriculture and the Farmers Movement in South Korea," *Korea Observer* 37, no. 1 (2006): 29–147.

4. To maintain rice production despite declining rates of consumption, the government has promoted the use of surplus rice in alcoholic beverage production such as *makgŏlli* and *soju*, as well as in bread and pastry production. Sunchul Choi, John Dyck, and Nathan Childs, *The Rice Market in South Korea* (Washington, DC: US Department of Agriculture, 2016).

5. Jaehyung Kim, "The Effect of Direct Payments to Rice Farming Households in Korea," MPA/MPP thesis, University of Kentucky, 2014.

6. Ministry of Agriculture Nature and Food Quality, ed., *Greenhouse Horticulture in Korea* (The Hague: Agroberichten Buitenland, 2016).

7. Food and Agriculture Organization of the United Nations, "Meat Production in Denmark and South Korea," Faostat, 2018, accessed December 1, 2021, http://www.fao .org/faostat/en/.

8. Korea Rural Economic Research Institute, *Agriculture in Korea* (Naju: Korea Rural Economic Research Institute, 2015).

9. Gitte Holmstrup et al., *The Lay of the Land, 2017* (Copenhagen: The Danish Society for Nature Conservation, 2017)

10. Ministry of Agriculture Nature and Food Quality, *The Korean Feed Market* (The Hague: Agroberichten Buitenland, 2016).

11. Holmstrup et al., *Lay of the Land, 2017*.

12. Ministry of Agriculture Nature and Food Quality, *Korean Feed Market*.

13. The size of agricultural fields in Denmark is still small compared with those in North and South America, but the change relative to previous field size is remarkable.

14. Philip McMichael and Chul-kyoo Kim, "Japanese and South Korean Agricultural Restructuring in Comparative and Global Perspective," in *The Global Restructuring of Agro-Food Systems*, ed. Philip McMichael (Ithaca, NY: Cornell University Press, 1994), 31.

15. Even though South Korea has been able to externalize feed production, the expansion of livestock production has had environmental effects in South Korea, most notably groundwater pollution and large-scale disease outbreaks such as swine flu.

16. Martin Hart-Landsberg, "Capitalism, the Korea-U.S. Free Trade Agreement, and Resistance," *Critical Asian Studies* 43, no. 3 (2011): 319–348; Byeong-Seon Yoon, Won-Kyu Song, and Hae-Jin Lee, "The Struggle for Food Sovereignty in South Korea," *Monthly Review* 65, no. 1 (2013), https://monthlyreview.org/2013/05/01/the-struggle -for-food-sovereignty-in-south-korea/.

17. John C. Beghin, Jean-Christophe Bureau, and Sung Joon Park, "Food Security and Agricultural Protection in South Korea," *American Journal of Agricultural Economics* 85, no. 3 (2003): 618–632; Penelope Francks, Johanna Boestel, and Choo Hyop Kim, *Agriculture and Economic Development in East Asia* (Abingdon, UK: Taylor and Francis, 1999).

18. Mindi Schneider, "Developing the Meat Grab," *Journal of Peasant Studies* 41, no. 4 (2014): 613–633; Tony Weis, "The Meat of the Global Food Crisis," *Journal of Peasant Studies* 40, no. 1 (2013): 65–85; Tony Weis, "The Accelerating Biophysical Contradictions of Industrial Capitalist Agriculture," *Journal of Agrarian Change* 10, no. 3 (2010): 315–341.

19. Weis, "Meat of the Global Food Crisis."

20. Schneider, "Developing the Meat Grab."

21. Derek Heady, *Anatomy of a Crisis: The Causes and Consequences of Surging Food Prices, IFPRI Discussion Paper* (Washington, DC: International Food Policy Research Institute, 2008).

22. Hart-Landsberg, "Capitalism"; Layne Hartsell and Chul-kyoo Kim, "The Global Food Crisis and Food Sovereignty in South Korea" in *Global Civil Society 2011: Globality and the Absence of Justice*, ed. Martin Albrow and Hakan Seckinelgin (Basingstoke, UK: Palgrave Macmillan, 2011), 128–133; Mi Park, "Framing Free Trade Agreements: The Politics of Nationalism in the Anti-Neoliberal Globalization Movement in South Korea," *Globalizations* 6, no. 4 (2009): 451–466.

23. Murray Johns, "The Beef Market in the Republic of Korea: Prospects for Demand Supply and Imports," *Occasional Paper* (Canberra: Bureau of Agricultural Economics, 1980), 12.

24. Hsiao, *Government Agricultural Strategies*; Burmeister, "State, Industrialization and Agricultural Policy"; Kym Anderson, "Growth of Agricultural Protection in East Asia," *Food Policy* 8, no. 4 (1983): 327–336.

25. Helen-Louise Brown, *Conceived in the Past and Raised in Modernity: A Study of the Korean Barbecue Restaurant* (Adelaide: University of Adelaide, 2010), 30.

26. Chong-dae Kim, "The Development of Commercial Poultry Production in Korea," *Extension Bulletin* (1994): 2.

27. Johns, "Beef Market in the Republic of Korea," 30.

28. Kie-jun Na, *The Development of Beef Cattle Production in Korea* (Taipei: ASPAC Food and Fertilizer Technology Center, 1994), 2.

29. Chul-Ho Yoo, "Problems of Beef Production and Marketing in Korea," *Journal of Rural Development* 16 (1993): 134.

30. One or two heads of cattle could provide upward of 10 percent additional income for a farming family. Johns, "Beef Market in the Republic of Korea," 36.

31. Larry L. Burmeister, "Korean Minifarm Agriculture: From Articulation to Disarticulation," *Journal of Developing Areas* 26, no. 2 (1992): 158.

32. Johns, "Beef Market in the Republic of Korea," 47.

33. Annual per capita consumption of meat increased from 13 kilograms in 1980 to 25 kilograms in 1990, and this rising demand was met primarily through the expansion of domestic meat production. US Department of Agriculture Foreign Agricultural Service, "United States Department of Agriculture Foreign Agricultural Service Production, Supply and Distribution Online, 2014," accessed December 10, 2021, http://apps.fas .usda.gov/psdonline.

34. "Big Agriculture Provides a Study in Raw Power," *New York Times*, October 12, 1993.

35. Jung-en Woo, *Race to the Swift: State and Finance in Korean Industrialization* (New York: Columbia University Press, 1991), 179.

36. McMichael and Kim, "Japanese and South Korean Agricultural Restructuring."

37. Burmeister, "Korean Minifarm Agriculture."

38. US Department of Agriculture Foreign Agricultural Service, "United States Department of Agriculture Foreign Agricultural Service Production."

39. Tim Josling et al., *Bringing Agriculture into the GATT, IATRC Commissioned Paper* (Davis, CA: International Agricultural Trade Research Consortium, 1994), 76–77.

40. Yong-Kee Lee and Hanho Kim, "Korean Agriculture after the Uruguay Round and World Agricultural Policy Reform," in *IATRC Conference: Agricultural Policy Reform and the WTO: Where Are We Heading?* (CAPRI: International Agricultural Trade Research Consortium, 2003), 5.

41. Yoo, "Problems of Beef Production and Marketing," 151.

42. C. Jo et al., "Keys to Production and Processing of Hanwoo Beef: A Perspective of Tradition and Science," *Animal Frontiers* 2, no. 4 (2012): 33.

43. Renee Kim and Milton Boyd, "Identification of Niche Market for Hanwoo Beef: Understanding Korean Consumer Preference for Beef Using Market Segment Analysis," *International Food and Agribusiness Review* 7, no. 3 (2004): 49.

44. J. G. Andrae et al., "Effects of Feeding High-Oil Corn to Beef Steers on Carcass Characteristics and Meat Quality," *Journal of Animal Science* 79, no. 3 (2001): 582–588.

45. Larry L. Burmeister, "South Korea's Rural Development Dilemma: Trade Pressures and Agricultural Sector Adjustment," *Asian Survey* 30, no. 7 (1990): 711–723.

46. Chul-kyoo Kim, "The Rise and Decline of Statist Agriculture and the Farmers Movement in South Korea," *Korea Observer* 37 (2006): 129–147; Hart-Landsberg, "Capitalism"; and Yoon, Song, and Lee, "Struggle for Food Sovereignty."

47. Francks, Boestel, and Kim, *Agriculture and Economic Development*; Kym Anderson and Will Martin, eds., *Distortions to Agricultural Incentives in Asia* (Washington, DC: The World Bank, 2009).

48. William Winders, *The Politics of Food Supply: U.S. Agricultural Policy in the World Economy* (New Haven, CT: Yale University Press, 2009).

49. Kie-Chung Pang and Michael D. Shin, *Landlords, Peasants, and Intellectuals in Modern Korea* (Honolulu: University of Hawaiʻi Press, 2005); Albert Park, *Building a Heaven on Earth: Religion, Activism and Protest in Japanese Occupied Korea* (Honolulu: University of Hawaiʻi Press, 2014).

50. KREI, *Agriculture in Korea* (Naju: Korea Rural Economic Research Institute, 2015).

51. Burmeister," Korean Minifarm Agriculture."

52. David I. Steinberg, "The Political Economy in Microcosm: The Korean National Livestock Cooperatives Federation," *Korean Studies* 18, no. 1 (1994): 158–170.

53. Larry L. Burmeister, "From Parastatal Control to Corporatist Intermediation: The Korean Agricultural Cooperative in Transition," in *Corporatism and Korean Capitalism*, ed. Dennis L. McNamara (New York: Routledge, 1999), 110–138; Yong S. Lee, Don F. Hadwiger, and Chong-bum Lee, "Agricultural Policy Making under International Pressures: The Case of South Korea, a Newly Industrialized Country," *Food Policy* 15, no. 5

(1990): 418–433; Larry L. Burmeister, "South Korea's Rural Development Dilemma"; and Steinberg, "Political Economy in Microcosm."

54. William Winders, *The Politics of Food Supply: U.S. Agricultural Policy in the World Economy* (New Haven, CT: Yale University Press, 2009).

55. This is not to argue that the agricultural sector did not suffer economically during the 1990s and 2000s.

56. Jung-Sup Choi, Zhang-Yue Zhou, and Rodney J. Cox, "Beef Consumption, Supply and Trade in Korea," *Agribusiness Review* 10 (2002): 9.

57. Hwan-il Park, "New Food Security Strategies in the Age of Global Food Crises," *Monthly Focus* (Seoul: Samsung Economic Research Institute, 2011).

58. KREI, *Agriculture in Korea*.

59. Park, "New Food Security Strategies"; Hwan-il Park et al., "Korea Needs Own Global Resource Majors," *Korea Economic Trends, Samsung Economic Research Institute Weekly Insight* 17, no. 22 (2012): 9–13; 이귀전 [Yi Kwi-jŏn], "4대 곡물 메이저와 '유통 大戰' . . . 식량주권 지키기 사활 [War with global four majors: Food security a matter of life and death]," 세계일보 [*Segye ilbo*], September 6, 2011; Sungwoo Park, "South Korea Starts Grain Venture in Chicago to Secure Supply," *Bloomberg*, April 29, 2011.

60. The strategy was put into law in 2012 National Assembly of the Republic of Korea, Overseas Agricultural Development and Cooperation Act, 270 § (2011).

61. KREI, *Agriculture in Korea*, 436.

62. 맹창호 [Maeng Ch'ang-ho], "물거품 된 '캄보디아 드림' ["Cambodian dream" wrecked]," 중도일보 [*Chungdo ilbo*], April 25, 2012.

63. This was much less than the five thousand hectares they had wanted.

64. Ji-Sook Lee, *Moving beyond Misconceptions: MH Ethanol—Case Study of a Korean Agro-Industrial Investment in Cambodia* (Pnomh Penh: NGO Forum on Cambodia's Land and Livelihoods Programme, 2011).

65. Kiyohiko Sakamoto, Yong-ju Choi, and Larry L. Burmeister, "Framing Multifunctionality: Agricultural Policy Paradigm Change in South Korea and Japan," *International Journal of Sociology of Food and Agriculture* 15, no. 1 (2007): 24–45.

66. Sakamoto, Choi, and Burmeister, "Framing Multifunctionality."

7. THE ECO-ZOMBIES OF SOUTH KOREAN CINEMA

1. Kiyah Duffey, Haeng-Shin Lee, and Barry Popkin, "South Korea's Entry to the Global Food Economy: Shifts in Consumption of Food between 1998 and 2009," *Asia Pacific Journal* 21, no. 4 (2012): 5.

2. Duffey, Lee, and Popkin, "South Korea's Entry," 5.

3. One famous example being Han Kang's 2007 novel *The Vegetarian* [채식주의자].

4. 이웃집 좀비 [The neighbor zombie], DVD, directed by Jang Youn-Jung, Oh Young-Doo, Ryoo Hoon, and Yeong Geon (Seoul: Kino Mangosteen, 2009).

5. 인류멸망보고서 [Doomsday book], DVD, directed by Kim Jee-Woon and Lim Pil-Seong (Seoul: Zio Entertainment, 2011).

6. 좀비스쿨 [Zombie school], DVD, directed by Kim Seok-Jung (Seoul: Peter Pan Pictures, 2014).

7. My use of the word nature is meant to imply spaces that *do not by default* necessitate human presence, despite there being no real separation between human and nonhuman. When I use the term "nature" in quotations, it is to refer to the cultural conceptualization of nature being separate from humans/human society.

8. Alexandre Kojève, *Introduction to the Reading of Hegel: Lectures on the Phenomenology of Spirit* (Ithaca, NY: Cornell University Press, 1986), 159.

9. Akira Lippit, *Electric Animal: Towards a Rhetoric of Wildlife* (Minneapolis: University of Minnesota Press, 2000), 18.

10. Lippit, *Electric Animal,* 18.

11. Sarah Juliet Lauro, "The Eco-Zombie: Environmental Critique in Zombie Fiction," in *Generation Zombie: Essays on the Living Dead in Modern Culture*, ed. Stephanie Boluk and Wylie Lenz (Jefferson, NC: McFarland and Company, 2011), 54.

12. Lauro, "The Eco-Zombie," 56.

13. Renee Kim, "Meeting Consumer Concerns for Food Safety in South Korea: The Importance of Food Safety and Ethics in a Globalizing Market," *Journal of Agricultural and Environmental Ethics* 22 (2009): 144.

14. Hyun J. Jin, "The 2008 US Beef Scare Episode in South Korea: Analysis of an Unusual Public Reaction," *Journal of Public Health Policy* 35, no. 4 (2014): 52.

15. Kim, "Meeting Consumer Concerns," 143.

16. Jin, "2008 US Beef Scare," 521.

17. Kwang-Ok Kim, "Rice Cuisine and Cultural Practice in Contemporary Korean Dietary Life," in *Re-Orienting Cuisine: East Asian Foodways in the Twenty-First Century*, ed. Kwang Ok Kim (New York: Berghahn Books, 2015), 75.

18. Seunghae Lee and Hae Sun Paik, "Korean Household Waste Management and Recycling Behavior," *Building and Environment* 46, no. 5 (2011): 1160.

19. Lee and Paik, "Korean Household Waste," 1163.

20. Julia Kristeva, *Powers of Horror: An Essay on Abjection* (New York: Columbia University Press, 1982), 2. Abjection defined as a breakdown of self and other can be applied to this system of waste repurposing in Korea, and Kristeva states that "food loathing is perhaps the most elementary and most archaic form of abjection."

21. Chin Thack Soh, *Korea: A Geomedical Monograph of the Republic of Korea* (Berlin: Springer-Verlag, 1980), 31.

22. *Wŏnangsori* [Old partner], DVD, directed by Lee Chung-ryoul (Seoul: Studio Neurimbo, 2008).

23. Graham Huggan and Helen Tiffin, *Postcolonial Ecocriticism: Literature, Animals, Environment* (New York: Routledge, 2010), 83.

24. Jong-Hyeon Park et al. "Control of Foot-and-Mouth Disease during 2010–2011 Epidemic, South Korea," *Emerging Infectious Diseases* 19, no. 4 (2013): 657.

25. Kim, "Meeting Consumer Concerns," 145.

26. 부산행 [Train to Busan], DVD, directed by Yŏn Sang-ho (Seoul: Next Entertainment World, 2016).

27. 김민규 [Kim Min-gyu], "영화 〈곡성 〉의 좀비영화코드 연구" [A study of the zombie code in "The Wailing"], 영상기술연구 [*Yŏngsang kisul yŏn'gu*] 27 (2017): 152.

28. *Okja*, directed by Bong Joon-ho, Netflix (South Korea and United States: Plan B Entertainment, Lewis Pictures and Kate Street Picture Company, 2017).

8. COMMUNAL ENVIRONMENTALISM IN THE HISTORY OF THE ORGANIC FARMING MOVEMENT IN SOUTH KOREA

1. At the same time, North Korea developed *Chuch'e nongpŏp* (farming based on the Chuch'e ideology). The cultivation of mountainsides and the intensive use of chemical fertilizers caused soil erosion and acidification and contributed to the outbreak of famine in North Korea in the 1990s.

2. The Green Revolution was a Cold War initiative of the US government to support the newly independent countries of the so-called free world and stop the spread of communism in Asia. Nick Cullather, *The Hungry World: America's Cold War Battle against Poverty in Asia* (Cambridge, MA: Harvard University Press, 2010), 70. The first high-yield rice varieties were developed at the International Rice Research Institute (IRRI) in the Philippines. Many Korean agricultural scientists were trained by the US Agency for International Development (USAID) in the 1950s and 1960s to develop rice breeding and

cultivation techniques. Larry L. Burmeister, *Research, Realpolitik, and Development in Korea: The State and the Green Revolution* (Boulder, CO: Westview Press, 1988), 51.

3. Kim T'ae-ho called these administrative and social schemes a "technological system of rice production" (增産體制; literally, production increase system). 김태호 [Kim T'ae-ho], "'통일벼'와 1970년대 쌀 증산체제의 형성 [The "t'ongil" variety and the formation of the 1970s rice production system]," PhD diss., Seoul National University, 2009, pp. i–ii.

4. Korea's international balance of payments improved after 1977, and the first steps to liberalize the domestic agricultural market were implemented in May 1978. 한국농촌경제연구원 [Han'guk nongch'on kyŏngje yŏn'guwŏn], 한국농정50년사 1 [50 years history of Korean agricultural policy 1] (Seoul: 농림부 [Nongnimbu], 1999), 59.

5. In 1975, Korea used 8,619 tons of pesticides; thereafter, the amount grew by more than a thousand tons annually, rising to 23,229 tons by 1987. "농산물값 올려야 농약공해에서 해방 [Food prices should rise to release farmers from pesticide poisoning]," 한겨레 [*Han'gyŏrye*], September 19, 1989.

6. For example, rice farmers sprayed about thirteen times a year, from early April to early September, which meant that farmers came into contact with pesticides once every ten days. "한국농촌의 오늘 [Korean farming villages today]," 한겨레 [*Han'gyŏrye*], October 29, 1988.

7. "농약중독이 늘고있다 [Pesticide poisoning is increasing]," 경향신문 [*Kyŏnghyang sinmun*], September 27, 1976.

8. Of the total, 51.1 percent had mild symptoms and 30.8 per cent had serious conditions. "국립보건원 조사 농민 82%가 농약에 중독 [National Institute of Health survey shows 82% of farmers suffer from pesticide poisoning]," 매일경제 [*Maeil kyŏngje*], December 4, 1982.

9. Specifically, the number of casualties was 1,186 in 1982; 954 in 1983; 1,135 in 1984; 1,561 in 1985; 1,391 in 1986; and 1,400 in 1987. "농약사망 해마다 1천명 웃돌아 [Over one thousand die from pesticide poisoning every year]," 한겨레 [*Han'gyŏrye*], February 28, 1989.

10. 원경선 [Wŏn Kyŏng-sŏn], "정농회강령 해설 [Explanation of Chŏngnonghoe's mission statement]," 정농회보 [*Chŏngnonghoebo*] 1 (1978): 14–19.

11. Baal was the name of the supreme god worshipped in ancient Canaan and Phoenicia.

12. The school was established in 1958 by Yi Ch'an-gap (1904–1974), a nephew of Yi Sŭng-hun (1864–1930), who founded the Osan School, a famous modern nationalist school in colonial Korea.

13. The Non-Church Movement (無教會主義, meaning, church for believers outside of church organizations) was a Japanese Protestant sect created by Uchimura Kanzō (內村鑑三, 1861–1930). It was brought to Korea by Uchimura's Korean students, such as Ham Sŏk-hŏn (1901–1989) and Kim Kyo-sin (1901–1945). The Non-Church Movement network between Korea and Japan directly influenced the creation of Chŏngnonghoe. Kotani Junichi (小谷純一, 1910–2004), an educator and Non-Church Movement evangelist who founded Ainōkai (愛農会) and the Ainō Agricultural School, was invited by Wŏn Kyŏng-sŏn in 1975. During his visit to Korea, Kotani apologized, as a Japanese, for the Korean people's hardships during the colonial period, and preached on why Christian farmers should practice organic farming.

14. The Osan School's ideal village movement was inspired by the Danish rural development movement led by Nikolaj Grundtvig (1873–1872) and Christen Kold (1816–1870). The Danish model was introduced to Japan by Uchimura Kanzō in his book, *The Story of Denmark* (Denmaruku koku no hanashi, デンマルク国の話) in 1913, and Uchimura's Korean students brought it to the Osan School during the 1920s. In Japan,

the Christian rural movement based on the Danish model continued within the Non-Church Movement group with the creation of Kōnō Gakuen (興農学園) in 1929 in Shizuoka Prefecture, and later in the Ainō Agricultural School.

15. Originally, Wŏn had run the farm as a commune for war orphans and homeless people since 1955; in 1976, he moved P'ulmuwŏn to a more rural area in Yangju, Kyŏnggi Province, to put Chŏngnonghoe's ideals into practice. 이선희 [Yi Sŏn-hŭi], "풀빛 일구어 온 삶 [A life that has grown the grass-green]," 샘터 [*Saemt'ŏ*] 20 (1989): 72–76.

16. 원경선 [Wŏn Kyŏng-sŏn], "나의 이력서 23 [My personal history 23]," 한국일보 [*Han'guk ilbo*], October 14, 2003.

17. Despite its commercial disadvantages, organic farming could be a viable option for farms whose goal was self-sufficiency, as it reduced the input costs of agricultural chemicals and relieved farmers from pesticide poisoning.

18. One Chŏngnonghoe member who farmed organic rice for six years recollected suffering his neighbors' hatred, which, he said, came largely from their belief that his failure to use pesticides would increase the insect infestations on their own farms. 백규현 [Paek Kyu-hyŏn], "무농약수도작 6년 [Six years of rice farming without using pesticides]," 정농회보 [*Chŏngnonghoebo*] 3 (1982): 19.

19. "Some call us 'reds' because we don't use pesticides. They ask why we decrease the national production, while all others try to increase it." 원경선 [Wŏn Kyŏng-sŏn], "믿는 자를 보겠느냐 [Will you see a believer?]," 정농회보 [*Chŏngnonghoebo*] 5 (1983): 9–18.

20. Specifically, police officers questioned whether ordinary country farmers could even think of opposing the government if they had not been instructed by North Korea. 김준권 [Kim Chun-gwŏn], "전도자로 살고 싶었던 원경선 선생님 [Mr. Wŏn Kyŏng-sŏn, who wanted to live the life of an evangelist]," 씨알의소리 [*Ssial ŭi sori*] 226 (2013): 37–38.

21. Kim Chongbuk taught at the P'ulmu School (September 1, 1969–February 22, 1972) prior to joining P'ulmuwŏn Farm. 풀무교육50년기념사업추진위원회 [P'ulmu kyoyuk 50-nyŏn kinyŏm saŏp ch'ujin wiwŏnhoe], 풀무교육50년—다시 새 날이 그리워 1 [50 years of P'ulmu education—Longing for the new day 1] (Hongsŏng: 풀무교육50년기념사업추진위원회 [P'ulmu kyoyuk 50-nyŏn kinyŏm saŏp ch'ujin wiwŏnhoe], 2008), 3611.

22. The lectures were punctuated by sermons and Bible reading throughout the program. Wŏn's personal network enabled him to invite prominent domestic and international lecturers, such as university professors, educators, and agricultural specialists from Japan and elsewhere.

23. 정상묵 [Chŏng Sang-muk], Personal notebook for the Short-Term Bible School (1979).

24. For example, gender relationships within the commune reflected the conservative culture of both the Korean Protestant Church and the rural society. Chŏngnonghoe was mostly led by male members, while their wives followed the Christian way and supported the patriarch.

25. Wŏn Kyŏngsŏn supported the idea of building a tofu-making facility within the farm to make the cash income necessary to run the farm and the classes. However, this for-profit business was seen as pursuing materialism, and some of the members left the commune for this reason.

26. 풀무학원 [P'ulmu Hagwŏn], "겨울 성서모임 [Winter Bible study group]," 새벽별 [*Saebyŏkpyŏl*] 86 (1978): 31–32.

27. 최성봉 [Ch'oe Sŏng-bong], in discussion with the author, January 15, 2015.

28. 홍순명 [Hong Sun-myŏng], "의도적지역사회론 [The theory of intentional community]," 새벽별 [*Saebyŏkpyŏl*] 88 (1979): 6–9.

29. Economic hardship drove many young people to the cities in the 1970s and 1980s. Many farmers lost their land and became tenant farmers or left farming altogether. "남의 땅 농사가 늘고있다 [Tenant farmers are increasing]," 동아일보 [*Tonga ilbo*], Febru-

ary 11, 1986. In the 1980s, land prices were rising rapidly, and urban people were speculating in farmland. Higher land prices encouraged struggling farmers to sell their land and become tenants. 조석곤 [Cho Sŏk-kon], "1980년대 자유주의 농정에 대한 평가 [An evaluation of the liberalistic agricultural policies of the 1980s]," 농촌경제 [*Nongch'on kyŏngje*] 27, no. 3 (2004): 59.

30. Accordingly, the number of Chŏngnonghoe's active members never exceeded two hundred.

31. The CCFM began to introduce organic farming to its members from 1978. While Chŏngnonghoe was a minor group within the Korean Protestant Church, the CCFM was a minor group in a movement within the Catholic Church. Compared to Chŏngnonghoe's organic farming movement, the CCFM's organic activities were more specifically a response to pesticide poisoning rather than a fundamental part of the CCFM's movement. Despite the division between the Protestant and the Catholic churches, some members of Chŏngnonghoe and the CCFM (and Hansalim) cooperated individually, sharing their knowledge and networks.

32. As of 2017, Hansalim included 54,000 consumer households (2.55 percent of all households nationwide) as members of one of its twenty-two local cooperatives across the country. Hansalim's products, which range from organic rice, vegetables, and fruit to organic processed food, are supplied by 2,159 farming households. Hansalim, *Together Again and Fresher: The 2018 Hansalim Story* (Seoul: Hansalim, 2018).

33. The "urban-rural community" was modelled after the *han* (班) system of the major Japanese cooperative group Seikatsu Kurabu (生活クラブ), following a Korean Catholic farmers and cooperative leaders' tour of Japan in 1984. Instead of *han*, *kongdongch'e* (共同體, community) was selected as a Korean term that embraces both farmers and consumers.

34. Tonghak (東學, Eastern Learning) was advocated in 1860 by Ch'oe Che-u (1824–1864). The Chosŏn dynasty regarded Tonghak's egalitarian (and revolutionary at the time) ideals as a threat, and executed Ch'oe Che-u in 1864 for deceiving people with heretical ideas. Ch'oe Si-hyŏng became the second leader of Tonghak and spread its organization nationwide. However, Tonghak lost its leaders and organizations after the defeat of the peasant revolution in 1894, and Son Pyŏng-hŭi, the third leader of Tonghak, fled to Japan. 노태구 [No T'ae-gu], ed., 동학혁명의 연구 [Research on Tonghak revolution] (Seoul: 백산서당 [Paeksan sŏdang], 1982).

35. 원주사람들 [Wŏnju Saramdŭl], "생명의 세계관 확립과 협동적 생존의 확장 [Establishing a worldview for life and expanding cooperative survival]," in 생명운동자료 모음 [A collection of the Life Movement writings], ed. 모심과살림연구소 (Mosim kwa sallim yŏn'guso) (Seoul: Hansalim, 2011), 285.

36. In August 1972, a big flood hit the South Han River basin, and Wŏnju was one of the most severely damaged areas, with one hundred thousand refugees. Chi Hak-sun, who was appointed bishop of the new Wŏnju diocese in 1965, followed the Second Vatican Council and actively advanced social work. Lacking enough priests, he invited laypeople including Chang Il-sun to carry out social work through the church. After the flood, Bishop Chi organized the Disaster Recovery Committee (DRC, 災害對策事業委員會, *Chaehae taech'aek saŏp wiwŏnhoe*) with these lay workers. Instead of distributing money to refugees, they invested in organizing and training people to be self-reliant. These activities continued until the DRC was reorganized in 1979. 김소남 [Kim So-nam], "1960~80년대 원주지역의 민간주도 협동조합운동 연구: 부락개발, 신협, 생명운동 [Research on the civilian-led cooperative movement from the 1960s to 1980s in the Wŏnju area]" PhD diss., Yonsei University, 2014.

37. Chang Il-sun (1928–1994) was a leading figure among the laity who inspired the young activists in the movement. As a former politician and local educator, he invited

young intellectuals like Kim Yŏng-ju, Kim Chi-ha, Pak Chae-il, and Lee Kyŏng-guk to form a working group and lead the rural movement. His previous support for peaceful unification of Korea had led to his blacklisting by Park Chung-hee's government, and he was forbidden to take part in any kind of political activity; Chang therefore took the indirect approach of starting a social movement through a religion by taking part in the Catholic Church's social work.

38. 정호경 [Chŏng Ho-gyŏng], 생활공동체운동: 생명의 농업 [The living community movement: An agriculture of life] (Daejeon: 한국가톨릭농민회 [Han'guk gat'ollik nongminhoe], 1985).

39. 이경숙 [Yi Kyŏng-suk], 박재순 [Pak Chae-sun], and 차옥숭 [Ch'a Ok-sung], 한국 생명운동의 뿌리 [The root of life movements in Korea] (Seoul: 이화여자대학교출판부 [Ewha yŏja taehakkyo ch'ulp'anbu], 2001), 197.

40. Women's movement groups played an important role in creating consumer communities. Early organizers like Lee Sun-ro, who was a member of Insŏnghoe (仁成會, Human Development Committee—Bishops Conference of Korea), created consumer communities by inviting their friends and neighbors to join them. More than 110 such communities were formed between 1987 and 1989, helping to establish the basis of the organic product market.

41. The Tano (端午) Festival in June 1989 (5 May in the lunar calendar) was attended by 103 consumer members and their families, one hundred farmers, and thirty others from outside Hansalim. Hansalim Board of Directors Meeting Minutes, July 8, 1989, Taech'i-dong Supply Center, Seoul.

42. 한살림 [Hansalim], 당신 덕분에 삽니다: 한살림 30년 백서 [We owe our living to you: Hansalim 30-year white paper] (Seoul: Hansalim, 2017), 348.

43. The Producers Council was only recreated on February 4, 2003. 모심과살림연구소 (Mosim kwa sallim yŏn'guso), 스무살 한살림 세상을 꺼안다: 한살림20년의 발자취 [20-year-old Hansalim embraces the world: Hansalim's footsteps for the past 20 years] (Hongsŏng: 그물코 [Kŭmulk'o], 2006), 81.

44. Organic farming shows steady growth. As of 2018, organic and nonpesticide farming accounted for 4.92 per cent of the total farmland. 한국농촌경제연구원 (Han'guk nongch'on kyŏngje yŏn'guwŏn), 2019 국내외 친환경 농산물 생산 및 소비실태와 향후 과제 [The production and consumption of environment-friendly and organic products in South Korea and foreign countries and future challenges 2019] (Naju: 한국농촌경제연구원 [Han'guk nongch'on kyŏngje yŏn'guwŏn], 2019), 2.

9. GOTJAWAL

1. According to the McCune-Reischauer, the Korean Romanization system, *kotchawal* might be the correct Romanization of this Jeju local term. However, *gotjawal* has been adopted and popularly circulated for introducing this particular forest to English-speaking readers. Hence, I opt for the more popular Romanization, *gotjawal*, in this chapter. In general, nongovernmental organization names, all personal names, and village names in this chapter are pseudonyms. The exceptions are public figures and intellectuals who have published books and articles.

2. "[제주] 제주의 허파 '곶자왈' . . . 원시림 속을 걷는다 [[Jeju] Gotjawal, the lung of Jeju Island . . . walking into the primeval forest]," 조선일보 [*Chosun ilbo*], April 26, 2010.

3. Geologists categorize lava flows into two types based on the viscosity: ʻaʻā and pāhoehoe, which are the Hawaiian names for those topographies formed by the two different types of lava flows. Pāhoehoe is a more fluid flow, while ʻaʻā lava flows more stickily and viscous. Pāhoehoe lava creates relatively flat surfaces, while ʻaʻā lava creates an uneven and bumpy topography. Song Si-t'ae, South Korea's first geologist who defined *gotjawal*, only considered areas created by ʻaʻā flows as *gotjawal* in his doctoral dissertation.

But later he expanded the definition to include some areas created by pāhoehoe flows. See 송시태 [Song Si-t'ae], "제주도 암괴상 아아용암류의 분포 및 암질에 관한 연구 [Distributions and lithology of the 'a'ā rubble flows on Cheju Island]," PhD diss., Pusan University, 2000; and 김효철, 송시태, 김대신 [Kim Hyo-ch'ŏl, Song Si-t'ae, and Kim Tae-sin], 바람과 돌이 빚은 숲, 제주, 곶자왈 [Jeju, gotjawal, forests shaped by the wind and stones] (Jeju: 숲의틈 [Sup'ŭit'ŭm], 2015).

4. On intimate knowledge, see Hugh Raffles, "Intimate Knowledge," *International Social Science Journal* 54, no. 173 (2002): 325–335.

5. Laura Ogden, *Swamplife: People, Gators, and Mangroves Entangled in the Everglades* (Minneapolis: University of Minnesota Press, 2011).

6. On multispecies ethnography, see Eben S. Kirksey and Stefan Helmreich, "The Emergence of Multispecies Ethnography," *Cultural Anthropology* 25, no. 4 (2010): 545–576; and Eben S. Kirksey, ed., *The Multispecies Salon* (Durham, NC: Duke University Press, 2014). Also see Anna Lowenhaupt Tsing, *The Mushroom at the End of the World: On the Possibility of Life in Capitalist Ruins* (Princeton, NJ: Princeton University Press, 2015).

7. Anna Tsing adopts the concept of "rewilding," which often refers to the process of returning wild animals to a habitat to enhance biodiversity, and extends the concept, as "auto-rewilding," to include plants and other organisms that are participating the rewilding activities in "human-disturbed landscapes." On auto-rewilding, see Anna Tsing, "The Buck, the Bull, and the Dream of the Stag: Some Unexpected Weeds of the Anthropocene," *Suomen Antropologi: Journal of the Finnish Anthropological Society* 42, no. 1 (2017): 3–21

8. On commons, see Elinor Ostrom, *Governing the Commons: The Evolution of Institutions for Collective Action*, Canto Classics (Cambridge, UK: Cambridge University Press, 2015 [1990]); and Jefferson C. Boyer, "Reinventing the Appalachian Commons," *Social Analysis* 50, no. 3 (2006). Also, on the history and the management of commons on Jeju Island, see Young-Sin Jeong, "Historical Evolution of Relations between Commons and Community: Focused on the Case of Dongbaek-Dongsan—Seonheul-Ri in Jeju Island," *Journal of Localitology* 17 (April 30, 2017): 119–163; and 윤순진 [Yun Sun-jin], "제주도 마을공동목장의 해체 과정과 사회생태적 함의 [The dissolving process of village pasture commons in Jeju Island and its social and ecological implications]," 농촌사회 [Nongch'onsahoe] 16, no. 2 (2006): 45–88.

9. 제주문화예술재단 [Jeju munhwa yesul jaedan], ed. 개정 증보판 제주어사전 [Dictionary of the Jeju language, revised and expanded edition] (Jeju: 제주특별자치도 [Jeju t'ŭkpyŏl jach'ido], 2009).

10. 제주문화예술재단 (Jeju munhwa yesul jaedan), 개정 증보판 제주어사전 [Dictionary of the Jeju language], 83.

11. To find recent publications on the resilience of nature or other-than-humans in the human-disturbed landscape in the Anthropocene, see Tsing, *Mushroom*; Anna Lowenhaupt Tsing, ed., *Arts of Living on a Damaged Planet* (Minneapolis: University of Minnesota Press, 2017); Andrew Mathews, "Landscapes and Throughscapes in Italian Forest Worlds: Thinking Dramatically about the Anthropocene," *Cultural Anthropology* 33, no. 3 (2018): 386–414; and also Bettina Stoetzer, "Ruderal Ecologies: Rethinking Nature, Migration, and the Urban Landscape in Berlin," *Cultural Anthropology* 33, no. 2 (2018): 295–323.

12. James C. Scott, *Seeing Like a State: How Certain Schemes to Improve the Human Condition Have Failed* (New Haven, CT: Yale University Press, 2008).

13. 제주문화예술재단 [Jeju munhwa yesul chaedan], 개정 증보판 제주어사전 [Dictionary of the Jeju language], 83–84.

14. Anna Lowenhaupt Tsing, *Friction: An Ethnography of Global Connection* (Princeton, NJ: Princeton University Press, 2005).

15. Tsing, *Friction*, 175.

16. I used the transliteration of Jeju native words to introduce the glossaries related to the concepts of forest or bushland. Each word in the Jeju language has its own quality that indicates a specific type of landscape, which I can only describe but cannot translate directly into English or even standard Korean.

17. There are regional variations: *mŏsengi, mŏch'e, mosi*. See 제주문화예술재단 [Jeju munhwa yesul chaedan], 개정 증보판 제주어사전 [Dictionary of the Jeju language], 353.

18. 제주문화예술재단 [Jeju munhwa yesul chaedan], 개정 증보판 제주어사전 [Dictionary of the Jeju language], 23.

19. 제주문화예술재단 [Jeju munhwa yesul chaedan], 개정 증보판 제주어사전 [Dictionary of the Jeju language], 536.

20. 제주문화예술재단 [Jeju munhwa yesul chaedan], 개정 증보판 제주어사전 [Dictionary of the Jeju language], 513, 538.

21. Jeong, "Historical Evolution of Relations," 119–163.

22. See 남도영 [Nam To-yŏng], 제주도 목장사 [A history of ranches on Jeju Island] (Kwach'ŏn: 한국마사회마사박물관 [Han'guk masahoe masa pangmulgwan], 2001); and also 김동전, 강만익 [Kim Tong-jŏn and Kang Man-ik], 제주 지역 목장사와 목축문화 [A history of ranches and the pastoral culture on Jeju island] (Seoul: 경인문화사 [Kyŏngin Munhwasa], 2015).

23. Interview, May 19, 2017.

24. Karen Barad, *Meeting the Universe Halfway: Quantum Physics and the Entanglement of Matter and Meaning* (Durham, NC: Duke University Press, 2007).

25. Jejudo, 제주도 중산간 종합연구 [A comprehensive study on mid-mountain areas of Jeju Island Jejudo] (제주도 [Jejudo], 1997).

26. Jejudo, 제주도 중산간 종합연구 [A comprehensive study].

27. Jejudo, 제주도 중산간 종합연구 [A comprehensive study].

28. 고기원, 박원배 [Ko Ki-wŏn and Pak Wŏn-bae], "제주도 지하수 조사 연구 발달 과정 [The path of development in the underground water research on Jeju Island]," 한 글저널이름 [*Jeju Development Review*] 9 (2005): 113–145.

29. 제주문화예술재단 [Jeju munhwa yesul chaedan], 개정 증보판 제주어사전 [Dictionary of the Jeju language].

30. Jejudo, 제주도 중산간 종합연구 [A comprehensive study].

31. Song, "제주도 암괴상 아아용암류의 분포 및 암질에 관한 연구 [Distributions and lithology]."

32. Later Song named "kotjawal lava" and added it to incorporated pāhoehoe lava along with 'a'ā lava that created the *gotjawal* topography. See Kim, Song, and Kim, 바람과 돌이 빚은 숲, 제주, 곶자왈 [Jeju, gotjawal, forests].

33. It is a single species in its own genus. See Byung-Yun Sun et al., "Mankyua (Ophioglossaceae): A New Fern Genus from Cheju Island, Korea," *Taxon* 50, no. 4 (2001): 1019.

34. IUCN, "Mankyua Chejuense: Son, S.-W., Kim, Y.-S. & Kim, H.: The IUCN Red List of Threatened Species 2016: E.T72136436A98368257" (International Union for Conservation of Nature, November 1, 2015).

35. On care and temporality, see Maria Puig de la Bellacasa, "Making Time for Soil: Technoscientific Futurity and the Pace of Care," *Social Studies of Science* 45, no. 5 (2015): 691–716; and, on the mode of living in troubled time, see Donna Jeanne Haraway, *Staying with the Trouble: Making Kin in the Chthulucene*, Series, Experimental Futures: Technological Lives, Scientific Arts, Anthropological Voices (Durham, NC: Duke University Press, 2016).

36. Jane Bennett, *Vibrant Matter: A Political Ecology of Things* (Durham, NC: Duke University Press, 2010).

10. SOUTH KOREA'S NUCLEAR-ENERGY ENTANGLEMENTS AND THE TIMESCALES OF ECOLOGICAL DEMOCRACY

1. "South Korea's Biggest Earthquake Triggers Nuclear Safety Concerns," *Reuters*, September 16, 2016. Notably, historical data prior to 1908 includes observations of earthquakes in Korea as early as the fifth century. See Kiehwa Lee and Woo-Sun Yang, "Historical Seismicity of Korea," *Bulletin of the Seismological Society of America* 96 (2006): 846–855.

2. Lee Keun-young, "South Korea Has World's Highest Density of Nuclear Power Plants," *Hankyoreh*, August 9, 2014.

3. John LaForge, "Defective Reactor Parts Scandal in South Korea Sees 100 Indicted," *Nukewatch Quarterly* 7 (Winter 2013–2014).

4. Dowan Ku, "The Anti-Nuclear Movement and Ecological Democracy in South Korea," in *Energy Transition in East Asia: A Social Science Perspective*, ed. Kuei-Tien Chou (London: Routledge, 2017). For an analysis of the political and historical context, see Taedong Lee, "From Nuclear Energy Developmental State to Energy Transition in South Korea: The Role of the Political Epistemic Community," *Environmental Policy and Governance* 31, no. 2 (2021): 82–93.

5. Robyn Eckersley, "Deliberative Democracy, Ecological Representation and Risk: Towards a Democracy of the Affected," in *Democratic Innovation: Deliberation, Representation and Association*, ed. Michael Saward (London: Routledge, 2003). See also Matthew Lepori, "Towards a New Ecological Democracy: A Critical Evaluation of the Deliberation Paradigm within Green Political Theory," *Environmental Values* 28, no. 1 (2018): 75–99.

6. See Joerg Chet Tremmel, *A Theory of Intergenerational Justice* (London: Routledge, 2009); Stephen M. Gardiner, "A Perfect Moral Storm: Climate Change, Intergenerational Ethics and the Problem of Moral Corruption," *Environmental Values* 15, no. 3 (2006): 397–413.

7. Vincent Ialenti, *Deep Time Reckoning: How Future Thinking Can Help the Earth Now* (Cambridge, MA: MIT Press, 2020). See also Gregory Benford, *Deep Time: How Humanity Communicates across Millennia* (New York: HarperCollins, 2000).

8. Vincent Ialenti, "Nuclear Energy's Long Now: Intransigent Wastes and Radioactive Greens," *Suomen Antropologi: Journal of the Finnish Anthropological Society* 3 (2013).

9. Lauren Richardson, "Protesting Policy and Practice in South Korea's Nuclear Energy Industry," in *Learning from Fukushima: Nuclear Power in East Asia,* ed. Peter Van Ness and Mel Gurtov (Canberra: ANU Press, 2017), 137.

10. "Locals Rejoice in Gyeongju's Selection for Nuclear Dump," *Korea Joongang Daily,* November 3, 2005.

11. Joseph Masco, *The Nuclear Borderlands: The Manhattan Project in Post-Cold War New Mexico* (Princeton, NJ: Princeton University Press, 2006).

12. Ialenti, "Nuclear Energy's Long Now," 63.

13. For a discussion of the heritage sector and the nuclear waste sector through the idiom of archaeology and the long-term future, see Cornelius Holtorf and Anders Högberg, "The Contemporary Archaeology of Nuclear Waste: Communicating with the Future," *Arkæologisk Forum* 35 (2016): 31–37.

14. Robert Oppenheim, *Kyŏngju Things: Assembling Place* (Ann Arbor: University of Michigan Press, 2008).

15. Jasanoff and Kim, "Containing the Atom: Sociotechnical Imaginaries and Nuclear Power in the United States and South Korea," Minerva 47 (2009): 119–146. See also Jacob D. Hamblin, *The Wretched Atom: America's Global Gamble with Peaceful Nuclear Technology* (Oxford: Oxford University Press, 2021).

16. Quoted in Jasanoff and Kim, "Containing the Atom," 133. For an analysis of the development of the nuclear industry in Korea, see Kim Seong-Jun, "한국 원자력 기술

체제 형성과 변화, 1953–1980 [Formation and change of the Korean nuclear technology system, 1953–1980]," PhD diss., Seoul National University, 2012.

17. Sung Gul Hong, "The Search for Deterrence: Park's Nuclear Option," in *The Park Chung Hee Era: The Transformation of South Korea*, ed. B. K. Kim and E. Vogel (Cambridge, MA: Harvard University Press, 2011), 483–510; Se Young Jang, "The Evolution of US Extended Deterrence and South Korea's Nuclear Ambitions," *Journal of Strategic Studies* 39, no. 4 (2016): 502–520.

18. Richardson, "Protesting Policy,"133–154.

19. Sung-Jin Leem, "Unchanging Vision of Nuclear Energy: Nuclear Power Policy of the South Korean Government and Citizens' Challenge," *Energy and Environment* 17, no. 3 (2006): 439–456. To compare with an analysis of how US activists successfully defeated plans for a radioactive waste incinerator in Livermore, California, see Hugh Gusterson, "How Not to Construct a Radioactive Waste Incinerator," *Science, Technology, and Human Values* 25, no. 3 (2000): 332–351.

20. Ku, "Anti-Nuclear Movement," 35.

21. Hyomin Kim, "Reconstructing the Public in Old and New Governance: A Korean Case of Nuclear Energy Policy," *Public Understanding of Science* 23, no. 3 (2014): 268–282.

22. Oppenheim, *Kyŏngju Things*, 6.

23. Myungseok Oh, "Cultural Policy and National Culture Discourse in the 1960s and 1970s," *Korean Anthropology Review* 1, no. 1 (2017): 105–129.

24. Tae-Hyun Kim and Hong-Kyu Kim, "The Spatial Politics of Siting a Radioactive Waste Facility in Korea: A Mixed Methods Approach," *Applied Geography* 47 (February 1, 2014): 1–9.

25. I. S. Roxburgh, *Geology of High-Level Nuclear Waste Disposal* (London: Springer, 1987).

26. Sun-Mi Wee, "Analysis of the Siting Procedure for Radioactive Waste Management Facility in Korea," MPP thesis, Korea Development Institute, 2012.

27. David von Hippel, Sun-Jin Yun, and Myung-Rae Cho, "The Current Status of Green Growth in Korea: Energy and Urban Security," *Asia-Pacific Journal: Japan Focus* 9, no. 44 (2011).

28. Ben Jackson, "The Myth of South Korea's World-Beating Nuclear Energy Exports," *Korea Exposé,* December 26, 2017, https://www.koreaexpose.com/korea-nuclear-export-power-energy/.

29. "Future of Nuclear Energy Bleak in Korea," *Korea Times*, April 21, 2017, http://www.koreatimes.co.kr/www/nation/2017/04/371_228046.html.

30. Ji-Bum Chung and Eun-Sung Kim, "Public Perception of Energy Transition in Korea," *Energy Policy* 116 (2018): 137–144.

31. Se Young Jang, "South Korea's Nuclear Energy Debate," *The Diplomat*, October 26, 2017, https://thediplomat.com/2017/10/south-koreas-nuclear-energy-debate/.

32. Su Young Choi, "Protesting Grandmothers as Spatial Resistance in the Neo-Developmental Era," *Korean Studies* 43 (May 2019): 40–67. See also Su Young Choi, "Resilient Peripheralisation through Authoritarian Communication against Energy Democracy in South Korea," *Environmental Politics* 30, no. 6 (2021): 1002–1023.

33. Observations are based on short-term fieldwork in Miryang and interviews with peace activists in Miryang, Seoul, and Jeju during 2015–2016 and 2018.

34. Drew Milne and John Kinsella, "Nuclear Theory Degree Zero, with Two Cheers for Derrida," *Angelaki: Journal of the Theoretical Humanities* 22, no. 3 (2017): 1–16; Timothy Morton, *Dark Ecology: For a Logic of Future Coexistence* (New York: Columbia University Press, 2016).

35. Hugh Gusterson, "Nuclear Futures: Anticipatory Knowledge, Expert Judgment, and the Lack That Cannot Be Filled," *Science and Public Policy* (October 2008): 551–560.

36. Bill McGuire, *Waking the Giant: How a Changing Climate Triggers Earthquakes, Tsunamis, and Volcanoes* (Oxford: Oxford University Press, 2013).

37. Rosemary Joyce, *The Future of Nuclear Waste: What Art and Archaeology Can Tell Us about Securing the World's Most Hazardous Material* (Oxford: Oxford University Press, 2020), 6; Ialenti, *Deep Time Reckoning*, 65.

38. Robert Jacobs, "The Visible and the Invisible when Considering Northern European Permanent Spent Fuel Storage: Forsmark and Onkalo," *Hiroshima Peace Institute Journal* 5, no. 13 (2018): 13–33.

EPILOGUE

Portions of this chapter were drawn from Albert L. Park, "Religion, 1876–1910," in *Routledge Handbook of Modern Korean History*, ed. Michael Seth (New York: Routledge, 2016); and Albert L. Park, "The Reshaping of Landscapes: Systems of Mediation, War, and Slow Violence," *Journal of Asian Studies* 77, no. 2 (2018): 365–368.

1. Aidan Farrow, Kathryn A. Miller, and Lauri Myllyvirta, *Toxic Air: The Price of Fossil Fuels* (Jakarta: Greenpeace Southeast Asia, 2020), 13.

2. Paul Costello, "Why Air Pollution Is Linked to Severe Cases of COVID-19," *Scope*, July 17, 2020, https://scopeblog.stanford.edu/2020/07/17/why-air-pollution-is-linked -to-severe-cases-of-covid-19/#:~:text=Studies%20are%20coming%20out%20that, areas%20of%20high%20pollution%20exposure.&text=This%20study%20and%20 others%20have,the%20COVID%2D19%20death%20rate.

3. Even though pollution from China is blamed as the main cause of air pollution in Korea, studies have shown that domestic factors play a significant role in producing air pollution and PM 2.5. See National Institute of Environmental Research (South Korea), "Introduction to the KORUS-AQ Rapid Science Synthesis Report," https://espo.nasa.gov /sites/default/files/documents/KORUS-AQ%20RSSR.pdf.

4. Jiaqi Chen, Zhe Jiang, Kazuyuki Miyazaki, Rui Zhu, Xiaokang Chen, Chenggong Liao, Dylan B. A. Jones, Kevin Bowman, and Takashi Sekiya, "Impacts of COVID-19 Control Measures on Tropospheric NO_2 over China, South Korea and Italy," 1–2, https:// arxiv.org/pdf/2006.12858.pdf.

5. Ko Jun-tae, "Clear Skies a Silver Lining of COVID-19?" *Korea Herald,* June 3, 2020.

6. Timothy Morton, *Hyperobjects: Philosophy and Ecology after the End of the World* (Minneapolis: University of Minnesota Press, 2013).

7. See Donna Haraway, "Situated Knowledges: The Science Question in Feminism and the Privilege of Partial Perspective," *Feminist Studies* 14, no. 3 (1988): 575–599.

8. See Albert L. Park, "Social Renewal through the Rural: Agricultural Cooperatives in South Korea as a Form of Critiquing Capitalism," *Global Environment* 9 (2016): 82–107.

9. On everyday militarisms, see Caren Kaplan, Gabi Kirk, and Tess Lea, "Everyday Militarisms Hidden in Plain Sight/Site," *Society and Space* 40, no. 3, https://www .societyandspace.org/forums/everyday-militarisms-hidden-in-plain-sight-site; on militarized modernity in South Korea, see Seungsook Moon, *Militarized Modernity and Gendered Citizenship in South Korea* (Durham, NC: Duke University Press, 2005).

10. See, among many other scholarly works on anti-base protests on Jeju Island, Andrew Yeo, "Realism, Critical Theory, and the Politics of Peace and Security: Lessons from Anti-Base Protests on Jeju Island," *European Journal of International Security* 3, no. 2 (2018): 235–255.

11. For more on the DMZ's ecologies, see Eleana Kim, "Toward an Anthropology of Landmines: Rogue Infrastructure and Military Waste in the Korean DMZ," *Cultural Anthropology* 31, no. 2 (2016): 162–187.

12. Robert Jervis, *System Effects* (Princeton, NJ: Princeton University Press, 1999), 6.

13. Kojin Karatani, *Transcritque on Kant and Marx* (Cambridge, MA: MIT Press, 2003), 19.

14. See Donald Worster, *Dust Bowl: The Southern Plains in the 1930s* (Oxford: Oxford University Press, 2004.

15. Worster, *Dust Bowl*, 6.

16. Courtney Bender and Ann Taves, "Introduction: Things of Value," in *What Matters?* ed. Courtney Bender and Ann Taves (New York: Columbia University Press, 2012), 10.

17. Bender and Taves, "Introduction," 13.

List of Contributors

David Fedman is associate professor of history at the University of California, Irvine, where he teaches courses on Japan, Korea, and environmental history. He is the author of *Seeds of Control: Japan's Empire of Forestry in Colonial Korea* (University of Washington Press, 2020), as well as numerous articles on the environmental history and historical geography of Japanese imperialism.

Ewa Eriksson Fortier had a thirty-year career within the International Red Cross Red Crescent movement, from which she retired in 2015. She has served abroad on long-term missions to Vietnam, Malawi, Bangladesh, and China; was the former Head of Country Delegation in Pyongyang, DPRK, in 2008–2009, for the International Federation of Red Cross and Red Crescent Societies; and has since returned to visit the DPRK Red Cross on behalf of the Swedish Red Cross.

Lindsay S. R. Jolivette holds an MA from the East Asian Studies Center at the University of Southern California and is currently a PhD candidate in the department of East Asian Languages and Cultures at the same university. Her research focuses on representations of the nonhuman other and horrific ecological manifestations in contemporary South Korean and Japanese visual media, with a specialization in cinema.

Eleana J. Kim is an associate professor of anthropology and Asian American Studies at the University of California, Irvine. She is the author of *Making Peace with Nature: Ecological Encounters along the Korean DMZ* and *Adopted Territory: Transnational Korean Adoptees and the Politics of Belonging,* both published by Duke University Press. Her research has been supported by the American Council of Learned Societies, Social Science Research Council, Wenner-Gren Foundation for Anthropological Research, the Fulbright Commission, and the Korea Foundation.

Nan Kim is associate professor of history at the University of Wisconsin–Milwaukee, where she directs the Public History program and is a faculty affiliate in anthropology. Her research addresses historical consciousness, trauma and memory, material culture, social movements, political protest, and transnational public history. She is the author of *Memory, Reconciliation, and Reunions in South Korea: Crossing the Divide* (Lexington Books, 2017), which won the Peace History Society's Scott Bills Memorial Prize. She is a member of the editorial board of *Critical Asian Studies*, and her work has appeared in the *Journal of Asian Studies; Verge: Studies in Global Asias; Asia-Pacific Journal;* and the *Routledge Handbook on Memory and Reconciliation in East Asia.*

Suzy Kim is a historian and author of the award-winning *Everyday Life in the North Korean Revolution, 1945–1950* (Cornell University Press, 2013). She holds a PhD from the University of Chicago, and teaches at Rutgers, the State University of New Jersey in New Brunswick, USA. Her latest book, *Among Women across Worlds: North Korea in the Global Cold War* (Cornell University Press, 2022), was completed with the support of the Fulbright Program and the National Endowment for the Humanities.

John S. Lee is an assistant professor in the History Department at Durham University in the United Kingdom. He holds a PhD in history and East Asian languages from Harvard

University. His research focuses on the environmental history of Chosŏn Korea, and he has further interests in comparative histories of preindustrial forestry and the long-term environmental legacies of Eurasian empires.

Marc Los Huertos is a faculty member at Pomona College's Environmental Analysis Program. He teaches introductory and upper division courses that focus on biogeochemistry, freshwater ecology, and sustainable agriculture. As an applied ecologist, his research addresses issues of water quality, greenhouse gas emissions, and soil nitrogen dynamics in row crop agriculture in California. He is the author of *Ecology and Management of Inland Waters* (Elsevier, 2020).

Sooa Im McCormick is the curator of Korean art at the Cleveland Museum of Art. In addition to her specialty in Korean art, her research encompasses crosscurrents in early modern East Asian visual culture. McCormick holds a PhD from the University of Kansas, with a dissertation titled "Comparative and Cross-Cultural Perspectives on Chinese and Korean Court Documentary Painting in the Eighteenth Century."

Anders Riel Muller (Yeonjun Song) is an associate professor in City and Regional Planning at the University of Stavanger in Norway, where he also teaches in the graduate program of Energy, Environment and Society. He holds a PhD in international development and global studies from Roskilde University in Denmark.

Hyojin Pak is a doctoral candidate at Leiden University's Institute of Area Studies. Her dissertation, "Laboring Waste, Wasting Labor: Waste Pickers and the Urban Periphery in Developing South Korea," looks into the labor of waste pickers at the intersection of informality, modern waste management, and urban spatial politics during South Korea's development period.

Yonjae Paik is a historian and Japan Society for the Promotion of Science Postdoctoral Fellow at Ritsumeikan University. He holds a PhD from Australian National University, with a dissertation titled "The Informal Life Politics of Community-Based Organic Farming Movements in South Korea."

Albert L. Park is the Bank of America Associate Professor of Pacific Basin Studies at Claremont McKenna College and the co-PI of EnviroLab Asia at the Claremont Colleges. He specializes in the histories of Korea, Japan, and East Asia, with a focus on the tension between authority and counter-authority. He is the author of *Building a Heaven on Earth: Religion, Activism and Protest in Japanese Occupied Korea* (University of Hawai'i Press, 2014), and his current book project looks at the origins of environmentalism and environmental movements in modern Korean history.

Joseph Seeley is an assistant professor in the Corcoran Department of History at the University of Virginia. He specializes in the histories of Korea, the Japanese empire, and East Asian environments and borderlands more broadly. His current book project examines the Yalu River boundary between northern Korea and China during the period 1894–1945.

Jeongsu Shin is a doctoral candidate in anthropology at the University of Illinois at Urbana-Champaign. She is completing her dissertation, "Worldly Ecologies: Landscape, History, and Environmental Politics on Jeju Island," which focuses on the environmental politics of Jeju Island, South Korea.

Index

Note: Page numbers in *italics* refer to figures.

Abelmann, Nancy, 7
abjection, 129, 218n20
acacia trees, 96, 213n42
Agenda 21, 85, 209n44
agricultural policy: bifurcation strategy, 112, 114, 115, 116, 119, 121; Chosŏn dynasty, 117, 185; in Denmark compared with South Korea, 110–11; intrasectoral politics, 117; investment in modernization, 115; North Korea, 183, 185; overseas development strategy, 119–21; protectionism, 116–17, 120–21; South Korea, 113, 139–40; state support of rice, 109–10, 118, 121; trade liberalization, 7, 114–18, 144, 219n4. *See also* agriculture
agriculture: chemical farming, 140–41, 148, 185; commercialization, 185; fertilizers and pesticides, 30, 88, 93, 96, 105, 140–41, 142, 185, 213n53; land, 13, 30, 110, 117, 218n1; markets, 114; meatification, 11, 112, 119, 121; North Korea, 88–89, 210n7, 218n1; schools, 141–42, 219n13, 220n14; small-scale, 117–18. *See also* agricultural policy; animal feed; organic farming; livestock farming; rice
Agriculture Promotion Public Corporation (South Korea), 158
Ainō Agricultural School (Japan), 219n13, 220n14
air pollution, 22, 63, 96, 179, 186, 227n3; "fine dust" (*misaemŏnji*), 178–79
alternative energy sources, 93, 96; solar panel use in North Korea, 101, 213n50
animal feed: and the bifurcation policy, 112, 114, 115–16, 119, 121; domestic production of, 110, 114; in *Doomsday Book*, 128–29; food waste as, 129, 130; imported, 110–13, *111*, 112, 113, 114, 115–17, 118, 119, 122; overseas production, 30, 107, 119–21; and quality grading of beef, 115
animals: commodification, 124; farm, 131–32; human/animal duality, 124, 126, 127, 130; rare and endangered, 10, 160; species, 28–30,

29; treatment, 131–32, 133; in zombie films, 131. *See also* animal feed; horses; livestock farming; meat consumption
animism, 186–87
Annals of the Chosŏn Dynasty, 9
Anthropocene, 162, 183, 186
anthropocentrism, 135. *See also* human/animal duality
anthropogenic landscapes, 149, 154. See also *gotjawal*
anti-base movement, 183
anticommunism, 140, 218n2
antinuclear movement, 166–67, 168, 169–70, 174, 177; United States, 226n19
antipollution activism, 8, 62
aquaculture, 53, 57–58. *See also* Sup'ung Dam
arable land, 21, 30, 45, 62, 90, 117
Arduous March famine (North Korea), 11, 88, 92, 117, 180, 218n1
Asian financial crisis of 1997–1998, 8, 182
Atwell, William, 66
"auto-rewilding" (Tsing), 152, 154, 156, 223n7

Baal, worship of, 141
Bankoff, Greg, 38
beef: and the Candlelight Protest of 2008, 106, 122–23, 127, 133; consumption, 30, 105–6, 107, 113; environmental costs, 106, 107; in the Global North, 105; imports and exports, 106, 122–23, 126; quality grading, 115, 116; South Korean beef culture, 105–6; in South Korean food policy, 11, 113, 126. *See also* livestock farming; meat consumption; meat industry
Bennett, Jane, "thing-power," 163
biodiversity, 28–30, 111, 150, 152, 160, 163, 185–86, 189, 223n7
"biological expansion of Europe" (Crosby), 196n5
bird life, 7, 28–30; distribution of crane and heron species, *29*
Blue Revolution, 57, 58

www.ingramcontent.com/pod-product-compliance
Lightning Source LLC
Chambersburg PA
CBHW041130280326
41928CB00059B/3313